PRISONER OF
DEATH

Patrick Stephens Limited, part of Thorsons, a division of the Collins Publishing Group, has published authoritative, quality books for enthusiasts for more than twenty years. During that time the company has established a reputation as one of the world's leading publishers of books on aviation, maritime, military, model-making, motor cycling, motoring, motor racing, railway and railway modelling subjects. Readers or authors with suggestions for books they would like to see published are invited to write to: The Editorial Director, Patrick Stephens Limited, Thorsons Publishing Group, Wellingborough, Northants, NN8 2RQ.

PRISONER OF DEATH

A GRIPPING MEMOIR OF COURAGE AND SURVIVAL UNDER THE THIRD REICH

GRAHAM PALMER

Patrick Stephens Limited

First published in 1990

British Library Cataloguing in Publication Data
Palmer, Graham
Prisoner of death.
1. World War 2 - Biographies
I. Title
940.548

ISBN 1-85260-305-4

Publisher's note
The author has requested that the royalties accruing from the sale of this book shall be paid to the British Red Cross Society.

Patrick Stephens Limited is part of the Thorsons Publishing Group, Wellingborough, Northamptonshire, NN8 2RQ, England.

Typeset by Burns & Smith Ltd., Derby.

Printed by Mackays, Chatham, Kent

1 3 5 7 9 10 8 6 4 2

Contents

We must never forget, or it will
happen again

Foreword

by
Philip Gardner VC MC
Captain (Rtd) 4th Royal Tank Regiment
Hon Sec of VC and GC Association

Many books have been written concerning officers captured during the 1939–45 War, but there is little or no mention of the experiences of 'other ranks', who without the privilege of officer status endured privation and conditions far removed from any 'Geneva Conventions', and I hope that this book will rectify this glaring omission.

Having experienced some of the minor hardships of life in a POW camp, during my own short captivity in both Italy and Germany, I could not stop reading this amazing work, *Prisoner of Death*, as Graham Palmer unfolds the incredible account of his survival while incarcerated for five years in both German and Russian prisoner of war camps and his many escapes and subsequent recapture.

It is almost unbelievable that anyone could have survived such inhuman treatment and I highly recommend this fascinating book to all those interested in the history of war.

1

The Execution

'I wish they would pull the ruddy trigger and get done with it', muttered an exceedingly disillusioned Thomas from under his blanket and who was standing in line at my side accompanied by two other pathetic-looking enemies of the glorious Third Reich. The line we were all standing in constituted in fact a pitiful row of four very dishevelled and beaten-up prisoners of war of the all-conquering German military forces, the Wehrmacht, standing disconsolately in a biting wind on a freezing cold morning facing the brick wall of a guard room in a prisoner-of-war camp in Poland with our backs to a firing squad which was not visible to us since our heads were covered by blankets. Lined up behind us in rows of five were the remaining occupants of the camp of about two hundred equally pathetic remnants of humanity, there at six o'clock in the morning to witness the fulfilment of the German camp commandant's threat to shoot any prisoners recaptured after attempting an escape. That early hour of the morning on the snow-covered plains of Poland could never be considered to rank as a hugely enjoyable environment, and on this particular occasion the circumstances did little to soften the bleak surroundings.

The year was 1940 and it was only some five months since the fall of France and consequential enslavement of thousands of remnants of the British Army who did not have the good fortune to escape from the clutches of the Germans at Dunkirk or subsequently from one of the other ports in northern France. The place was a small town called Hohensalza in Central Poland where a forced labour camp had been set up by the Germans to keep their captives fully occupied, and the fundamental reason for Thomas's utterance invoking an early opportunity for us to meet our Maker was the assault upon our bodies, not at that moment by German guards but by battalions of lice.

The lice were the inevitable consequence of months of privation, lack of food, above all water, which became too precious to use for washing and in very short supply even for drinking, and lack of any hygiene facilities at all. Labouring at some of the filthiest tasks our captors could find for us, such as demolition works and emptying sewage cesspits, did not improve our state of uncleanliness which had progressively worsened during these past five months.

'For God's sake, pull the ruddy trigger and let's get done with it,' was my only fervent wish and earnest back-up to Thomas's own supplication. A year earlier, I would never have thought I could wish my life away so earnestly. There was no future for us now anyway; the Germans had to all intents and purposes won the war, France had been overrun and capitulated and the SS Führer, the top Hitler representative who would occupy Buckingham Palace after the King had fled to Canada, had already been named and was no doubt preparing himself for the joyous task of being overlord representing the great Adolf himself in his shortly-to-be annexed colony of Britain. So what better ending for these miserable captives than to be quickly despatched to a hopefully more joyous world and, we hoped, cleanly shot through a heart which was getting pretty fed up with beating anyway and which was beginning to carry out the operation rather erratically, and to put an end to the immediate agony and spare us maybe many years or indeed a whole lifetime of slavery in foreign lands. Life is precious to those who have hope and something to live for in freedom. Today we are, of course, aware that the duration of that war was to be finite, but at that particular time there was no guarantee of an end date to our future period of captivity. At that moment even the most hopeful of our doleful quartet could not summon any optimism, and the only apparent beneficiaries of our continued existence were the little brutes who were tucking into various parts of our bodies.

Through the haze of consciousness, barely believing that this was happening to me and that my life would end so inauspiciously, I somewhere heard the engine of a car. There was little else to be heard in a field some two or three miles from the nearest town at early dawn on a November day other than the continuous raucous shouting and screaming of uncouth, bombastic German guards, and a vicious lecture which was being delivered by a very irate camp commandant at full scream in an unaccustomed tongue to the assembled prisoners, advising them in no uncertain terms that escaping was the greatest crime in the book and punishable by death, which was what they were about to witness. His night's enjoyment of the unwilling but attractive maiden from the local village had been ruined by these English pigs, and he was in no mood for dishing out pleasantries to the barbarians assembled before him.

Geneva Convention requirements laid down in previous years for the humane and correct treatment of prisoners during warfare were, at that stage in the war, so much eye-wash, and whilst the Convention expressly disallowed the shooting of prisoners except when refusing to submit after being apprehended following an escape, in 1940 this was regarded by the German camp commandants as quite unnecessary to comply with in view of the imminent conquering of the world by the all-powerful Wehrmacht, and the indiscriminate shooting of a prisoner of war was of no more consequence than the necessity of getting some other prisoners to dig a trench and dispose of the body.

But pull the trigger they did not, and live to tell the tale my three compatriots and I certainly did. No doubt our earnest supplications to the Deity to put an end to our misery went unheeded for some very good reasons which completely escaped our understanding at that time. No doubt we mere mortals were there to suffer and not to question the reasons, and the Deity must have decided that we had many more good years of suffering in us before finally permitting our release from the treadmill.

Together, the four of us had attempted an escape from this working party camp, and thanks to a certain amount of co-operation between one of the inmates of the barn in which we prisoners were housed, a little Welsh gentleman, and his German captors, information on the hole in the brick wall of the barn which we had been so carefully making during our nights of incarceration was leaked to the guards, and on the particular night we had arranged to break out the first one through the hole was duly pounced upon by a guard who was waiting outside the wall. Simultaneously and to our utter horror and amazement guards entered into the building and called out my name and the names of the other three involved in the diabolical attempt to escape from the clutches of the Wehrmacht (the German Command), indicating their quite obvious prior knowledge of the full details of the escape, and we were all led immediately to the camp guardroom. We later discovered that the Welsh gent referred to was subsequently removed from the barn for his own protection and was later seen working in the German guards' quarters, frequently being photographed by the guards polishing their boots, and no doubt carrying out all sorts of other menial tasks for a slight improvement in rations or for an opportunity to ravenously clean up any left-overs from his masters' plates. Such photos must have immensely buoyed up the spirits of those relatives of the German soldiers in the Fatherland who were already savouring the first delights of victory over France and numerous other European nations. To see pictures of Britons in such subservient postures must have enormously added to the already rapidly growing narcissistic attitude the Germans had readily adopted consequent upon their military successes.

This had all occurred during the night, as we had carefully planned an escape for about 2 a.m. to coincide, so we had hoped, with the least watchful period of the night by our guards, and as we were subsequently led from our prison hut to the camp guard room following apprehension by the Germans we surely must have presented an appearance which would have qualified as the most dejected sight one could possibly imagine. It was very cold, we were very tired from the general circumstances arising from captivity and from the five months of extreme deprivation following battles we never had a chance to recover from, but to add to all that the utter dejection and resultant frustration of our attempt to escape, as we were marched out of the barn which had been our home for a month or two, we really imagined that we had reached the end of life's road. Anyone attempting to escape had been threatened by the authorities with execution and clearly this was to be the fate awaiting us. I did not, in fact, have any hopes that I would be returning to my native land, and a rough and ready burial in Polish soil, committing my defunct body to the earth propelled into the ditch by the toe of a German jackboot was not what I might have wished for in happier days.

Anyway, we had been kept in the guardroom for what seemed an interminable period, probably two or three hours, sitting on a bench with hands resting on head and unable to do anything to alleviated the continual biting by our unwanted friends, the lice, not to mention an adequate supply of bed bugs, fleas and the like. They all really had a banquet, but the aggravation occasioned to the four miserable recipients of the ceaseless biting was indescribable, mixed with the considerable degree of apprehension as to our future and the further intentions of our captors. It had previously been so very clearly indicated by the German commandant and guards that shooting would be the fate to be meted out to any prisoner who attempted to escape, and that seemed to represent the sum total of our future destiny. Besides, we had already witnessed such treatment on many occasions in the past six months, prisoners shot dead without any prior warning, for stepping out of line whilst marching, or failing to keep up as a result of illness or injury.

Such happy deliberations which represented our general view of life as we sat uncomfortably in the guardroom were suddenly and rudely interrupted by a vicious crash of a rifle butt against the side of the head of one of the four, Peter Reeves, an advertising agent from Richmond, Surrey.

'What the hell was that for?' questioned Peter rather uselessly to a bunch of German-speaking guards.

'*Schweine, verdammte Schweine*,' came the unhelpful reply. 'Pigs, bloody pigs' which seemed to summarize the Germans' view of the biological category of their prisoners, and at the same time afforded some more cruel-minded stalwart of the Super Race an opportunity to vent his feelings on one of those who had the misfortune to be born into the lower echelons of humanity.

Ultimately the final hour arrived and we were ordered to file out of the guardroom at about dawn and were lined up against a wall, facing the wall and about two feet away. The whole time we were covered by guards liberally equipped with rifles and machine guns pointed at us and blankets were put over our heads. That indeed seemed pretty ominous, although we had nothing to look at anyway except some uninteresting Polish brickwork. We could not, of course, see what was happening behind us on the parade ground but later we learned that all the inmates of the camp were lined up to face the villainous four. Whether the intention of the commandant was actually to shoot us or only to frighten the other inmates with this macabre performance, no one will ever know, but we four certainly assumed, as did the spectators, that it was for real. We stood there awaiting the arrival of the piece of explosive steel which would put us out of our agony once and for all, whilst another lecture was delivered to our assembled colleagues by the furious commandant on the inadvisability of escaping and emphasizing that punishment would be shooting.

However, at that very moment, and this was then about six o'clock in the morning, a German staff car entered the camp gates. Who was in the car and what transpired, such lowly creatures as prisoners shall never know, but shortly after its arrival the four of us were led back into the guard hut to resume our earlier positions on the bench, together with the accursed lice, whilst we heard our comrades, who had been paraded for hours watching us, being dismissed and returned to the barn to prepare to march to the day's work after their interrupted night's rest. We were then left to endure a further period of unequal battle against the lice, who were winning hands down, and the long period of sitting on that bench being bitten and awaiting a decision from the camp commandant, or his newly arrived superior, on what to do, we found most uncomfortable and nerve-racking, to say the least.

Just to show how helpful fate can be, one of us had previously picked up a key in the gutter when marching to work through the town – this key had been taken away when we were searched – and now came a vicious cross-examination about the wretched key, for it transpired that it belonged to a store in the town where ammunition was kept, so the vigilant guards immediately assumed that the escapees had been negotiating an uprising with the very depressed Poles in the town. Nothing was further from our minds, as no one even knew what lock the key fitted – but try telling that to Jerries who only wanted an excuse to shoot us.

'Where did you get this key from?' came the harsh demand of the blotchy-faced young guard who acted as interpreter and had learned his English apparently at a special school organized by the Hitler Youth Organization, and who greatly relished his sudden advancement to a position of power, at a very young age, over the English swine.

'We found it in a gutter on our way to work,' I replied, speaking for the benumbed group.

'Don't be so dumb. You think we Germans will believe such idiotic replies? We are the most superior race in the world and you think we will believe these stupid lies of yours? You were conspiring with your friends the Poles to rise up against us.'

'That is nonsense,' I insisted. 'We did find it in a gutter, and we have no idea what lock it fits. In our position, you must know that we would pick up anything in the hopes that it might be edible or eventually become useful for something. We just picked it up at the side of the road and my mate here put it in his pocket,' I said, indicating Peter with a nod of the head – the only thing remaining to me that I could move. 'There was no attempt at any uprising and such an idea is quite ludicrous. None of us can speak Polish and we are not enabled to speak to them, so how can we possibly organize an uprising?'

The logic of the argument finally struck home, for I was addressing a member of one of the most logical-minded of races, and ultimately the Commandant realized that an uprising by a bunch of half-starved prisoners in conjunction with Poles whose language none spoke or understood, would be a little preposterous. So the matter fortunately was left at that and the lice just went on biting.

The events that led to this unhappy encounter with the hated Hun, approaching perilously close to termination of my eighteen years of mixed fortune, had commenced for me before the formal declaration of hostilities on 3 September 1939. They had been accentuated by the devastatingly rapid assault through France by the well-equipped and carefully trained German forces which left this particular starry-eyed young man, as I could only at that time have described myself, much the worse for wear and exceedingly apprehensive as to what the future might hold in store for him.

It is, therefore, to the immediate pre-war days – that joyous, warm and carefree summer of 1939 disturbed only by the persistent raucous bellowing of one Adolf Hitler countered by successive umbrella tricks performed by British Prime Minister Neville Chamberlain – to which I must return to establish just how I got around to participating in this macabre performance in freezing Poland some fifteen months later.

2
The Adventure

When I went with my Territorial Army unit to France early in 1940 it was strictly on the understanding, at least a unilateral understanding on my part, that I would participate in a 'phoney' war, not an exceedingly real one. Nothing had, of course occurred since September 1939 to upset the generally accepted belief that the impregnable fortresses of Maginot and Siegfried would never change ownership, and the primary intent of the ordinary uneducated, cloth-eared squaddy amongst whose very serried ranks I had taken up a position, was just to enjoy oneself in a foreign country.

The great Maginot line of concrete bunkers and tank traps extending up to the Belgian border seemed secure enough to defend France. The great brains of yesteryear seem to have ignored the possible ability of the Germans to wander round the top of it, through a virtually defenceless Belgium. The German Siegfried Line remained, of course, in mint condition, to coin the philatelic terminology.

For someone who had, to that time, spent his one 'adult' year from leaving school at sixteen, in an office in central London counting up strings of meaningless figures appearing on a quantity surveyor's dimension sheet (without the assistance of a calculator!) for nine hours per day and for a remuneration of ten shillings per week, the opportunity of actually travelling overseas, and indeed the very fact of a Declaration of War, was of immense excitement and importance; it was the only sign of relief on the horizon from an otherwise thoroughly boring present and apparently equally dull future. As a member of the local Territorial Army which at that particular time all the patriotic and bored young men of this country were rushing to join, urged on by a rather precarious political situation on the foreign front and on the home front by a desire to enjoy some action, some comradeship and some beer (not necessarily in that order!), this presented me with a unique opportunity of release from staring all day at the wrong sort of figures, coupled with an immediate chance of a visit to a foreign country and, who knows, the possibility even of studying at a closer range the sorts of figures which to that point of time had only been dreams or clandestinely observed in sordid magazines or upon occasional visits to the Gaumont cinema.

My military training up until then had not been impressive and could not readily be considered as adequate preparation for the non-professional youth of the nation to engage in armed combat against the efficient military machine which the rather belligerent Adolf Hitler had been preparing over the past decade. I had joined the Territorials in the spring of 1939 because it was generally anticipated that a war with the bellicose Hitler regime was very much on the cards, and the patriotic and noble thing for any right-minded young gentleman of the day was to 'join up', which we all flocked to do, largely through boredom with our station in life, partly through a lemming-like desire to imitate one's peers and probably as much as anything 'for the beer'. There seemed to be a growing spirit of comradeship floating about the place at that time, and despite Neville Chamberlain's umbrella tricks and brief courtship with the dreaded Führer at Munich, most people in their heart of hearts had a pretty sound premonition of doom being around the corner. We were all of course children of another war, 'the Great War', which had ended only twenty years earlier, and we were very war-conscious.

So the Territorials did their best to provide an answer, at least on land, to Hitler's rather better-trained and armed Panzer divisions. That answer was, however, pretty pathetic, probably best described as 'too little, too late', and our preparation consisted in the main of attendance once or twice a week at a Drill Hall, for which I was let off work a little earlier than usual by a no doubt reluctant employer too embarrassed to refuse such a noble cause, and which handsomely made up for any inconvenience and made it all worthwhile. At the Drill Hall we attended lectures about apparently non-existent weapons, for whilst we were shown many drawings and pretty pictures of such unobtainable items as 'Bren' machine-guns and a terribly complicated thing called a personal anti-tank gun, it was some time before they materialized for our inspection and admiration. The anti-tank gun incidentally did not in fact earn much admiration from me, for when I eventually took very temporary possession of one, I found the darn thing was so heavy it was almost immovable although intended to be carried as a personal weapon. Rumour had it that the recoil after firing was so powerful that unless you had the shoulders of an ox you stood in definite danger of having the upper part of the body shattered, which presumably was to be regarded as a reasonable sacrifice for knocking out a German tank, if this was what it could do, a fact which I and many of my colleagues greatly doubted.

However, after all the training received at the Drill Hall and subsequently at a military camp at Lyme Regis in Dorset to which I was sent in August to replace the usual family summer holiday at Bexhill, I could honestly say that before going to war, the total amount of weapon training I had received, apart from the theoretical, was to fire about six rounds of .202 from a standard British Army rifle on one unique visit to a firing range; all the rest of the training seemed to be in the polishing and boning of boots to a most fantastic shine (rubbing the toe caps with a piece of bone to obtain a glittering finish - for the uninitiated), and similarly the polishing of brass buttons so meticulously that it would wear away the regimental insignia embossed on them and make the wearer look, at the tender age of seventeen, like an old soldier! We were, of course, taught to march smartly, salute with great dignity and fervour, and shout as loud as our poor little larynxes would allow, none of which attributes, as we subsequently found to our cost, were to impress the German armoured divisions in the least respect. I could only suppose that the sole benefit of that training period was that we got to know each other as individuals, to understand the strong and weak points of our motley assembly, for the recruits came from just about all walks of life, rich, poor and indifferent, labourers, butcher boys, clerks and bankers' sons, so the training really was a matter of acclimatization to a very changed set of circumstances in a social structure which had up until then been pretty static and to establish new records in beer-drinking, something I found at that early time to be quite exciting and at which I think I can say, without undue boasting, I was quite good; this cultivated a certain bonhomie amongst the odd assortment of civilians in military uniform, which was probably of some very small ultimate benefit to pit against the German might.

There is little doubt that the Territorial Army served this country as an absolutely essential stop-gap to preserve the Regular Army and hold the fort for a short time whilst the 'powers that be' got around to assembling together a few more Bren guns and other probably more vital equipment which, in the pre-war years successive British governments had ditched or failed to replace in the sacred cause of Universal Disarmament, a game played by many but not unfortunately by friend Adolf. Anyway, the whole so-called preparation for active service was so pathetically futile that at the end of the intensive training period which lasted from just before the outbreak of war to about the end of the year, the reluctant trainees had not really succeeded in achieving any realistic battle training, acclimatization to weapon fire either directed against or by them, or any of the the other rather basic requirements needed to support a front line soldier in times of need.

I was promoted to the elevated status, first of lance-corporal and within a few weeks to full corporal, probably because no one else wanted the job, or maybe because I needed the extra money more than the others to buy all that beer. My qualifications for attaining the second from lowest rank in the British army were virtually none, except for a moderate ability to shout quite loudly, but seldom did I know what to shout and have much to shout about.

However, life had become really very enjoyable, and the evening sing-songs in the pubs of Richmond were a far cry from the previous mundane existence. The surge of power I felt in walking about in uniform with two very clean white stripes on each arm, amongst the more timorous (but I secretly suspected, more intelligent) civilians, was ample reward for having to put up with the occasional night exercises in Richmond Park, which were not, contrary to my hopeful expectations, carried out in the company of the local belles.

Any possibility of becoming bored with the public houses of Richmond and Kingston was unhappily removed by a thoughtful Command which every now and then sent groups of us off to guard certain strategic locations from attack – not from the Germans but, even in those far-off days, from the IRA. I spent many an unhappy hour trudging around the oil tanks at Port

Victoria, a place I had previously never heard of and nobody else seemed to have heard of either (instead of being situated in some exotic spot like the West Indies, it transpired it was to be found in the Isle of Grain in the Thames Estuary – a grave disappointment). Standing on Rochester railway bridge watching the trains go by may be all good fun to the young train spotters, but marching up and down the wretched thing in full equipment and saddled with a heavy rifle and standing jammed up against the buttresses whilst express trains whizzed by at great speed some six inches from my nose was not the height of enjoyment, even though I may have been instrumental in preventing the IRA from blowing it up, which I doubt. The pleasures to be had in exploring public houses in parts of the world as far distant as Chatham and Gravesend, however, was indeed compensation for any slight discomfort occasioned. I was even sent to guard German civilian internees at Lingfield Racecourse, which was then being adapted for the incarceration of foreign nationals and prisoners of war, and this was indeed an odd quirk of fate in view of the future which confronted me.

But these diversions soon came to an end (the IRA didn't) and I was eventually returned to Richmond for more intensive beer-drinking and some additional training in boot-polishing, and then all of a sudden, completely out of the blue, sent on embarkation leave.

The whole performance was really just one of assembling sheep for the slaughter, albeit quite willing sheep, and trying to kid them that they were being made capable of devouring a wolf which had already succeeded in making mincemeat of the probably better equipped and certainly more enthusiastic military strength of Poland and various other nations before them.

I did, however, find the embarkation leave a bit of a mixed blessing. On the one hand, it presented me with an opportunity to augment at no cost to myself, my daily intake of beer, purchased with unstinting generosity by masses of relatives and friends who seemed to think I should be provided with as much false cheer as they could stuff down my throat. Presumably they felt, and correctly so too, that my future opportunities for beer-drinking may be considerably curtailed; but also no doubt they were personally a little relieved to see so many volunteers going off to defend the old country, thereby putting back by a few months or years maybe, the demand which in the end would no doubt be made upon themselves.

The tricky part, however, lay with the placating of my own parents. I had been given a form by my regimental office to get completed by my parents, and upon careful study of the form in between pints, I had realized that I had to procure their agreement before I could be sent overseas on active service – the result of my tender years. I realized that this just had to be signed by my parents; in no way could I now back out on my mates and leave my battalion in the lurch without their most valuable corporal – indeed it would be most embarrassing to have to say to my regimental sergeant-major, as a full blown corporal, 'Sergeant-Major, my mummy won't let me go to war.' It was quite unthinkable, but the ghastly possibility did present itself to me.

In so far as my father was concerned, it did not appear to be too difficult, for he was quite sure that a little bit of war would probably do wonders for the boy, mature him a bit and bring him out. After all, that's what wars were for, weren't they? But all my more realistic mum could see was the gathering together of the shattered pieces of what was to her the most beautiful body in the world – a leg here and an arm there blown off by the nasty Germans, and the shell which shocked her little boy's brain into a gruesome but very real imitation of a cabbage. Sightless, limbless and senseless, she could see her little darling being returned to her, albeit with a quite useless medal pinned to the remains of his shell-torn chest. How horribly realistic mums can be if they are allowed full scope for their imaginations.

Clearly I had to work hard on my dad during those ten days of furlough, and in the end got my way. The important little piece of paper was duly signed, and much relieved I went down to the pub with my father for another pint; and mum cried her eyes out, as they always do.

The parting was no less emotional. On Sunday at seven in the morning we had to be back in barracks, and my father obliged with a lift in the family car. Mum said her goodbyes at the house; she could not face having to give way to her emotions in front of 900 stony-faced men, and the final hug would be the last one she would be able to provide for her son for the next five years. A quick press of the hand from dad at a convenient spot not too near the barracks (in case anybody saw the car, and passed caustic comment on this status symbol) and Hey presto! I was a man, a very young one at that, completely on my own for the first time in my life.

So the ultimate march through the centre of the regimental home town of Richmond and embarkation on a steamship to France were events of unparalleled significance to the adventurous seventeen-year-old, and showed the unlimited possibilities this new life held for me.

I experienced some qualms when ascending the gangplank up into the quite aged commandeered passenger liner which was to take me and a few more thousands over the sea for the first time. There seemed to be so many troops, soldiers everywhere and masses of equipment and everyone seemed to be so acclimatized to it all and I was not. There were sergeant-majors screaming their heads off, officers with pretty red bands round their caps saluting and being saluted all the time, and apparently doing little else and thousands of resigned looking troops, all years older than me, who looked as though they had been putting up with this sort of performance on countless earlier occasions.

I felt lost. When some nut merrily shouted out, 'Hope Jerry doesn't send a torpedo our way', I must say I had some slight misgivings for the first time about the sagacity of my enterprise. It had not really struck me that there was actually an enemy somewhere gunning for me. This condition and realization did not improve as Southampton receded into the distance and I did, for the first time in my young life, seem very much alone, whilst surrounded by the teeming thousands from whom I could not expect, in total, one fraction of the love I had left behind with my parents.

Arrival in the fair land of France at the port of Le Havre did, however, considerably improve my view of the future, since after settling in to a pleasant camp site in an orchard near a charming small town somewhere near Rouen I and my colleagues were lectured daily, not upon the military requirements of fighting, but on how to distinguish those ladies in the local town with whom one may consort without fear of unpleasant consequences and those who were 'unfit for human consumption'. Fortunately there was no talk or even thought of fighting, just an acceptance that there were Germans tucked up somewhere in Germany and chasing Poles all over Poland, and a vast expanse of territory dividing us from the nearest area of conflict. Our concentration was undivided from the consumption of French cheeses and wines, and those 'consumables' amongst the female French local populace who seemed to be readily available for our delight, at a price.

The starry-eyed one was rapidly becoming much impressed with the very great potential this new life seemed to offer. I suppose one of the great advantages of youth is that it is a time when one can see no further than the end of one's nose!

3
The Battle

There was no apparent break in this idyllic situation as my colleagues and I soaked ourselves in best French wine and gorged hunks of Camembert and other delights which had formerly been just names, and I greatly enjoyed my first view of a foreign country. In those comparatively spartan days any opportunities for travelling overseas were restricted to multi-millionaires, cranks or government officials and this free tour of *La belle France* was a terrific treat for this particular young hero. What a wonderful thing war was, that provided the youth of a nation with unlimited opportunities for free travel as well as the chance of performing noble deeds in defence of one's homeland.

We enjoyed an especially pleasant stay at a 'resort' called Fécamp, where my unit was posted to theoretically to guard a port, against what no one ever knew nor much cared. Presumably the view of the masters was that the Germans might suddenly appear in the harbour entrance with a few warships, completely unannounced, and my six valiant men and I would shoo them away with the Bren gun we had at last taken possession of; why exactly the French could not provide a defence for their own ports I never could quite understand. Maybe we were there to deter the occasional German agent from planting an odd bomb or two around the place, although I am not sure I would have recognized one if I had come across it (bomb, that is, nor in fact agent). However, we were invited by the monks in the local Benedictine monastery to partake of as much of their local brew – the well appreciated Benedictine liqueur – as we could consume, just in case the unthinkable should happen and it fell into German hands. What a good idea and what charitable monks to prefer the thought of it upsetting British heads than German, for the offer was accepted with alacrity and to the extent that when awakening each morning and seeking the customary mug of hot tea, I found myself feeding on a mug of Benedictine. I had a cup of Benedictine for breakfast, mid-morning break, lunch, tea and supper. The whole platoon guarding this particular post were drunk continuously for about two consecutive weeks, so I really could not rembmeber much about it other than that it was a new and novel experience to be actually non-compos-mentis for such a long period. The days were passed very happily in a haze of Benedictine and unsuccessfully chasing French belles around non-existent bollards on the quays.

'Out on guard, you bleary-eyed pot-bellied bunch of b.....ds' would come the raucous bellow of my own particular pot-bellied, red-faced, beer-swilling ignoramus of a sergeant when the time came round for my section to do guard and march or stagger precariously down to the quay of the little harbour to ensure that the Germans did not make a sudden landing. It is astonishing that none of us, in our highly inebriated state, finished up in the harbour, and just what we would have done had a German appeared from nowhere can only be left to the imagination.

I have never been able to face a glass of Benedictine since, but it served as an illustration to me, not only that I should always endeavour to avoid drinking or partaking in any similar unhealthy pastime, which may in fact have been the indirect intention of the wise monks in the first place, but also not to rely upon such delightful episodes in one's life as being everlasting; this extremely light-headed approach which we were then adopting to the obviously serious performance of carrying on a war seemed to be the generally accepted manner amongst all those with whom I was concerned at that particular time, but it was very foolhardy of us to assume that this carefree approach was all there was to war. I hoped of course that it might indeed be the case, but I soon came to realize how wrong I could be. Still, with the Germans presumably safely locked up in Germany or in Poland or some such place and the theoretical requirement of standing on guard duty at a port on the north coast of France being no more than a very tiresome theatrical performance between drinks, life was good.

One day, however, a rather more urgent and less raucous series of grunts came from the normally bellicose sergeant. The bombshell landed in our smoke-filled Benedictine-impregnated billet like a bolt from the blue.

'Pack up your gear – we are going up to the front.'

I suppose our immediate reaction was that Pot-Belly was playing a very sick joke on us, and after a brief look up at the sergeant from the heavily laden card table, we instantly resumed the absorbing game of pontoon. However, a repeat command uttered with no small degree of urgency, obliged us to pay more serious attention to the bloated one. Viewing the serious and obviously meaningful intent written all over the sergeant's exceedingly unattractive countenance, we suddenly realized he was not joking, and time suddenly stood still in the marquee posing as a canteen. You could have heard the proverbial pin drop, if there had been a floor.

My heart dropped about four feet into my boots, which did not leave it much further to go before it would be flat on the ground, and I regarded my colleagues who looked at each other in disbelief.

'Not us, mate, you've got the wrong lot.'

Gradually and unbelievably it impressed itself upon us that we were actually being called upon to go to war.

'Christ, you can't mean it, sarge,' said an utterly shattered ex-bank clerk from behind a mug of Benedictine. None of his erstwhile bank colleagues, when pushing him off with a farewell party in the pub on Richmond Green had ever said anything about going into a Front Line to fight.

'Get your bloody arses off your cots, pack and be outside in full marching order in fifteen minutes,' came the very sobering response. I am not sure whether Pot-Belly was enjoying this, or whether he too had serious misgivings about the future.

The astonished members of my platoon were not slow to give full vent to their views on the unutterable injustice of this sudden interference with the very pleasant routine which had been followed at Fécamp, but having regard to my elevated status as a section commander, I had little option but to set a good example and struggle to put things together, in particular to sober up, find bits of equipment and eventually ensure that within an hour or so my section emerged from the hut as fine figures of fighting men, albeit unwilling, still slightly intoxicated, psychologically shattered and no doubt with some belt or strap fixed on the wrong way round, shortly to be joined by the rest of the furiously muttering platoon, all of whom were hurling abrasive invectives around the orchard which would be sufficient to sour the fruit for many years to come.

'They can't really mean it,' growled an ex-dustman. 'What the hell has happened to all the regular soldiers who are supposed to be guarding the flaming country?'

They did mean it.

I had never really catered for this turn of events in my own mind. I had heard of front lines, nasty muddy things where you got bogged down for maybe years on end, hurling shells at each other and not daring to put a head above the level of the ground for fear of getting it blown off. Surely they could not mean that I was going to have to take part in some performance like that. It had never escaped my thinking that there was some element of danger involved in the course I had voluntarily undertaken, but it was only other people, and in story books, that chaps actually got killed, ended their lives in fact, or continued them with essential parts of their anatomy missing or irretrievably damaged. That could not possibly happen to one so young as I. Damn it, I had hardly started my life – in fact it had only started when I got to the fair land of France – and now there was the most distinct possibility that it might suddenly end. That was hardly fair and not in accordance with the rules of the game.

The Maginot line was impregnable, that was for sure. I had read all about it in the papers and it was quite clear the Germans would never be able to get past it. So how come we were now required to enter into the fray when there was a whole British Expeditionary Force up in Belgium and north of the Maginot to deal with any German attack in that area?

'Maybe we are only a relief unit – you know, going up for a few days' tour of duty and then back here to the Benedictine,' hopefully put forward one equally shocked lance-corporal. 'After all, we are only Territorials, surely they don't expect us to fight! Anyway, we haven't got anything to fight with.' The last statement was more or less addressed to some invisible umpire as though appealing for 'bad light' to put an end to the horrific nightmare which had so suddenly appeared.

It was a sad fact that this was the sort of feeling which predominated in our minds as we organized ourselves to board the dark green 30 cwt trucks making up the battalion convoy. The loading up of emergency rations and all available weapons and ammunition did little to reduce the tension, and the exchanges which passed around the barrack room at the same time indicated the distress we found ourselves in.

'I've got a date with that blonde bird from the tavern at eight – what the hell do I do about that?'

'Do you think we'll get any post up at the front? I'm waiting for a letter from my bird – said she was putting on weight or something – don't like the sound of it – she was going to a doc. Now how the hell do I find out what happened?'

My own fleeting thought was for my parents who themselves had probably never imagined that such an eventuality may occur. My mother would no doubt shed a few more tears, and I expect my father might even have thought it was going a bit too far. Our whole peaceful existence had been shattered in a matter of the few seconds it took Pot-Belly to scream out his instructions to get moving, so it was very upsetting when trucks eventually got going to take us nearer a front line we had only at that point of time vaguely heard of from a great and safe distance.

We set off appearing to travel east for an uncomfortably long while and after three or four hours' travelling we all began to feel a certain growing apprehension as we saw, first a few and then ever increasing lines of civilian refugees blocking the roads to the east. As is evidently customary in the British Army, no one at any level had any idea of what was going on, where we were going or what the future held, but these refugees struck the first strings of foreboding in my heart that all was not perhaps as it should be, and there was a much more serious side to this business of war after all. In fact the refugees who had to make way for our transport, indicated by their glances at us that they knew quite well we were heading in the wrong direction, the right one being west away from something they had no wish to be further involved with. That impression was given devastating support at a place near Abbeville where we arrived to find that the Germans had just bombed a troop train in the station containing about 2,000 men, and probably killed at least half of them. This was certainly the most dramatic tragedy I had to that time ever encountered and I could never properly express my horror at the sight which met our eyes and represented a terribly sudden introduction into the very sordid realities of war, so much so that our convoy had to turn around immediately and retreat a little way towards the West, much to our great relief.

The destruction we briefly were witnesses to, the mangled corpses, burning sheds, buildings and twisted metal and the hysterical confusion and noise and piteous screams of the wounded that reigned during the few minutes we were in the proximity of the station was a very short but exceedingly sharp first lesson in the horrors of warfare, many moons removed from the placidity of Fécamp and light years from the pubs of Richmond. I had never before seen a steam engine sticking up perpendicular from the ground on its cab with steam surging out all over the place; railway carriages derailed and strewn about the station entangled with the steel framework of the station building; destruction on a, to my mind, vast scale and accompanied by the much more horrifying screams of the wounded and sight of the suddenly lifeless corpses hurled about and left in weird and terrifying positions.

It was a sudden mental jolt to us, which served to awaken us from the cancer of lethargy which had until then governed our participation in the war. Although our convoy turned about immediately to put as much distance as we could between the ill-fated station and ourselves for fear of further air attack and to avoid unnecessarily clogging up the roads in the immediate neighbourhood, thereby hindering rescue work, we saw enough to ensure that we would depart from the scene well aware that we were in a war, not a drinking spree. The tragedy of the many hundreds who had died in those few moments of bombing bore ample testimony to the fact that we were in the vicinity of a well-equipped and merciless enemy, and we were the victims of unpreparedness – the result of pre-war efforts to foster peace and goodwill amongst men some of whom were not prepared to play ball. There was clearly absolutely no protection for our troops from aerial attack, and without such protection it was abundantly clear we were completely at the mercy of Hitler's well-trained Luftwaffe. We rapidly came to realize that there is no more devastating position to be in than that of being ground troops completely devoid of any aerial support or protection. There appeared to be no RAF to oppose the Luftwaffe's monopoly of the air space.

We then started a round of 'taking up positions' and relinquishing them almost immediately after. The 'taking up' consisted of digging some trenches, siting our Bren machine gun in some suitable position covering a bridge or crossroads and brewing up tea, supposedly but not necessarily in that order. Fortunately for us, however, at the positions we took up nothing much came our way, and ultimately after forty-eight hours or so we were ordered back on to the lorries like sheep into a pen for a retreat and welcome jaunt off to the west. The only notable event that came my way before I left, which was very early in the morning, was that a herd of cows which had been in a field adjoining the orchard in which we were all trying to get some hour or two of sleep suddenly panicked and took fright from the gunfire and ran through the orchard. I awoke to see the udders of a flying cow passing over me at great speed, which was more disturbing at that time than the proximity of the German Panzer.

Henceforth the wretched man Rommel wreaked havoc with the British front lines. Things happened which starry-eyed youngsters had never even remotely dreamed about. I retain a general impression of living in a perpetual state of fear of being annihilated by dive-bombing Stukas (the principal German fighter-bomber of the time) at any moment, of living through days and nights without any scheduled or undisturbed sleep period, be it only a matter of a couple of hours, and eating an occasional bite of anything reasonably edible which came my way, again very irregularly. The whole business of living became very haphazard and uncertain.

We seemed to move from place to place apparently defending odd points that might ultimately be a location where German armoured units might appear – corners of bridges, intersections of roads etc. – but what exactly we were supposed to do if they did appear remains to this day a complete mystery. We had anti-tank rifles, those great heavy things which we lugged around and which were euphemistically called 'personal weapons', but we did not of course have any ammunition for them. Wherever we went we were strafed by German Stukas against which there was absolutely no defence; various brilliant governments at home in the thirties had extolled the virtues of disarmament to the point that Germany now remained the only country to have an effective air force, and so became king of all it surveyed. Shadows no doubt of 'Unilateral Disarmament' policies of the future.

This chasing around defending strategic points got very tiring and unsettling. We never seemed to eat, except an occasional can of Machonicies (which, again for the uninitiated was a robust Argentinian tinned stew which may have dated from World War I) washed down liberally with the inevitable mugs of stewed sweet tea also of uncertain vintage. I got so tired that, after having no sleep at all for about four days, I fell asleep eventually whilst actually walking off guard duty in the middle of the night in a forest somewhere, and walked straight into the corrugated iron side of a Nissen hut. The resultant clang of my rifle against the iron sufficed to wake not only our own encampment but probably the whole adjoining German lines, wherever they may have been. It was one of my less popular performances.

Whilst lying in a ditch somewhere awaiting the passing of Stukas, I looked up to see a sign nailed to a gate saying 'Private – College d'Eu'. An extraordinary coincidence, as my father had been sent as a boy to school at the College d'Eu in France, and, as far as I knew, was ultimately expelled with another British lad for chasing French girls. It was obviously not an hereditary trait since I had little opportunity to follow my father's footsteps but in any case on the occasion of my visit to Eu there appeared to be a distinct shortage of girls to chase.

Wherever we went there were the inevitable swarms of refugees, none of whom could be trusted since the Germans had infiltrated 'fifth column' agents amongst them. The fifth column was organized by the Germans originally pre-war through long term indoctrination of French civilians with a view to enlisting their eventual support in the event of a war between the two countries. It was based on the theory that France would fare better by being an ally of the powerful new Germany than siding with the British who had historically been the enemy of France and would only let France down in a war against Germany, and defend their own island shores. It had many supporters amongst the French, especially in the North where there was a noticeable shortage of sympathy for the British following the devastation from World War I, and events which were to follow may have, at least in the short term, provided some credence to the views.

The fifth column was now considerably stepped up, and as the Germans advanced into France they set up a network of captured French civilians who would then join the lines of French refugees, frequently accompanied by disguised German Intelligence officers, passing through the forward Allied positions, and radio back information on the disposition and strength of the

British units. Such refugees were impossible to distinguish from the genuine article and an encounter with groups of refugees at one of the positions we had taken up adjoining an important cross-roads where a small group of five civilians approached the strategic position being guarded by my section of six braves and myself, went something as follows:

Me: 'Halt. Who goes there?'

Refugee: 'Comment?'

Me: 'Who goes there?'

Refugee: 'Qu'est ce que ce Hugo There.'

Me: (Getting slightly irritated and feeling a little helpless) 'Who the hell are you?'

Refugee: 'Comment?'

Me: 'Oh, get to hell out of it.'

Refugees shuffle on and move into the distance, whence is faintly heard, *'Fritz, hast Du etwas zu rauchen?'* ('Fritz, have you got a smoke?') It was hopeless trying to stem the continual infiltration of French traitors and German soldiers through a front line which in any case had no specific delineation and the whole point of manning these strategic points seemed quite lost on us, and for that matter, on my superior NCOs and officers. But anyway we were ever mindful of the sole duty of His Majesty's soldiers which was to obey without question; which is what we did, but it seemed to fail miserably in the general attempt at stemming the flood of German troops into north France.

The actual plight and horror of the lines of those refugees has stayed with me ever since, and especially in a world today where civilian refugees appear to be evident only too frequently, for it appears the civilians do the suffering in war now and not the military. 'If only the persons who were responsible for starting this wretched war could now see the fruits of their labours' I thought as I encountered the real impact of the refugee problem at its worst. Somewhere on a main road leading, of course, from east to west, our convoy had been confronted with a line of refugees which must have stretched for five or six miles. Obviously it had a devastating effect upon the lines of communication for the defending army, since our convoy had been required to slow down our journey to the east and in fact halt at the wayside to allow time for our very harassed military police equipped with motor-cycles to try and clear a way through the milling mob. Whilst we were so stopped we did of course become very vulnerable targets to air attack by the ever-present Stukas, who held complete control of the skies in the absence of Allied planes of any sort.

The lines of refugees proceeded on foot, on bicycle, by horse and cart and for the more affluent, in the family car. In a reasonable sized bus you could of course take the whole village. All were laden to the skies with all the family goods they could carry with them; even cookers, fires, chairs and other furniture were strapped and tied to the tops of magnificent American motor cars, and carts filled with all the household goods that could be loaded on to them, with Grandma perched precariously on top of it all, would be drawn by one puffing horse which resisted with all it had, which was not a lot, the continual persuasion of its master to hasten it and its cargo to greater effort towards safety.

Every so often the whole sad convoy of hopeless and despairing humanity would be suddenly thrown into utter confusion and chaos as the dreaded Stuka dive-bombers would fly down low over the lines of refugees with screaming engines and the horrific and deafening noise of the rat-tat-tat of countless machine guns firing at the helpless civilians who would be forced, in the questionable desire for survival or maybe just as an automatic reflex, to scatter into the ditches at the side of the road for what shelter from the rain of death they could find; and then, with the passing of the harbingers of death from the sky, they would reform in the road to count the dead and wounded, amongst the piteous sounds of wailing as each family discovered its particular loved ones, even pets, who had been mown down and left either mercifully dead or less mercifully badly wounded to suffer the searing pains of such wounds with no available medical resources to aid them; Grandma mercilessly gunned down from her perch on the wardrobe surmounting the cart load of family goods and now left to die in agony in the adjoining ditch under the smashed remnants of family goods and chattels; and all this amongst a mass of wrecked trucks, carts, dead horses, personal and domestic goods littered everywhere, resulting in even more chaos than existed to commence with for the poor victims of the egotistic military aims of Adolf Hitler to have to endure further. The Germans would have explained away the attacks by coldly stating that there may have been Allied troops amongst the refugees, and in fact there were very many French soldiers hastening west away from the conflict who had abandoned their weapons and tell-tale uniforms and now used their greater agility and strength to overtake the slow moving mass. Maybe it was part of their strategic plan to cause chaos in the lines of communication to the front to delay reinforcements passing along the roads. This they succeeded in doing, but any sane, thinking person would be repulsed at the performance and horrified to find that there was apparently no point at which the attacker would stop the mindless slaughter of innocent civilians in the single-minded effort of achieving a so-called victory.

It was when we were stopped in the shelter of some trees near a village that a red-faced warrant officer of considerable stature and little charm took advantage of the plight of the refugees to improve his own lot and relieve his own terrible suffering – lack of 'crumpet' (Army slang for 'birds', not the flying type). A large American car had stopped near us, full of men, women and children and laden as usual to the skies, and a young woman, in fact not more than a teenager, had walked over to our truck and asked for some petrol. Clearly I could not let her have petrol, otherwise we would finish up having to supply the whole refugee column, so I refused reluctantly and the girl went back to the car.

'What's she want?' the red-faced one had asked.

'She wanted to buy some petrol,' I replied, quite innocently.

'Nice-looking bird' the red-faced one had said, looking very thoughtful and staring hopefully at the American car, the occupants of which were also staring hopefully at our truck.

'I think I'll go over and talk to them,' said red-face, as though having come to a great decision about something, and duly strode off in the direction of the car. A rather long drawn-out conversation seemed to be in progress and I was surprised that red-face, who spoke no French, seemed to be getting along so well, but it subsequently turned out that the conversation he was engaged upon did not really require a great knowledge of the French language. He returned with the piece of crumpet and carrying the two cans, and it was fairly obvious that a satisfactory deal had been negotiated.

'All of you out of that truck,' he peremptorily ordered the three of us who had remained in the truck whilst the rest were on guard somewhere ensuring we were not suddenly attacked by a squadron of tanks.

'Quick, out of it.' Red-face could hardly contain himself and assisted with great pleasure the young girl into the back of the truck, where spare five gallon cans of petrol were kept. He then very carefully closed the rear tarpaulin cover to ensure privacy, and with a knowing wink, instructed his corporal to make sure that no one entered the truck. Some twenty minutes or so later a satisfied and even redder-faced creature emerged and following him a wide-eyed young French maiden who may have lost any virginity that may have remained to her before entry into the truck, but had gained two gallons of petrol which may well have helped her family put forty miles more between them and the advancing savages. I was thus able to learn rapidly the value in life of being in a strong bargaining position when undertaking such delicate negotiations.

The full enormity of the horrific plight of these refugees only became completely apparent to me when I translated the situation into much more personal terms. As a spectacle, the machine-gunning of defenceless refugees remained a blandly overawing, stupefying, tragic act, from which we soldiers would, with some luck, get back into our lorries and drive away from; we would never truly understand the full drama being played out on that dusty minor road overladen with distraught, tensed humans trying to cross an open space without being so unfortunate as to appear within the sights of a brave German Luftwaffe officer seeking the rewards he would surely have heaped upon him for causing the maximum human suffering which he could at that moment inflict. But to really understand the resultant human tragedy one had to exchange places with the terrified and hapless victims.

Where on earth did all this human flotsam come from? Who are these people who are reduced to offering their daughter's virginity in exchange for a can of petrol and suffer endless slaughter from the skies? How did this state of humiliation ever arise for people who seemed to be no different in outward appearance to me? Could I imagine my mother and father loading the family Rover up with all the household goods it would carry, topping it up with my grandmother, and then leave our home full of our possessions, clothing etc. which really constituted our very existence open to any old marauders who lacked the moral convictions to prevent them from stooping to loot other people's property, and then taking to the road to be suddenly machine-gunned and bombed from the air and for my mother to emerge from the nearest ditch to find my father with one arm blown off? I shuddered at the very thought of it. One may be forgiven for thinking that such dramas always happen to the other person; it may be more realistic, however, to appreciate that some time, maybe not this time round, it may happen to you, and let's hope you are ready for it when that day comes.

These French and Belgian refugees were just the same sort of people as I and my own family, and had been living at peace with their neighbours and under whatever security their respective politicians had been able to negotiate for them, having the same hopes and personal problems as their counterparts in England; and now, thanks to the inability of their elected representatives and the single-minded vicious and unopposed dreams of a mad German ex-painter and corporal, their lives had been almost instantaneously left in ruins and they themselves reduced to the most degrading and humiliating suffering, a seemingly unending assault upon their bodies from the skies by persons unknown.

One may be forgiven for trying to trace the connection between the politicians surrounded by the ultimate in personal comfort who, after a satisfactory lunch at the club, ordered the war to commence and the real victims, these refugees, who are the ultimate recipients of the dubious benefits of that command. Presumably whilst there continue to be aggressors in society, and aggression is an important element in human nature, there must likewise be those whose misfortune it is to pay the cost of such aggression – not just politicians and the militia but the defenceless civilians who can do little more than place their faith in their leaders (and in God) that they will not become victims of the screaming, hysterical rabble-rousing aggressor capable of issuing a sufficiently plausible argumentation to establish a following of like-minded morons known often as 'nationalists'. Obviously, in this instance, the politicians let them down (and God). Maybe next time (may the same God forbid) the democratic process may have become so powerful throughout the land that the general public may demand to be invited to vote before a military assault is undertaken. If the real results of war are sufficiently known to the voters, the verdict of such a vote would, I am sure, be a foregone conclusion. But then memories tend to be pretty short, and propaganda in these days of instant communication can be very convincing, especially if the recipient is given little time for reflection and is not educated to think for himself.

The spasmodic 'taking up positions' continued for several days (or was it weeks?) and only on one occasion did I actually get round to firing a Bren machine gun in earnest. I fired into a wood where German troops were allegedly about to attack our positions which were providing cover for yet another retreat. The wretched gun made a ghastly noise, and although I aimed it in the general direction of the woods, my innermost thoughts retained the hope that I missed actually hitting any poor soul. I am not too sure that I am made of the stern stuff that the best warriors are made of – I would take little delight in killing or even wounding or maiming an animal, let alone one of my own species and this out-of-character display of aggression was probably brought on solely in a reckless attempt to avoid slaughter by one or more of my own species who appeared to consider my presence in turn a threat to them.

Once again we were relieved from this position, so uncomfortably adjacent to the theoretical front line, and loaded back on to the 30 cwt dark green army Bedford trucks to enjoy a brief journey which we were all pleased to notice was in the general direction of the west. However, this was not to be for long, and we soon got heavily caught up again in the ever-increasing lines of refugees, as we turned about and travelled again east, ultimately reaching Amiens and the Lille areas and seeing names of places that conjured up considerable fear into our little hearts. They were the names of famous World War I battles where similar slaughter had been enacted only some quarter of a century earlier. Very clearly these places were now facing a new battle but a battle of a very different type to the long drawn-out trench warfare and sieges of World War I. No longer was there any evidence of a static line with gains being made by one side or the other amounting to a few yards at a time. There now seemed to be a new set of rules operating whereby no one seemed to be allowed to know where the front line exactly was if, in fact, there was any such thing as a front line. The introduction of a new word, *Blitzkrieg*, said it all, for now the front line was where the *Blitz* or lightning happened to strike and that was a completely unknown element and like the proverbial lightning, it never seemed to strike twice in the same place. The Panzer column attacks by Rommel's spearheads, combined with an effective fifth column support inside France, obviously had rendered traditional battle line tactics useless.

Everywhere there were troops, British, French and some remnants of other nationalities and the whole atmosphere was very far removed from the cosy corner at Fécamp. We heard incessant gun fire which seemed to come from all directions, but it was clear that a heavy battle was raging to the north of us. We were ordered into a variety of different positions, mostly at road intersections and bridges, and commanded to shoot up any tanks or German troops who might appear, but we were not then made aware of the fact that an enormous troop evacuation was taking place at Dunkirk just north of us and some fifty miles away, and that we were supposed to be a sort of far perimeter guard for the evacuation. We were unaware of the vast operation taking place on the coast, for where we were there did not appear to be any great excitement to relieve the monotony of deserted and uninviting woods, digging personal trenches and filling them in, loading up and unloading etc, although we kept on being promised action at any moment; maybe I should say 'threatened', for we were not all that keen on becoming heroes, especially dead ones so early in our lives. We built barricades which probably would not have stopped an Austin 7, let alone a tank, built camouflaged shelters and organized some sort of base. Then as soon as we had made ourselves comfortable with a mug of tea and a tin of stew, off we would go to start the same performance again elsewhere.

We would of course have been very much more concerned had we known that at that particular time the rest of the British Army, and in particular the Regular Army units in France, were being loaded on to ships at Dunkirk and removed altogether from the European mainland, to leave the defence of France to the remnants of the French Army and a few highly unqualified units such as we ourselves represented. The French have been critical of this evacuation in historical narratives published since the war, and those of us who were situated in the outer defence perimeter around Dunkirk had no idea, at least at our level, of what was going on, and if we had known, we would probably have been no more overjoyed at the 'victory' of Dunkirk than the French critics ultimately were. The best that can be said was that it all turned out all right in the end, but we were patently unaware of that fact at that time. Doubtless it was a great evacuation, but we and our French allies seemed to be the sacrificial goats.

The mystery as to why the German forces, advancing with such fantastic speed from the south and east towards Dunkirk and the Channel Ports, inexplicably halted about 22nd May to give enough time for the evacuation of Dunkirk to be organized and substantially completed, remains a mystery to this day. War historians have proffered various theories, ranging from German concern as to the vulnerability of exposed flanks to Hermann Goering's desire to annihilate the British army from the air at the evacuation ports, thereby saving the German army some effort and loss of life and for further assaults in the future (and no doubt to enhance Goering's own considerable stature). One thing must be certain and that is that if those German Panzer commanders had realized what a pathetic ill-equipped bunch of 'civilian' soldiers were holding the territory between them and the ports, they could not possibly have found it necessary to halt the advance for a couple of days to get fresh wind. If they had just kept the steam roller going it would have flattened us, and there was, in fact, no one to threaten their flanks.

However, it may just have been that this apparently ridiculous 'taking up positions' all over the place giving some sort of appearance of considered activity on the British side of the front line, wherever that may have been, gave a semblance of military manoeuvre, no doubt related back to the German Army Command via the 'fifth column' and other espionage systems and probably grossly exaggerating the true strength and ability of our forces and may well have influenced the Germans in halting their advance, thereby enabling 350,000 trained soldiers to return to the United Kingdom and fight another day. If it did, well and good, and there were certainly many courageous rearguard actions to support that view, but I for one, not included amongst the 350,000, would probably have felt pretty cheesed off about it all if I had known at that time that the cream of my army was being removed back home and I and my Bren gun, without any ammunition, was being left in its place. I suppose that it was fortunate for the 'lambs' that they did not know they were already at the door of the slaughterhouse.

Eventually we took up a more permanent position on the outskirts of a wood, and were told that this was to be our final defensive position. My section was allocated an area to defend of apparently several acres at the edge of the wood overlooking open fields, and an officer came around and solemnly warned me, as section NCO and leader of the motley group of seven men good and true, that we were to remain at our posts come what may 'to the last man, the last round of ammunition'. Very impressive, especially since we did not have many men or much idea of where an attack was likely to come from, and my seven brave men were hardly able to cover a front line defensive position of several acres. Nor did we have many rounds of ammunition, and as the officer departed in his jeep I somehow felt that he had delivered a sentence of death upon us. This was in fact just about what he had done, if he had been taken seriously, but I felt a bit too young at eighteen to die, and so did my mates. Our motley assembly, consisting of a dustman, a theatrical technician, a butcher's boy, a surveyor's clerk and a couple of building labourers, did not seem to be of the stuff from which heroic 'last ditch' stands are made. My whole section began to feel a little less patriotic and not quite so brave as we had previously felt when at Fécamp. Any last trace of glitter which may appear to have been attached to these particular martial arts had long since worn off and been replaced by deep scepticism, even amongst such young innocents as we undoutedly were. This grand theatrical speech, 'to the last man and the last round of ammunition' which were the officer's actual words, seemed so incongruous and impractical when issued by an ex-bank-under-manager to our squad of youthful cannon fodder. It seemed like something out of a story book from the First World War.

'Do you think he means it?' timorously queried George, one of the building labourers, who no doubt at that moment would have preferred to be standing holding the ladder steady at a building site, with a nice cup of tea in the offing, rather than having just had an effective sentence of death passed on him.

'Of course he bloody well means it,' I replied as sternly as an eighteen-year-old inexperienced 'rooky' could muster. After all, I was solely in charge, and was obliged by military code of discipline to carry out my superior officer's command, however inane, and had at least to show a bold front, even though my teeth may have chattered whilst issuing immediate orders.

'Start digging trenches, stack arms and ammo, check food stocks,' I imperiously commanded. The verbal responses should not be printed, but despite the rather obvious unwillingness of the participants in the charade, we dug ourselves a very fine communal trench or main hole and a couple of slit-trench outposts, covered them with branches of trees and foliage and shortly became fairly invisible and most uncomfortable. The local rabbits must have wondered who their new neighbours were.

Time went by and nothing much happened. There was the ominous and incessant sound of warfare going on all around us, shelling, machine gun fire, etc, and the inevitable dive-bombing attacks, but nobody came our way and the Stuka shells fortunately missed. We spent the whole night in our various trenches, hardly daring to make too much noise, and arguing fairly silently but nonetheless formidably, over the division of the very sparse amount of rations which we had been left, and which we consumed virtually in the course of the first banquet.

By the following morning, nothing had happened.

'We can't bloody well stop here forever,' complained a very nervous theatrical technician who no doubt would have found life more enjoyable at that time ringing up the curtain at the Kingston Empire.

'Look, Corp,' (the unsavoury abbreviation for corporal!) 'if we bloody well stay here forever, the Jerries could go right past us and we would get cut off from our unit.'

Good thinking, from one whom I am sure would go far, at least in the all-important matter of self-preservation. But we had been ordered to stay put until the last drop of blood had been shed, so stay put we must. Or must we?

Suddenly all hell broke loose in the area, and we were strafed (attacked by dive-bombing German Stukas which were used to wipe out forward positions before the tanks moved in to attack on land), bombed, machine-gunned and generally unpleasantly dealt with by our Teutonic cousins for some hours. Eventually, after a particularly vicious succession of attacks by Stukas who seemed to be singling out inoffensive trees as their prime target, and equally vicious mortar fire somewhere in the immediate, in fact far too immediate, vicinity the fracas died down a bit. My section, who still all seemed to be there, emitted a variety of 'Bloody Hells' and 'Christ Almighty' and various other fervent supplications to the Deity and some less pious and more obscene expletives.

When it comes to the crunch, I do not quite understand how any Territorial volunteers, like our little bunch of seven dedicated civilian beer swampers and card players, could have been trained to withstand the impact of the actual 'Front Line' assault for the first time. Admittedly we had little with which to defend ourselves against armoured vehicles or fighter aircraft but the actual experience was something I had never really cottoned on to. When considering such an eventuality previously, I had envisioned muddy trenches and nasty Germans shooting at your head when it appeared over the top of the trench; possibly, and at worst, a horde of the same nasty Germans jumping into your trench and attacking it with bayonets fixed, revolvers, etc. This was 'Front Line' war as portrayed by the various films and story books I had read since 'the Great War', and this was more or less what we expected. All the field training in Richmond Park was based on the same sort of premise.

What had just occurred was a vastly different experience. The noise of attacking Stukas with machine guns blazing and swooping down directly at us, the noise being accentuated by some mechanical device which I gather was attached to the planes' weapons to increase the impact of the attack and to transform an ordinary rat-tat-tat into a thunderous and deafening onslaught to terrify the recipients on the ground which it did with great efficiency, together with the noise of exploding shells crashing apparently all around us and millions of tracer bullets providing additional evidence of their deadly existence by means of white tails illuminating their trajectories all over the place, was all something we just had not imagined nor bargained for. The impact on our nervous system was horrific. I don't care how courageous a soldier is normally expected to be, he would have to be an absolute idiot not to be terrified of this lot, and as a fairly normal bunch of young butcher boys, building labourers and surveyors' clerks, this bunch were simply not geared up to withstand this sort of treatment. I think it was probably the noise more than anything else which was most terrifying, since in fact none of us was even scratched. Maybe the Stukas were not actually aiming at us or maybe they were just pretty bad shots, but no one seemed to suffer any damage. The explosions of shells etc. seemed to be very close, but again nothing actually landed on us. At this time on the edge of the wood, as later on under similar circumstances of 'Front Line' confrontation, it seemed to me that it was the noise, above all else, which was most demoralizing, not the actual thought of being on the receiving end of a missile. The noise seemed to effectively break down any rational thinking processes and produce an immediate and urgent desire to 'get the hell out of it'.

'We can't bloody well stay here,' whined the bank clerk, very reasonably. 'Do something, Corp.' As though I were able to raise my arms as some modern day Moses and bring down the wrath of God to crush the offending German Stukas and Panzers to smithereens.

However, very precariously I ventured forth from my position and together with one other member of the section crept down a short way along a track at the edge of the wood; we kept our heads well down, for on one side were open fields and the other the dark mysterious forest. At a distance of about 300 metres we suddenly came upon the most horrific signs of butchery and carnage that can be imagined. Apparently all the bombing etc. had been directed not at us, but at a French artillery unit which had been passing down a road at the end of the track. When I got there, accompanied very appropriately by my stalwart the butcher boy, there was an eerie silence and nothing stirred - it could not stir for everything was dead. There were numerous dismembered carcases of horses, numerous French corpses all in horrific stances, and a most ghastly stink of death. For both of us, surveyor's clerk and butcher, it was a scene not only to turn our stomachs but to shatter the nervous system completely. This was a close-up of death en masse, and a far cry from the mundane office in Central London for which I would happily have exchanged my present situation and from the acceptable earlier experiences further west in France. Those poor magnificent horses - why should they have to suffer so abominably for the follies of men? The starry-eyed one was beginning to see that some formerly cherished and accepted views about the sagacity and goodness of his fellow humans may not be quite so well founded.

This must have been a French artillery troop of about fifty or so men having artillery pieces drawn by horses. Now the whole unit was shattered and must have received several direct hits from the bombing attacks which had left both horses and men splattered amongst the trees and the guns and carriages so much scrap metal.

There was nothing we could obviously do to assist, for the dead appeared to be terrifically dead, and there was no knowing whether any advance German snipers or patrols may be in the area, so we turned round with some alacrity and retraced our steps, if that is the expression for breaking into a rapid gallop to return to the relative safety of our trench and foxholes.

Having safely got back to the rest of the section from this carnage, and feeling at my tender age the first strains of responsibility creeping up, I really began to wonder whether I was right in complying too rigidly with the officer's command and fight to the last drop of someone else's blood like a good soldier would. Maybe I should use a modicum of common sense and preserve, at least for another day, the lives of my six noble colleagues and even my own. Being motivated, regrettably, at all times, by rational instinct rather than noble intent and not really being able to understand how seven virtually unarmed young men could withstand the well-heeled forces that Adolf Hitler had been busily preparing for ten years to murder us with, and spurred on by yet another Stuka attack and lack of anything to eat or drink, I gave the no doubt cowardly and dastardly order to up anchor and get to hell out of it, much to the relief of my section of warriors, especially the dustman! I do not feel that the course of the war would have been very different if we had remained in our position, and I was quite sure the course of our own lives would have been substantially shortened.

Unfortunately I was not at all certain in which direction to lead my charges and a certain amount of democracy, unacceptable though it may be according to the Army Manuals of Conduct, entered into the decision, with every member of the section simultaneously indicating his views, all of which differed. We did not actually resort to a ballot, for I autocratically put my foot down and led the still furiously debating group off in the direction I thought looked farthest removed from the position where the unfortunate French artillery men had met their fate. It was indeed a lucky guess for it apparently led us back to where we had first disembarked from our company trucks. Not that there was any longer any evidence of trucks or indeed any sign of life. To cap it all, when we arrived eventually at where I believed our company HQ to be, it was completely deserted, and all had fled, which made me feel decidedly better about the whole thing.

After a lot of trudging around and eventually coming across other units and stragglers, we did ultimately and quite accidently track down our company. I reported somewhat sheepishly to my platoon commander who, despite his earlier instructions to me to remain come what may at our post, seemed nevertheless reasonably happy to see us again. He told me that they had sent a dispatch rider to tell us to evacuate our position but the poor chap had not been seen since, presumably killed. I felt I had best believe that, for dispatch riders were certainly at that time the most vulnerable of our forces and seemed to be sitting ducks anywhere near the front line, perched on their motor bikes and providing good target practice for the many German snipers concealed in the woods and in the treetops around.

After procuring some sort of a meal and thirty-five winks, we then took off at nightfall, in full company transport of about ten to fifteen trucks, towards the wonderful west, with slight hopes in our breasts of something better for the future. These hopes were somewhat rudely shattered when, whilst travelling down a very narrow road in the middle of the night, we encountered some vehicles travelling in the opposite direction. Normally no great disaster and one which may be eventually satisfactorily overcome by the usual exchange of expletives and altercations between the drivers of the opposing transports, with the gentlemen amongst them giving way; the trouble however, this time was that the opposing transport happened to be a section of German Panzer. Why exactly it should have been travelling from west to east – that is, from the rear British lines towards the British front line we had no time to enquire, but no doubt this was a very clear indication of the state of uncertainty which then existed amongst those whose job it was to draw up the battle lines.

The result was chaos of the first order. The Germans opened fire with all they had, which was a lot, and the occupants of the trucks, including my braves and I, just jumped off and fled across an adjoining field, pursued by millions of rounds of tracer bullets and all kinds of other high explosive missiles. This was my first record run, to be beaten shortly in another thrilling 1,000 metre world record attempt, but it was amazing how fast I moved across that field, having no idea of where I was going except that it was definitely in a direction away from the all-powerful tanks and their reign of death. We all ran and ran, and the whole company was completely split up and disintegrated, everyone charging off in different directions. All we could see in the distance in the pitch darkness was the red glow in the sky from our blazing trucks which the Germans had fired before the tanks nonchalantly pushed them to one side, quite casually carrying on with their journey; and a continuous stream of tracer bullets and explosions lit everything up all around us and it was very obvious, at a glance, that there no longer remained any effective centre of control for our company; in fact, there did not appear any longer to be any company.

There were fields stretching both sides of us and woods beyond, and with a sea of tracer and machine gun fire being very apparent in all directions, the only sensible course left was in a direction well away from the burning trucks and the road, which by now was of course, very definitely in the hands of the enemy. The only possibility left to us was to distance ourselves from the scene of the holocaust, in the sacred cause of self-preservation. The whole unit was completely split up in different directions, and very many killed, and it was quite obvious that no re-organization of the unit was anymore possible at that location. Whatever happened to my own particular section I had no idea. Everyone went their own way on a mission of survival and there was no opportunity amongst the hail of bullets and shells to order a roll-call and inspect arms.

Now I really was on my Jack Jones. I had no idea where I was or what to do on a pitch black night in a field somewhere in northern France, with no living creatures appearing anywhere around. I stumbled across many ditches, barbed wire, filled my boots with best quality French cow dung and generally got into a right mess physically and even worse mentally before I eventually arrived at a road along which after a while came a truck moving

slowly without lights. I waved it down, which was a very precarious thing to
to do in view of the fact that it had no lights and appeared to be driven in
pitch darkness and very likely to run one down; and moreover I had no idea
whether it was British or German. It turned out to be French, and a
sympathetic bunch of French soldiers, furiously on the retreat, allowed me to
join them in the back.

I had no idea whether they knew where they were going, but at least it was
their country and they must know something about the place, which was a lot
more than I did.

We crept along through the night and as it got lighter towards dawn we
speeded up, being occasionally the subject of machine gun attacks which
ripped holes through the canvas sides of the truck and somewhat unsettled us
all, but whether the machine guns were British, French or German, who
knows?

The intentions of my new-found French colleagues was to reach a port,
Calais, Boulogne or what have you. This seemed a generally pretty good idea
to me too, so I stuck with them giving vent to my best school French which
must have mixed rather incongruously with the loud and very verbose and no
doubt rather coarse cursing and swearing which seemed to represent the
main drift of the conversation between my new comrades.

After a lot of driving, and at about nine o'clock in the morning, we arrived
outside some coastal town called St Valéry-en-Caux. And boy! was there or
was there not chaos in this place. My heart dropped well below my knees at
the scene which confronted me. We had driven as far as we could, which was
an open field overlooking the town and port, and there we dismounted to
make further progress to the port on foot, which was the only way left to
proceed. In front of us the roads into the town were completely blocked by
countless thousands of British and French army vehicles of all types – mostly
rendered useless by smashed vital parts before their occupants had departed
on foot to the port to see if there was any hope of getting on a ship. St Valéry
is a small port and surrounded by cliffs. It was thus extremely vulnerable to
military attack. In a vain attempt to seek any sort of ship or even rowing
boat, many thousands of hopefuls had entered into this trap and were now
caught up in a bowl of death and destruction as the Germans, holding the
advantageous cliff-top positions, picked off their ensnared victims at their
ease.

I went down a road which led into the town and harbour, the road itself
being completely blocked with smashed army vehicles, three abreast jeeps,
three tonners, artillery tractors; you name it and it was there, and my little
heart sank exceedingly low to see such wanton destruction and wholesale
abandonment of British war material. The immobilizing of these vehicles
was of course the last duty of the drivers before abandonment, but I
presumed that eventually the Germans must have got a pretty good haul of
captured trucks and vehicles generally.

The town had been taken over by the remnants of the 51st Highland
Division and there were literally thousands and thousands of British and
French troops around, looking for boats or anything that would float sixty

to seventy miles across the Channel. I gathered that one or two small ships had got away before I arrived, but there was nothing there at that time which would float, just many thousands of soldiers caught in a bowl with German mortar and machine gun posts on the overlooking cliffs and tanks further out driving more and more troops to the slaughter, and slaughter it was.

I came across a sort of cave in which were huddled a hundred or so French and a few British. One of the British was an officer who was injured severely in the leg, and due to the vast overcrowding people were continually bashing into the injured leg, so I took up position as protector of the leg for a while, but then felt that this was an unsatisfactory situation because (1) a shell may explode in the mouth of the cave and we would all be buried alive, and (2) it was not in the vocabulary of a brave British soldier to act as nursemaid to a wounded officer, and, anyway, was I not funking it by not going out into the general mêlée and slaughter and getting wiped out with the rest? It was probably the former consideration which made me ultimately move from the cave, which by then had become a repository for sick, wounded and dead and was stinking to high heaven, so out I went. I had to leave the officer with an improvised shelter for his leg and the hope that he would be able to keep it out of harm's way, but what then would be the fate of the poor man and his leg one could only leave to the imagination.

In the town, or what was left of it, were groups of soldiers of all nationalities running about trying to shelter from the incessant downpour of shells and machine gun fire. I took shelter in an abandoned house which had been and was still then in the process of being ravaged by soldiers. Each room had been entered into, and private goods, clothing, etc. were strewn all over the place. I was astonished to find that people had so much concern to steal other people's property when they themselves were facing imminent death or at best incarceration. Anyway I left the marauding mobs to it and followed a route to the beach which was being taken by the less mercenary majority.

The beach at St Valéry is a miserable affair and is simply a stone and pebble strip at the foot of cliffs some 200 feet high or more, rising sheer at the side. When the tide was fairly high, as it then was, the available beach was not more than some 30 to 40 feet wide from the foot of the cliffs to the water, and there was just no way up those cliffs from the beach. I had gathered that there was a vague possibility that a ship or ships of some sort lay off the coast of the adjoining town and harbour to the north called Veules-les-Roses and if one ran along the beach at the foot of the cliffs to this town, one could maybe get on a boat of some sort. The town was rumoured to be about two or three miles away. This therefore seemed to me to be the only practical way forward, since it was abundantly clear that by remaining in St Valéry I would only ultimately become a victim of the shells or machine gun fire, or both.

So off I went on the second most notable run of my short life. The trouble was that the beach was covered by German machine gun posts located on an adjoining cliff top which had the whole run of the beach in its sights as far as could be seen. So I moved very, very fast indeed along the beach, frequently passing less fortunate young men who had succumbed to the relentless machine gun fire. What fun those Jerries must have had, I thought, so well and comfortably situated with nobody to fire at them and no aerial attack to contend with (for the British did not appear to have an air force) and serving with considerable relish their Fatherland by mowing down a pretty defenceless enemy, whilst the miserable vanquished did not have an earthly chance to retaliate. War must be great if you are winning, although I also felt that even then it must have its moral shortcomings, if not physical; it is pretty uncomfortable, however, if you are virtually defenceless. Relentlessly mowing down scores of young men may be a joyous pastime to some, especially to those who had been sufficiently indoctrinated by propaganda to hate and to kill, but if I had been in that position I think that the task of some obviously killing with such awful ease would have left me in later years with substantial misgivings about the whole horrific performance. I suppose each of those German machine gunmen may have derived enormous pleasure from his efforts on that day, or maybe they just shrugged their shoulders and said, 'It is my duty to the Fatherland', but I wonder whether any of them got around to questioning to himself, 'What am I doing?'

Anyway, in a frenzied attempt to evade the furious onslaught, I ran on and at one spot, where the cliffs adjoining the beach formed a projection, I had to circumnavigate the pile of dead corpses of those who had gone before but got no further. An ever growing pile of young men who did not want to finish their lives in such a useless and untimely manner, left lying on a beach in north France in a variety of horrific stances which would have torn to shreds the hearts of many loved ones at home had they been able to see the dreadful end to which their nearest and dearest had been subjected. Not a pretty sight, but one which no doubt the proud and efficient manufacturers of German machine guns would have been satisfied to observe. The pile must at the time I reached it have consisted of at least fifty to a hundred bodies (I did not stop to count!) and no doubt the number grew as the machine guns trained on the spot continued their merciless onslaught. It was at this spot where I accelerated to a four minute mile pace, and amazingly enough, made it round the gruesome pile of human debris. Having passed this impediment, if a mound of dead and wounded young men could be so termed, I ran on, and lo and behold, there before me and round the bend a small ship came into view, lying just some hundred yards or so off the coast.

How foolish one can be in desperation and panic. It was a ship, a thing that usually floats on the water and could presumably float in the direction of Blighty if so propelled, so everyone made a dive for it – but it was pretty obvious the ship, maybe a 500 ton or so vessel, was not going anywhere until the tide came up, and by that time it was going out. However, it presumably floated and was the only possibility I or any of the teeming thousands around me could see of travelling closer to our homeland, so I half waded, half swam out to it and clambered on to a deck littered with all manner of human flotsam.

I found a place on deck with difficulty and lay down exhausted next to a French officer one side and a French civilian on the other, wedged up like sardines. Despite our proximity, no word passed between us. Under those sorts of circumstances, conversation just does not take place; it all goes unsaid although obviously each recognizes the other's plight. There is no need for further expressions of fear or hope and despite the many story book tales to the contrary, not even any wisecracks or other attempts at humour. We just lay next to each other, on the hard wooden deck of the ship, tightly jammed up against each other, understanding it all and fearing the worst.

And worst it was.

I had just got myself geared up for a nice long rest until the tide came up, when a tremendous, ear-splitting explosion shattered the reveries in which I and my new-found colleagues were no doubt engrossed, reveries which surely included foaming pints of beer and thick chunks of bread liberally covered with Cheddar cheese and butter, or no doubt involving wine and Camembert for my neighbours and other delights which reputedly fascinate in particular the Frenchies. When the smoke, dust and flying debris had settled a bit I looked at the French officer and saw that his stomach had now been deposited neatly on to his chest. A shell had registered a direct hit on the ship and the result can only be imagined – best not described.

My neighbour the French officer, who was now writhing in agony, had had the misfortune to receive a piece of shrapnel which all too neatly cut his stomach open and placed the innards on to his chest. The civilian had been blown some few feet away from me, and I knew no more as to his fate. The ship rapidly went on to its side, settling down into the shallows, and completely destroyed by the direct hit which had found it amidships, and the result was an obviously very large number of casualties, the dead being the luckiest, the many wounded being without any means of assistance. Amongst those who remained alive and reasonably whole, it was a matter of everyone for themselves. I did not wait to see any more and with whatever remaining alacrity I could muster, jumped or fell off the remains of the ship and swam or paddled ashore. Regrettably I was not joined by many others – the accuracy of the German gunners was such that the number of casualties was extremely high, and I did not see a lot of whole bodies about.

That was, thank God, virtually the end of that particular nightmare, because when I again reached the beach, after wading rather laboriously and half dazed through the shallow water, I gathered that some very sensible gentleman, sadly misnamed General Fortune, had called an end to the unsavoury proceedings, realizing the hopeless position his troops were in, and had raised the ignominious but very welcome flag of surrender, so the remainder of the shattered army in that particular vicinity where I was clambered up a steep path up the cliffs into captivity.

In the usual manner of defeat, we were immediately required to throw down our rifles – something I was in fact very happy to do since I seemed to be one of the very few idiots who had retained a weapon whilst performing the athletic feats on the beach and indulging in the two short swims, etc. – and place our hands securely on the top of our heads. In this ultimate position of humility and taking a first look at our erstwhile (and future) tormentors, who aligned both sides of the path we ascended and who glowered at us with triumphant glares, well armed and regaled with all manner of vicious-looking weapons and who did not appear to have taken part in a battle at all, we clambered up the steep path to the top of the cliff to face a barrage of German tanks, screaming officers and a future which did not appear to contain one single ray of hope. The transformation of the starry-eyed one into an extremely cynical and disillusioned young man was now fully in progress.

What I would then have given for a pint at the Roebuck on Richmond Hill or even a Sunday afternoon tea on the lawn at home! We never do really appreciate the good times until it's too late – now it was far, far too late.

Note: The 2/6th Battalion The East Surrey Regiment

It may be considered that I have been somewhat flippant in my comments on the unpreparedness and lack of war preparation that existed in as far as my battalion was concerned, at the time we were set against Rommel's armoured divisions in France in May and June 1940. As I hope I have succeeded in indicating, I personally as a non-commissioned officer, had very little idea as to what was happening anywhere on the war front, in fact those back in England who listened to the BBC would have known much more, and I am pretty sure the same could be said for the other non-commissioned officers and men in our unit and probably for the officers too. If the officers did know what was going on they certainly did not hasten to keep their underlings informed, but I'm pretty sure that they had little more knowledge of the general deployment of our own and enemy forces than did the butchers, refuse collectors, builders etc, or even I who was part of one of the sections, of one of the platoons, of one of the four companies, of which the battalion was constituted. I think, therefore, a few actual facts and details which have subsequently emerged may be of assistance in measuring any element of flippancy which may be contained in my remarks.

The 2/6th Battalion was a Territorial Army battalion, which originally was a part of the ill-fated 12th Division which came to grief in Belgium, on the Saar, but at that time our battalion was employed in fairly routine coastal defence operations mainly in the Dieppe area, hence my sojourn at Fécamp. The 2/6th then joined an organization called 'Beauforce' which on 20 May tried unsuccessfully to get up to Boulogne by road to help in the defence of the port. As a result, they were then put back into the 12th Division and became involved in the fighting around Abbeville, and upon the disintegration of the 12th Division, became attached to the 51st Highland Division in the hopeless task of stemming the advance of Rommel's many armoured divisions which became involved in a pincer-movement towards the southwest and then sharply turning to the north to cut the division off at St Valéry-en-Caux.

At the time of seriously getting involved in the front line fighting, I understand that our commanding officer made known to the higher authorities his objections to the involvement of the junior Territorial battalion in the front line activities, the objections being based on the fact that we were hopelessly ill-equipped and ill-prepared for front line fighting, and many of our soldiers had never fired a shot from a rifle and should not be thrown in the deep end of the ferocious front line fighting which followed the German break-through into France.

It is obvious the authorities, however, must have taken the view that a few hundred butchers, bakers and candlestick-makers (and a reluctant surveyor's clerk!) were presumbaly better than nothing at all to put in the way of Rommel's tanks.

I now understand the battalion had 500 rounds of ammunition for its twenty Bren machine guns, no mortars, carrier transports, revolvers, compasses or binoculars and virtually no signalling equipment, which was not a lot for a front line battalion. Despite this serious lack of equipment, I understand we succeeded in putting many of Rommel's tanks out of action almost manually, by climbing on to the tanks and dropping grenades through the hatches and other primitive methods. We had some anti-tank rifles but the ammunition for those never appeared in the same place as the rifles.

It was at Aumale, twenty-five miles south-east of Dieppe, that we met the German tanks in a country lane, the tanks being spearhead units of the German 5th Armoured Division, and at that confrontation my whole company were overrun.

Eventually, at St Valéry, only fifteen officers and 261 other ranks remained of the whole battalion. The battalion had apparently served an important and vital function in providing ground cover for 2-pounder artillery gun emplacements and in defending various major road intersections, bridges etc. Whilst neither I nor anyone around us seemed to have any idea as to what was happening, it subsequently transpired that the battalion had discharged its duties, despite the handicap of unpreparedness and lack of equipment, with full honours.

I add this note since this information has only come to light since the end of hostilities, and only long after the end of the war did I have any idea as to what we were supposed to have been up to in Normandy in 1940.

4

Captivity

'*Immer fünf Mann, Ihre bläde Schweine*' which very roughly translated may result in 'Get into rows of five, you bloody pigs' came the relentlessly repeated welcome from our hosts. 'Get knotted' or something stronger and equally uninformative came the response from the British mob, who were not in the best of moods for polite conversation. The young, bewildered but victorious German warriors were overwhelmed by the number of prisoners they had suddenly been confronted with and frustrated by the mutual inability of both races to understand each other's vicious expletives which resonated around the fields on the cliffs overlooking the English Channel without much impact.

The Germans, in an effort to foster an aura of trust and forgiveness amongst their conquered adversaries, resorted to passing out British cigarettes by courtesy of Messrs John Player & Sons which had been previously looted by them from captured British Army stores, with the soothing 'Cigarette, comrade' which seemed to represent the only two words of international exchange which could convey any meaning to anyone. Their 'comrades' however, emanating from an island race educated over countless generations to be suspicious of the bearers of free gifts, especially when they emanated from the continent of Europe, were still not impressed by this attempt at hospitality. Anyway, cigarettes were no longer a priority and although the more seriously addicted were happy to try and let the problems of the moment go up in smoke, the great mass of captured soldiers were more concerned to obtain water, as the first general priority on a hot summer's day, and bandages, and treatment for the sick and wounded as an overriding priority where needed.

Assembled on the cliffs at Veules-les-Roses adjoining the remains of St Valéry were the many thousands of remnants from British and French fighting units; a more disillusioned and despairing congregation could not be conceived. Amongst them, what does a young man of barely eighteen do when faced with such a situation? In one direction, home with mum and dad and security; in the other, man-eating Boche. The sea looked almost inviting on a hot June day – only seventy miles or so to swim, and then the nightmare would be ended. The farthest I had ever swam before was about 100 yards. The prospect, whilst being unutterably daunting and quite impossible when considered in the normal light of day, was nevertheless given the most serious consideration by me and by very many others amongst that unhappy gathering on the cliff top. The huge open expanse of fields in which we were all gathered under a hot sun seemed to be filled with dishevelled exhausted dirty men or relatively smart grey-blue uniformed well-disciplined members of the victorious Wehrmacht.

A watery grave looked to be the better alternative, but better because it represented almost certain suicide rather than being taken into captivity by an enemy who had never appeared to show great sympathy for those who were unfortunate enough to fall into their clutches.

The watery grave lost the unhappy vote by a reasonable margin, but certainly not by anything like a unanimous verdict. There were many amongst those gathered on the cliff top who jumped over the cliffs to join, several hundred feet below, the already considerable number of those who had fallen victim to the German machine guns, mortars, etc., rather than face an indeterminate period of captivity in the hands of the cruel and slave-driving taskmasters of Europe.

The word 'despair' is so inadequate. I would find it difficult now to consider that moment of time in my progress through this earthly paradise without recourse to an involuntary shudder; it must be remembered that the period of captivity I had just entered was not necessarily a finite period. It is now known that it was to be for five years, but then that relatively happy thought was not available to me. Ahead lay an indefinite period, perhaps till ultimate release in death, or slavery under clearly vicious German rule. The Czechs, the Silesians, the Austrians, the Poles had all been put under German domination and no release was evident – why should we fare better? And to cap it all, I had only an utter futility of a war to look back upon. When one goes to war one expects to fight, and if one gets killed, at least that is an anticipated alternative and some competitive struggle has been enacted. Nobody ever suggested that my only role would be to stand defenceless with no effective weapons and no training as a temporary human barrier against well-equipped and trained fighting units to await inevitable collapse whilst the responsible politicians who had put me there could have time to work out some salvation for themselves and the nation, in that order.

There was of course, thanks be to the Almighty, one politician at least in whom the remaining faith of the British could ultimately rest and who would be able in the end to give the lie to this statement; one Winnie, more accurately the Right Honourable Winston Churchill, bless him!

But the whole thing had been such a farce. Dunkirk had not been any victory; it had simply been a testimony to the inadequacy of those who for many years previously had ruled Britain, preached unilateral disarmament and consequently reduced it to a defenceless and pitiable laughing stock. It was only the individuals who participated at Dunkirk and in all the subsequent débacle who could be considered as worthy of any respect, not the Ramsay MacDonalds, Chamberlains, etc, and many French politicians who had reduced us to this pathetic state.

As we stood miserably on that cliff top and considered what had happened

No. *R/403 Wing/ES/.1097*

(If replying, please quote
above No.)

Army Form B. 104—83A.

Infantry Record & Pay Office, Record Office,

ASHFORD, MX, Station.

13 SEP 1940 19

SIR ~~OR MADAM~~,

I have to inform you that a report has been received
from the War Office to the effect that (No.) *614002*
(Rank) *Cpl.* (Name) *Palmer G C.*
(Regiment) *2/6 Bn.* EAST SURREY REGIMENT,
is a Prisoner of War *at Stalag XXIB*
Germany.

Should any other information be received concerning him, such
information will be at once communicated to you.

Instructions as to the method of communicating with Prisoners of
War can be obtained at any Post Office.

I am,
SIR ~~OR MADAM,~~
Your obedient Servant,

G.W. _____

for Officer in charge of Records.

IMPORTANT.—Any change of your address should be immediately notified to this
Office. It should also be notified, if you receive information from the soldier above, that
his address has been changed.

Wt.30241/1250 500M. 9/39. KJL/8818 Gp.698/3 Forms/B.104—83A/b

*The War Office notification sent to my parents advising that I was a
POW. I was captured on 12 June 1940, but this notification was not sent
until 13 September, three months later. A worrying time for parents, no
doubt!*

to us and to our war, we felt very, very bitter. We could understand how a boxer may feel, put into a ring with one hand tied behind his back, to receive the inevitable slaughter and be unable to retaliate. We had been cheated out of a fair fight and now faced a diabolical future, a reward for our nation's ineptitude. No medals nor fancy demob suits would ever make up for our humiliation and for the inhuman treatment we were now about to receive from the swaggering conquerors.

Needless to say, the Germans took full advantage of the disaster which was the British Expeditionary Force. They photographed the prisoners in the most humiliating positions – begging for water and so on – and the younger Germans took considerable pride in strutting about screaming useless invectives in an ineffective foreign tongue and booting and striking with their weapons injured, slow or otherwise shattered prisoners, which description just about covered the majority of us. Noticeably the older Germans, who 'had been there before' were more sympathetic or at least did not take immediate advantage of their new-found power over the human dross.

Obviously the Germans were overwhelmed by the vast quantity of prisoners they had taken. No provision was made for feeding or even more important, water or sanitation, and of course in the middle of a hot June day, after many hours and in fact many days of nerve-racking and tortuous experiences, everyone was gasping for water. Some had water bottles still, and these were in great demand; some had equipment (very few) but most had only the clothes they stood up in, and many not even those since they had futilely embarked on a swim to England, or had been on a minor craft of some sort and of necessity returned or been sunk. Very many were injured from shrapnel and machine gun bullets and all were utterly exhausted and had had no proper meals or drinks for weeks – and had no immediate prospect of getting any now. Only the radiant sun provided any solace, and that was drying us up too! The nervous tension under which most of us had lived for some days or weeks made further demands upon our parched tongues for liquid intake which was not forthcoming.

I stood there with the rest, in rows of five and took stock of my position. There was no further chance that my father would suddenly roll up in the Rover and bail me out and take me back to England. The chances of seeing my home in the immediate or distant future, or maybe ever again, were remote. I had possession of my wits, which were not in too bad shape, though probably a little dulled or more dull than usual; my general health, which had been in very good shape, had received a temporary setback from the activities of the past few days, which had blessedly and quite astonishingly left me reasonably unscathed with only a few cuts and bruises and a small shrapnel wound in the right upper arm, a uniform albeit stinking but mostly there except for a few tears, shirt and underclothes which could have been beneficially replaced several weeks earlier, a watch of little value, about 12/6d in English money and a few francs, and not an apparent friend in the world. The only thing I could shout about was that, apart from some grazes and the piece of shrapnel in the arm, which was not of great consequence, and the few cuts and bruises, I was physically sound, and in the surroundings I now found myself, a good physical condition would clearly be of the greatest importance, as well of course a rational mental state. My reactions as far as the senses went seemed to be just the same as they were before the affray. What ultimate effect upon the innermost workings of the mind the recent happenings would have remained, of course, to be seen in the future. The thing which had taken the greatest battering was that intangible but vital prerequisite to life – hope for the future; hope now seemed to be something which had existed only in the past, for the future appeared at best not a subject for contemplation.

Eventually we were gathered together in rough groups and viciously coerced by a mixture of kicks, bayonet prods and assorted blows to various parts of the anatomy to start walking in a general direction away from the cliffs, one could only describe it as 'walking' – it was in fact a mixture of marching, walking, stumbling and being half pushed and fully encouraged by our energetic and jubilant captors. A pretty miserable melancholy parade of humanity, blood-stained and bandaged wounded, some sightless ones being led, others being fully supported by their mates and generally dragged or urged along; it was made abundantly clear by the new masters that any who could not make it would be left for dead or shot on the spot – any theoretical nonsense about the captors providing medical assistance to their injured captives was strictly for the birds.

'*Immer fünf Mann, immer fünf Mann*' continued the excited German guards, as they prodded the unwilling human wrecks into lines of five to get the groups started on marching in some very vague semblance of order.

'Water, water, for God's sake, water, Comrade,' came the entreaty of those who hoped for some response from their new masters to their pitiable requests. Offers of English and French money and even valuables were accepted by the Germans with requests for water, but water was not forthcoming. The struggling bodies, dried up from the burning sun and from nervous exhaustion as well as from the physical efforts of the immediate past few hours, had never been so dehydrated before, and the minds of the confused and desperate sufferers were becoming somewhat crazed as a result. Visions of frothing pints of beer passed before the eyes like mirages in a desert, and we gradually became more and more dehydrated to the point where the thought of liquid refreshment excluded all other rational thinking.

We were marched past a group of top-ranking generals and staff officers whom we were given to understand by the Germans were Rommel, accompanied by the misnamed British Major-General Victor Fortune, and various other high-ranking officers who had collectively contributed to the pathetic state to which their once loyal and upstanding soldiery had now been reduced. However, the top brass all looked quite comfortable and did not appear to be suffering; although I imagined the British general was feeling pretty humiliated, I was quite sure he was able to get a glass of water. The officers were of no further interest to the defeated troops and no longer could they berate us to 'fight to the last man' and all that nonsensical paraphernalia of the schoolboy hero books. The truth was out, it was all just a damn great sham and the general with his red tabs was the focal point of the whole senseless charade.

So we started a march which was to remove us out of France and take us through Belgium and south Holland to eventually embark (what a posh word for a kick up the rear!) into the hold of a barge to travel down a canal and river ultimately to arrive in Germany. The march started on 12 June 1940, the day we were taken prisoner by the Jerries, and rather surprisingly I was able to record all the daily journeys on a piece of paper which to this day I still retain.

The journey went as follows:

June	12	St Valéry	June	21	St Pol
	13	Yvetot		22	Béthune
	14	Forges		23	Seclin
	15	Formerie		24	Tournai, Belgium
	16	Legionnères Châtel		25	Renaix
	17	Airaines		26	Ninove
	18	Doumatre		27	Aalst
	19	Doulons		28	Lokeren
	20	St Pol		29	Moerbrike

which completed the march (or stumble) of about 250 miles averaging about fifteen miles a day.

I soon acclimatized myself to the routine of each day's march for they all followed a similar sort of pattern. Long lines of mentally and physically shattered men struggling to walk at all; turned into a field at night-time to virtually graze, because that was about all there was to eat. The actual ration, if you got it, consisted of a bowl of chicory at about 5 a.m. and then on the road with nothing more. When the marching, or rather struggling ceased, about mid-afternoon, having been put into the field, we were eventually provided with a piece of bread and maybe if lucky some potato or swede soup from which the potato or swede had been instantly removed after insertion. And that was our lot.

I had plenty of time, whilst marching along the endless roads of France, to comtemplate my current situation and to observe the new circumstances under which my life henceforth was to be led. To that point of time in my brief experience of life, people had been reasonably predictable in as much that, with the exception of a pretty small minority, the reaction of one's fellow creatures could be reasonably ascertained by general intuition and people behaved in a logical and for the main part, honest and straightforward manner. The indoctrination instilled on the school cricket grounds suggesting upright and rational sporting behaviour had not yet worn off.

Now, however, I was faced with an entirely different set of circumstances. I was surrounded by a mass of people who seemed to be far more experienced than I in the all-important battle for basic survival. To win that battle, all the old rules and regulations of life had to be set aside. If your boots fell to pieces through wear and tear, you stole the boots of the sleeping man next door to you (if the chap was idiot enough to take them off). If there was food anywhere in the offing you rushed at it and knocked anybody who got in your way to the ground, and then took the maximum you could grab. If it was necessary in the cause of obtaining an extra morsel of bread, to 'shop' or split on your comrade, then you shopped him and took the proffered morsel. If it was necessary to kill for an egg, then that was the 'going price' of an egg.

It seemed to my innocent observation that the great majority of those who could now be dubbed 'my comrades' had been practising these tactics over a period of many years. Not having been acclimatized to resorting to such extreme measures I found myself at a considerable disadvantage in adopting an 'after you, kind sir' attitude. Apparently the great mass of prisoners I now joined seemed to be so well trained and experienced in these arts, that at first I found it difficult to switch my moral code of conduct, which was more automatic than the result of personal enlightenment, to adopt the same drastic measures in the sacred cause of survival, but I caught on and caught on quite fast. I may have been a rooky to commence with, and was shattered and disgusted to see what people would do to ensure their personal survival, but I ultimately realized with regret, that if I was ever going to see my home and homeland again I had better give at least serious consideration to the adoption of this new set of rules. In fact the problem was alleviated to some extent by groups of prisoners of a like mind, not being prepared to sacrifice all moral scruples, allying themselves together and forming gangs joined together to ensure the survival of the whole gang, which was at least some improvement over the 'winner take all' attitude.

The long lines of prisoners marching down the streets and country roads of France were kept under control by marching guards with machine guns and more guards in trucks, and anyone, just anyone who fell out of line for any reason – illness, calls of what was left of nature, etc. – was punctiliously shot on the spot, no questions asked; no thought of Geneva conventions or any of that rubbish. At one spot, one day, I spied some rotten chunks of bread in a ditch at the side of the road. I could not resist the temptation and jumped out of line to grab the mud-encrusted but succulent and inviting morsels and succeeded, but others who followed my lead were relentlessly mowed down by the nearest guard; I shudder to think at what cost my mouldy bread was eventually eaten, but the example showed the dire straits to which the prisoners had soon been driven, and the callous manner in which our guards would react.

On several occasions I tried to eat grass, but discovered that it was just not possible to get the wretched stuff to go down – it is too light and airy. Presumably cows have different digestive mechanisms. Eventually I hit on the idea of mixing the grass with mud, which at least made it go down but not stay down. However, always it was water which was the necessity most distressing to be without, and the prisoners consumed vast quantities of water very unfit for human consumption – from ditches, etc., which probably laid the foundation for the eventual mass diarrhoea and dysentery and would have been a sound basis for a horrific outbreak of typhoid, cholera, etc, had we not all been so well inoculated against such problems when preparing to go overseas. I guessed that I had not washed for about three weeks at least from the date of capture and another two weeks could be added for the period prior to capture, and even such delights as toilet paper were unheard of or at an enormous premium, with the result that grass or dirty paper had to be used, the former giving rise to diseases such as worms etc.

Inevitably the black market commenced operations, and many of the prisoners still had personal goods to barter, watches, rings, gold tooth fillings, etc, and the ever keen guards were quite prepared to become involved in clandestine trading operations at such little cost to themselves (a full water bottle for example for a solid gold watch). They could and did take the watches without giving anything in return; in fact my own very cheap ten shilling watch went that way, simply ripped off my wrist by a young German guard. Presumably giving a little water occasionally in exchange soothed their conscience – if they had any.

The blackmailing of one's own comrades in times of such distress did not, of course, know any moral or national boundaries. Whilst the Jerries would profit, so would those in position of authority in the ranks of the prisoners – cooks, who were the new millionaires, sergeants and top NCOs who were allocated by the Germans to positions of responsibility to keep a semblance of order in the absence of officers who had all been taken off separately somewhere, and the French who sometimes had some local advantage seeing they were in their home territory and rather naturally took every opportunity to benefit from being on home ground. In a political world to-day in which some not small group of people devote themselves to the pursuance of a theory of equality for all, with a theory of fair distribution of resources, one fact from my experience in prison camps stands out very clearly, and that is that in whatever circumstances or wherever a group of people are congregated without any apparent wealth and with considerable demand for basic necessities, a hierarchy of privileged classes will ultimately emerge. Inevitably there will in the end always be those who have and those who have not, and that had absolutely nothing to do with inheritance, public school education, knowing the right people or any of that claptrap. The political lesson to be learnt was that you always had one smaller section of the community capable and willing to consort together to become better off than the remaining larger section, no matter what colour you may call it. There had to be a leader, and he had to have aides, and the leader inevitably had to have some privileges or he could not establish any authority within which to lead; and there had to be people who handled the basic necessities – food, water, clothing, etc, – and these people always ended up as mutually trading groups who profited from controlling and stealing from the remainder, and I very soon realized that you don't have to be Karl Marx to work that simple fact out. The cooks pinched food which they sold or gave to the camp leaders for favours such as better quarters, no dirty duties, etc, so that an eventual privileged class emerged at the expense of the rest, and it is so patently obvious that the same rules equally apply to-day under capitalist or communist or socialist governments.

It is clearly a part of the survival inheritance of our breed, but it is not nice to see or have to admit since the privileges so obtained are not usually utilized for anything but personal gratification and gain, and this gain was achieved during those days of severe hardship during this march across France at a very great cost to others, the price being additional suffering by the unprivileged many.

Our basic existence during the eighteen days of the march became simply a major feat of survival. I have no idea how many died, but I was exceedingly grateful that as a child and during boyhood I had had the advantage of being fed on good nourishing foods that presumably had built up protein and bone marrow reserves which were now fully called upon. Never before had my body been called upon to survive for days the rigours of a forced march with little or no intake of food or liquids and little or no real sleep, and exposed continuously to the elements. I have no doubt those resources built up during happier times now played a large part in my own survival.

The amazingly indomitable spirit of my fellow countrymen also showed up in a very good light, and whilst the British contingent in the vast accumulation of many thousands of French, Belgian and other nationalities was invariably the last to get started in the morning, moaning and muttering unmentionable strings of expletives, by the evening they were well ahead of the rest of the field, having kept together in a reasonable formation and united in keeping up their spirits. I was in fact very proud and pleased to be one of the British contingent and pitied those other nationalities who did not seem to have the same survival abilities. Maybe it is something to do with being an island race, for De Gaulle was quite right – the British just are not the same type of thinkers as those on mainland Europe. There appears to be something slightly different, not necessarily better but just different, and this showed up very clearly in their behaviour during those daily forced marches which the lines of weary men had to undergo. They even appeared to exhibit comradely bonhomie and mutual assistance (when there was no food about!) and despite my previous views upon the ability of my compatriots to put personal survival first, which I came to accept as rather natural, there existed a certain amount of decent behaviour which drew the line at allowing one's fellow sufferers to expire if this could be avoided without too much personal discomfort.

On one occasion, when we had stopped for a while in a town called Moerbrike in southern Holland, I was singled out for unusual treatment. A very important-looking SS officer appeared opposite the section of prisoners where I happened to be standing, penned into the courtyard of a school adjoining the road. He was presumably important because he had Iron Crosses hanging off his whiskers and all the guards immediately hastened to do his bidding and bowed and scraped all around him. Somewhat apathetically we glared through the iron railings dividing us from the road at the obsequious performance of our guards towards the new arrival, but our screams for water, bread and the general clamour continued undeterred.

'Silence, pigs,' came the order from the guard commander to the interested prisoners. 'Is there anyone here from the county of Sussex in England?' he demanded in German.

Whilst the assembled group of prisoners were still trying to work out what he wanted, and had only caught the word 'Sussex' repeated many times, my own rather limited school German allowed me slightly faster comprehension, and I hastened to make it known that I was from Sussex. In all probability, since the group of prisoners I was then with was mainly remnants of the 51st Highland Division, it was a fairly good bet that very few of them hailed from Sussex in any case, but when volunteering for anything strict adherence to the truth was not blindly followed. Anyway, I thought there might be a reasonable chance of a bun in it at the end of whatever may be in store, and took the risk of volunteering, for risk indeed it may well have been, for the Germans may just have been looking for a scapegoat for some unknown reason, but when you have absolutely nothing to lose, who cares?

The guards then hustled me out of the main barbed wire improvised gate and I was marched off by a SS gent and at least four obsequious guards from the compound to a magnificent Mercedes car which had been pulled up in the street opposite. In the Mercedes sat an even more important-looking man who could not have been many executions behind the Führer in the unholy hierarchy. The man was fairly young and probably handsome in the tall fair-headed and cruel blue eyes sense of Teutonic good looks, and absolutely weighed down with Iron Crosses and other impedimenta, and clearly was a very high-ranking officer. I noted, amongst other important items of regalia, the inevitable SS badges on the lapels of his tunic which was black to contrast with the dull Wehrmacht grey. I was duly led, in considerable trepidation, up to the car and the young god inspected me from his seat, observing a pitiable filthy dirty, stinking, half emaciated wretch little resembling a human being at all. He then got up and descended from the car amidst much extravagant holding open of the car doors, clicking of heels and '*Heil Hitlers*' at the rate of twenty per second, etc, in which performance I did not participate. When the fuss had died down, the officer and I were left facing each other, surrounded by his numerous minions.

'You are from Sussex, my friend?' he started and I nearly collapsed, not only as a result of the unaccustomed word 'friend' but because his English was so fantastically good. 'You are surprised I speak English,' he continued. 'I was educated at Marlborough College and Cambridge, so I have had plenty of opportunity to speak your tongue. Tell me, my friend,' (there were beginning to be too many 'my friends' for my liking) 'have you lived in Sussex long?' This seemed to be developing into a sort of cosy teatime chat and I was worried especially in view of some of the tales I had heard of homosexuality being rife in high places in the Nazi leadership, although what on earth could attract him from my filthy appearance I could not imagine. I explained however, that I had lived some ten years near Eastbourne on the coast, and as I said it I wondered if I had put my foot right in it. I bet he wants to cross-examine me about defences on the south coast. No doubt the German victory in France was only a stepping stone on the way to England, and he probably wants to know where the Martello towers were situated, or something equally vital to the German advance.

However, it soon transpired that my fears were unnecessary. I was duly asked a whole pile of questions about local councils. 'Who is the present Mayor of Sussex?' he wanted to know.

I explained that Sussex had no mayor, towns had mayors, which made me wonder how it was he had not gleaned such information whilst at Cambridge. He asked a number of inane questions about the roads to London and the rail links to the capital, answers to all of which I would have thought he could have quite easily got from a children's atlas and railway timetable, but in the course of the twenty minutes or so of questioning, he did not appear to be seeking important classified information, not that he would have got it anyway, but just seemed to want to set eyes on someone from Sussex, or to practise his English.

Clearly he saw the puzzled look in my face, and as if to clarify the whole ridiculous performance in one simple statement to be followed by my dismissal, he said, 'You see, the Führer has appointed me *Gauleiter* [overseer] for Sussex when our victorious Wehrmacht [army] has conquered Britain, which will of course be very shortly.' And with that he turned round and shot back into his car.

I, on the other hand, was returned under escort minus the first SS officer, and unceremoniously pushed back into a pen, without as much as a crumb from my 'friend', let alone a bun. What the score was with the very senior young officer in the Mercedes I had no idea. His statements did not tie up for I could not understand why an ex-English University man should want to ask such inane questions about nothing of any importance of a prisoner from Sussex. I could only think that there was some much deeper significance to the charade or else the young officer was just besotted with power and felt he should assert his authority as an SS officer in an area which was definitely the prerogative of the Wehrmacht. Whatever it was, there was no bun, not even any thanks, but the real disaster occurred as I was being pushed back through the gate to the prisoner's enclosure.

As I was crossing the pavement and was about to enter the gate with a guard prodding me from behind, a woman, no longer young and a fairly typical-looking Dutch housewife, who was standing near the gate lunged forward and thrust into my arms a long loaf of bread. It was a magnificent gesture, but not at all to the liking of the Huns. The guards immediately seized the woman and led her off screaming all manner of abuse to somewhere down the road, and I shuddered to think where. The loaf of bread was immediately snatched away from me, and I received several blows from rifle butts for having received it. The nett result of this little expedition was that I lost two teeth and suffered a number of sores and bruises from kicking and punching. The trouble was that I knew that once inside the pen there was no medical aid available, and not even a lot of sympathy since everyone else was fully occupied with their own problems and had little strength left over to offer solace to others. In fact I did find a dentist or dentist's assistant who looked at my mouth and made sympathetic noises, if nothing else, but astonishingly enough he found some ordinary cement with which he filled a tooth adjoining the one knocked out, and that cement filling remains still there to this day!

I realized that the real point behind the savage attack by the guards upon me was really that the Germans just could not bear to witness any mutual sympathy or understanding between the British and the peoples they had just conquered. Regrettably, I did not think they found much difficulty in turning the French prisoners against us by referring to the evacuation of British troops at Dunkirk and implying that the British had left their French allies in the lurch. I was pretty sure, however, they never succeeded in alienating all the Dutch, the Belgians, nor the Poles from a mutual alliance despite the traitorous few who hastened to do the Nazi tyrant's bidding for personal gain, and all those nationals would happily take the opportunity to spit on the ground as a Jerry walked by. I shudder to think however what happened to the poor, generous-hearted Dutch woman. The sound of some rifle shots nearby shortly after the episode augured ill, but there were sporadic shots being fired most of the time, so I can only hope she was not the recipient.

It would not have been difficult at this stage to have escaped from one of the temporary compounds we were kept in, and outside there was enough local help to keep an escapee going for a while. However, by so doing one would be certain to involve the local nationals in an extremely dangerous exercise for them of hiding and helping us. That they may have been willing to help would probably be a 30/70 chance against, for they too had to look to their survival, but what was pretty certain was that the escaped prisoner must surely become a heavy burden of responsibility and embarrassment to them. It was only practical, perhaps, for the few RAF or senior technical personnel at officer level. The British Government would soon establish, at no small cost, proper escape lines, and pay well for the services rendered at such enormous risk to the local nationals. Such generosity was not, however, really available to the likes of me, and the risk imposed upon the local inhabitants was so onerous that an escape seemed quite unreasonable.

During those seventeen days I did not see the inside of a building or any form of shelter and it was fortunate for the thousands of pitiful wrecks partaking in the march that it was mid-summer. In fact we frequently got drenched sleeping at night under the stars, without even a greatcoat since few were carrying such luxuries when captured in the middle of June, and then to march the following day with our clothes gradually drying on us. No wonder I suffered ultimately in later years from the odd rheumatic pain. To say that hygiene facilities were poor was a vast understatement, they were usually non-existent and at best just a large ditch or hole dug in the corner of a field with probably no cleaning facilities, so when we arrived ultimately at the town of Ennerich in Holland to be herded on to barges for the journey into Germany, we were in a pretty sorry state. I was minus two teeth which had been knocked out during the encounter at Moerbrike but otherwise was not too badly off physically though probably stinking to high heaven and morally pretty disenchanted with humanity in general. However, the progress from the starry-eyed state to intense cynicism was well under way.

Each one of those eighteen days of marching had been a day of personal effort in survival for every individual involved. No one really knew whether they would be alive to face the next day; the marching itself was not a slow meander. The Germans kept us going at a military pace and if you could not keep up you knew very well that the result would be the bullet. There were no medical facilities available and such trivia as blisters, sore feet, etc, were of no greater consequence than a wound daily becoming worse from infection and ultimately gangrene. When the marching stopped for the obligatory five minutes' rest in every sixty minutes, required under German army discipline, to stop marching was bliss, but to start again, after the all-too-short break was absolutely hell; the poor feet which had suddenly received brief respite from continuous plodding, had to be literally forced back into operation again. The body was very, very unwilling but the mind knew, only too well that there simply was no alternative. I found I just had, each time regularly once per hour, to force myself to stand an exhausted body up on very painful feet and oblige it to propel itself along despite all the tortuous aches and pains, otherwise I would have to accept the alternative of saying adieu to this blessed life. The alternative way may well have provided an easy way out, but there is something which just makes one go on. Death is really so very final and very much a last resort, especially in the view of an eighteen-year-old, even though he may not have a very rosy future ahead of him.

5

The Exodus

The barge-holds used for the transport of prisoners and into which we were herded at Ennerich were not the last word in luxury. They had no provision for human occupation at all and were simply the holds which usually accommodated coal, and the thirty-six hours we were to spend in them far exceeded the pinnacles of misery we had till then experienced. The new experience we entered upon must in fact have been very reminiscent of the Black Hole of Calcutta fame. The holds were absolutely jam-packed tight with bodies standing, so if anyone was foolish enough to try and lie down, chaos would result and the recumbent one would soon be crushed to death. There must have been at least 300 men to each hold and other than a small piece of bread before embarking, the Germans provided no food and worse still, no water. Furthermore, there were initially no sanitary provisions.

After some considerable period of distress, the Germans arranged for a few buckets to be lowered to cater for our, by then, extremely pressing sanitary needs, and similarly some buckets of water were lowered. However, this was completely useless amongst the large numbers, and rarely did the water get much farther than the point at which it was lowered, and I was not unfortunately at one of the favoured watering holes. The prevalent diarrhoea produced its inevitable disgusting consequences and the dire straits of extreme thirst to which many men were driven forced them to the ultimate depths of degradation in partaking of their own urine as an ultimate resort, although this was one particular delight I did not feel obliged to participate in.

After much screaming, pushing and shoving, we eventually got going on what must have been one of the most uncomfortable journeys any of us had ever had the misfortune to be involved in. We could not of course see where we were or what was happening above the level of the top of the hold. Our world was going on in a floating dungeon for whilst these same barges were no doubt customarily employed in carrying lumps of coal down to the industries of the Ruhr district, we had now replaced the lumps of coal and were just a living consignment of potential energy to be transported into the depths of the Reich to provide fuel for the vast German industrial complexes supporting the German war machine.

I doubt very much that the Germans would have moved their cattle or farm animals in this cruel and inhuman manner, and any view that may have remained that the German army might treat their captives as captured soldiers and extend to them facilities similar to those enjoyed by their own troops at the hands of the British was very obviously so much balderdash. Our existence in those holds was indescribable and could only be considered as sheer hell, and whilst the Germans may have believed it to be an expeditious manner of transporting a considerable number of prisoners, I will always feel that there existed a sad lack of human sympathetic sincerity in the German make-up to enable such suffering and hardship to be experienced by so many completely defenceless people who had laid down arms upon the apparently false assumption that they were surrendering to a civilized nation, which had truly accepted the provisions of the Geneva Convention.

Needless to say, there was great relief when, accompanied by much banging and crashing, the barge eventually came to final rest at a quayside somewhere, and the hold covers were opened up to enable some sun and air to reach us and we were finally allowed to disembark and join the human race again.

I felt however, that I and my colleagues were not really looking our best upon arrival in Germany at a place called Bucholt. It was pretty obvious that the Germans were purposely producing a situation where their captives would look their worst, filthy, exhausted, variously covered in mud, blood and even human excreta, undernourished to the point of starvation etc, so that when we were paraded through the streets of this old border town, which was very German to the core, the locals would appreciate how superior they, the Master Race, really were, and what an inferior and pathetic race the British were – really no better than pigs. We had in fact become temporarily unwitting and very unwilling victims of the callous, efficient German war propaganda effort.

This comparison with pigs or criminals was evident on many occasions to me when my fluency at the language had sufficiently improved to permit me to fully understand the German guards, especially at camps in Poland where the guards frequently pointed to Polish or Jewish captives who were of course suffering in the extreme and deprived of everything, saying, 'Look, they are just animals.' So would the 'Master Race' be if they were locked up in the packed hold of a barge for days on end without water or food, or in train trucks made for 'Eight Horses or Forty Men', and filled with 60 to 80 men, and deprived of all means of eating, drinking and cleansing. I felt sure, however, that the average German actually began to believe in this distinction between the Master Race and the rest, *Menschen* and *Untermenschen* as the Germans themselves referred to it. Their territorial gains in Europe over virtually undefended countries, or nations unwilling for clear and rather good reasons to take up again the cudgels which they had hopefully left to rest after the horror and devastation of World War I and again fight bloody battles, had in fact led them first to believe, and now to see, the evidence for this nationally-held view being happily paraded in front of them – that they were the Master Race and contented products of Adolf Hitler's bully-boy tactics and the theory of the pure Aryan stock being the unquestionable foundation of their egoistic principles would remain undisputed.

The march through the streets of Bucholt was very degrading and humiliating for us and we were liberally pelted with rotten vegetables by the inhabitants, who lined the streets. This would not have been so bad if we could have caught the missiles and consumed them, but we were prevented from picking anything up whilst marching upon pain of being machine-gunned down, and they were hurled with rather too much force to allow us to catch the delicacies. The local citizens were, of course, completely assured by their leaders that Germany had won the war, as were all the guards, and the fall of France would involve an immediate capitulation in Britain and occupation of Buckingham Palace by Hitler's henchmen and leave the Germans as conquerors of the whole of Europe.

I only hope someone threw rotten vegetables back at the noble citizens of Bucholt after the war, although I doubt very much that British troops would stoop so low, or bother,

Since the war, there has been much talk of how the German civilian population really did not support the Nazi régime, and were forced to succumb to bully-boy tactics. There was no evidence of such enforcement that day in Bucholt as we were paraded before the joyous townsfolk. The civilians lined the streets without any apparent coercion to extract every last drop of satisfaction they could by humiliating an enemy they seemed to be very happy to let their troops at the front send back as prisoners for their especial enjoyment and upon whom they could give vent to their sadistic feelings of hatred. I doubt, however, whether the fighting troops themselves would have behaved so shabbily, but judging by the turn-out at Bucholt that day, the Nazi Party seemed to have supporters in almost one hundred per cent of the local population, and any efforts since the end of the war to make it appear that the civilian populace, other than the Party members and SS, were innocent victims of propaganda and unreasonable coercion would seem to me to be largely poppycock; that the civilian population may have questioned the advantages of blindly following Nazi propaganda in later years, from 1942 onwards, may be true, but on that day in 1940 in Bucholt it was very evident that the whole nation was fully backing the Party activities so ably enforced by the SS.

At Bucholt we remained a couple of miserable days in a field and then it was entrainment for journeys much farther east. At the local station we were unceremoniously crammed into cattle trucks at between 60 and 80 men per truck, the last few men entering with the help of a jackboot in their posteriors. Then the sliding-track door was closed and barred and only the small slits at roof level remained for ventilation. We were provided with a bucket per truck for sanitation, and this had to be emptied via the slit, bad luck for the chap who bagged the available space near the ventilation, since he was frequently the recipient of some part of the contents of the buckets when being emptied out of the swaying train.

The very fact that I was now travelling towards the east and therefore further away from my homeland only served to increase the utter despair and despondency with which I and no doubt my fellow sufferers were afflicted. With every revolution of the trucks' wheels our position became even more hopeless; the security, pleasures and love which had existed in the past became a thing of the past, and never likely to be repeated, and I suppose that every one of us lying on those hard wooden floors of the very bumpy truck must have been fully engrossed, not by his own physical pains, but by the anguish of the final separation which was being enacted.

Food consisted only of the occasional cup of chicory or some similar brown looking liquid grandly called coffee, or potato or swede soup (not that there were any cups – you had to improvise a container and if you had no container, bad luck!) and then only when provision could be made by the no doubt harassed German supply officers, and we soon got the feeling that we were not very high priority for the available supplies. But again, it was not food so much as water that was the problem. Occasionally the train stopped, and this was only very rarely and under strict surveillance of numerous troops liberally supplied with machine guns, we were allowed out of the trucks for a very brief respite and had an opportunity to get some water and to have a sorely needed leak and take care of any other natural functions, but most had nothing to carry any water in and tins were at a premium and not always watertight, so the dehydration augmented by the hot stuffy conditions in the truck went unrelieved, and the diarrhoea continued its relentless and disgusting course.

At one station where we briefly stopped but did not disembark, a British staff sergeant in my truck induced a civilian on the platform by signs and gestures through the narrow slit to fill his water bottle for him and I watched him pass over in return to the civilian the whole of the regimental mess funds he was carrying, which we subsequently discovered was about £6,000. An expensive way of quenching your thirst but an example of the extremes to which thirst can drive one. We were literally being driven out of our minds. Incidentally, the civilian disappeared with both water bottle and money, not to be seen again.

Going hungry – developing with tedious finality into starvation – is not only a physical discomfort, it is primarily a mental concern, graduating from an increasingly severe desire for a bite to a delirious demand for sustenance to enable one's organic functions to continue. In between these extremes there is a period of agonizing deterioration, both physically and mentally, accentuated in some who may have become acclimatized previously to a greater interest in feeding and less emphasized to a point of annoyance by those who usually consider the basic necessity of eating as rather a bore. Both categories of sufferer however, ultimately came to realize that without food, and more especially without drink, the internal physical organs of the body may perish or commence to decay from lack of use, and therefore the basic and urgent survival fears take over; it is not very long after that one's whole mental observation of the objective world begins to become severely distorted and the customary ability to string facts and events together coherently becomes impaired to the point where fantasy enters into the picture; despair and resultant depression are inevitably followed by a basic lack of desire to physically continue the fight for existence although the superior innate natural demand to survive at all costs seems to persist to the bitter end. To say that one's whole attitude to life becomes disorientated is only to pick out one part of the process. It continues up to the point where the sufferer is in danger of being driven completely out of his mind and to the ultimate stage where the one great resistance factor, hope, fades. We seemed to be in immediate danger of entering deeply into this process. I understand it is possible to survive several days without food, but just try going without water in an overcrowded cattle truck under a flaming July sun and under severe nervous tension; that following weeks of severe tension was a trial indeed.

The weather in Central Europe in the middle of July was, of course, exceedingly warm and this added considerably to our distress. A march undertaken years later in captivity in Eastern Europe occurred in mid-winter under extremely cold conditions. It is hard to say which climatic condition was the most agonizing, but I will always remember thirst as being the greatest burden to endure, and that comes with heat, emphasized by the nervous tension inherent in the situation. Although no one actually died in the truck that I was in as far as I could see (I am not too sure, for many looked almost dead!), there were many deaths resulting from this utterly inhumane treatment by the Germans, who no doubt thought they were acting in a truly practical German style in transporting as many prisoners at lowest cost in fuel for the very long journey right across Germany to end up in Western Poland. We were locked up in those trucks from 6 July to 8 July; sometimes around midday the train would be halted for a while and the temperature in the unventilated crowded trucks under the mid-day sun must have reached well into the 100° Fahrenheit mark, or maybe much more.

We arrived on the 8th at a place called Schubin on the East German/Polish border in the province of Upper Silesia. Upper Silesia, or the Gau (District) of Upper Silesia as it was correctly termed by the Germans, had earlier in its chequered career been a part of the Reich (the German Empire) but was separated from Germany after World War I and became a part of Poland which was invaded and recaptured in 1939. Together with the Warta Gau and its capital Posen, it was now again separated from Poland and the inhabitants appeared to be regarded as 'Quasi-Germans', not quite the real thing. Their loyalty was forcibly to Germany, but not a hundred per cent.

This was to be my first taste of a prisoner-of-war camp proper, and was a converted old military camp containing a number of single storey corrugated iron huts and central more permanent buildings as establishment headquarters for the Commandant and guards.

The camp Stalag XXI B had been used in the 1914–18 war as a prisoner-of-war camp and for other military purposes since that date, and was old and totally inadequate for the large number of new residents now to be housed there. There was a very obvious lack of proper sanitation and many of the huts had only been recently and rapidly erected and were barely wind and weather proof. However, they were buildings that at least represented shelter from the elements, something we had not been used to for several weeks, but that did nothing to raise our spirits as we entered the well-protected courtyards after passing through the German headquarters compound, and some very substantial walls of barbed wire overlooked by the traditional sentry towers manned by guards well provided with machine guns and searchlights.

The fences at the perimeter were some ten feet in height with the accompanying guard towers at all corners and intermediate stages, and this all served to make me appreciate the fact that my liberty, something I had taken for granted all my life, had suddenly disappeared and been replaced by complete loss of freedom to move or do what I wished, possibly for the rest of my life. Worse still, it had finally removed any last remnant of personal individuality that may have remained with me. We were now sheep firmly enclosed in a pen, and just like sheep we would act exactly as the good shepherd, the square-jawed, slit-eyed balding German camp commandant with the look of a Prussian cavalry officer, would command. We could say goodbye from now on to any element of individuality which may have remained in our personalities and to any privacy which we may have wished to cling to. Every action, every word would henceforth be in response to the dictate of the mass or in compliance with the demands of our masters and would be entirely public.

The camp was occupied by prisoners from all the services, but there was a separate compound for navy personnel, marines, RAF, as well as for prisoners from other nationalities. At this time in the war the Germans had not made much provision for prisoners and it was really a sort of transit camp. The camp was, I believe, eventually transferred elsewhere, and closed for military purposes, which would have been no great loss to the prisoner fraternity.

As soon as we all got into the huts, jockeying for positions of strength commenced amongst the inmates, and the inevitable Black Market chain of authority got going. Unless you were 'in the swim', you simply became the victim of a chain of corrupt internal authority instituted by your 'comrades' in addition to being the butt of aggressive captors. I was by now becoming less reticent and shy about adopting extreme measures to survive, but could never out-manoeuvre the more experienced regular soldiers in finding the cushy jobs and best places. This was a skill reserved for a certain type of specialist and required many years of training to become fully adept. The scrounger, the crawler and the bully seem to be specialist types to be found in all sections of 'other ranks' of the permanent armed forces, although the army seemed to attract by far the largest element. One could only be led to the conclusion that this was an art experienced and practised by the armed forces prior to the present débacle in which we all found ourselves. This situation no doubt always occurs when people who are defenceless and useless, such as prisoners, refugees, etc, are assembled together and are forced to submit to these overriding pressures; noble deeds and intentions are all very well if you can afford them, but at a time like the present in those camps, any mug who tried to behave according to the gentleman's code of conduct would not survive long. The principles by which I was obliged now to play the game were self first, at all times, and do to others as they would do unto you, but do it first. If you left it too late, you could never recover. If you occasionally came across the unusual specimen of humanity who continued to play by the rules of good moral conduct, then it was indeed a rare event which had to be fleetingly accepted and enjoyed, and I did in fact find some groups who even under the prevailing adverse conditions were able to continue to consort together like human beings and communally share what little there was to share and not slit each other's throats for the bigger portions. It appalled me to think that such animal-like behaviour should be demonstrated before the very eyes of an enemy who had been themselves accused of barbaric treatment of their fellow men and were ultimately, following the exposure of the treatment of Jews and Poles, to be categorized as unfit to be accepted amongst the ranks of the so-called civilized.

Obviously we were all very weak, dirty, undernourished and dejected and it was quite clear that the Germans enjoyed their prisoners being in this pathetic state which deterred us, as a result, from making any efforts to escape or become any sort of nuisance. It was probable that at that time escape was far from anyone's mind for there just did not seem to be anywhere to escape to and no very obvious means of traversing the barbed wire enclosures. I was in a camp for non-commissioned officers and men and this was very different from the officer camps and RAF camps where the conditions for living were probably superior and the standards of comfort and general facilities were much higher and on a more gentlemanly plane; of course there was no compulsory work for officers and they and the occupants of RAF camps must have represented a gathering of men having a range of joint intellectual ability higher than that possessed by the ordinary common cannon fodder. A further disadvantage to the ordinary soldier in escaping was that it appeared to us that all escape organizations were geared up to assist in the escape of 'valuable' officers and RAF personnel, and that no one in Britain was really concerned at recovering an imprisoned 'squaddy' or Army other rank, so I felt from the first that the odds were stacked against me in even being able to participate in a well organized escape.

If I was going to escape at all it would have to be on my own or in the company of one or two of my mates, but we would not be able to rely upon any help from the usual escape organizations which would eventually be set up in the occupied territories of Europe. I was told, however, that as an NCO below the rank of sergeant, I would be sent out to working camps, and apparently escape from the working camp would be a very much easier proposition than from the well-guarded Stalag.

The Germans did not keep us long at Schubin. This was a main reception and transfer camp and we were only intended to be there for a brief visit pending being sent out to work in the inevitable stone quarries, coal mines, building sites, etc, which would keep the many ordinary prisoners and civilian internees and natives of the conquered territories fully occupied for the war years.

All sorts of rumours circulated as to the places we might end up working at, and these varied from the more salubrious thoughts of farms and farm girls to the rather bleaker vision of the coal mines of Silesia. In fact parties went to both such destinations and to many other varied types of labour camps, but for the moment it was 'hit or miss' as to where one would end up. In fact the Germans made a theoretical point of trying to find out the previous occupation of the prisoners and fit them in to work places accordingly, which is probably why former piano tuners would end up in stone quarries, but in the main no more than lip service was paid to this procedure.

An essential part of the stay in the 'Reception Centre' was to get a bit cleaner. To this end, all prisoners had their heads shaved clean as a whistle. It was, of course, summer, so the immediate effect of the draught did not worry us unduly, but at first I had great difficulty in even recognizing my own mates. We seemed to look entirely different with no hair, and facial features were severely accentuated so that one stopped and stared at people at first until becoming acclimatized to the new look. In fact I found that the shearing of the head, whilst producing profound displeasure at losing that integral part of the facial features which had been there for so long, did ultimately assist in matters of hygiene and I felt better for it. It also assisted the Germans of course in recognizing prisoners both in the camp and on the run. However, it soon became my view, as well as the view of many of my fellow internees, that there were great advantages to enforced baldness, something which probably the younger generation today would not agree with.

It was also at this camp that we recieved our first introduction to the *Holzschuhe* or clogs as we and the Dutch know them. Most of the boots in which we had travelled through France, and subsequently existed in patched up as best as one could and frequently tied around with string etc, had by now given up the unequal battle to support us, and many had no boots or shoes at all, wrapping blistered and severely punished feet with old newspapers and anything which would afford some protection. However, at Schubin we were duly issued with wooden clogs, presumably purloined in vast quantities by the Germans from Holland.

The clogs were, at first, a nightmare. Without thick socks, they wore away the skin from the sides and tops of our feet, and we found them in fact quite difficult to walk in and extremely uncomfortable. However, as time and circumstances demanded their use, we grew accustomed to them, and with a vast amount of filthy cloth wrapping around the feet before insertion into the clogs, we soon found they were quite comfortable and in the winter were really very warm. They did, however, tend to severely slow down our movement, obviously a considerable advantage to our captors as this precluded any possibility of running. To see a group of newly shod prisoners negotiating their clogs en masse on parade was like watching ducks waddling around a pond.

But our major problem was that the dreaded bug had got hold of the inmates at almost all camps and despite continuous trips to the delouser, lice were now the single most absorbing discomfort we had to contend with. All over the camp, wherever you looked, you could see men squatting on the ground picking lice out of shirts, vests, trousers, etc, as the wretched things got into every available seam and were not easy to find. They bit, produced little pin-prick wounds and carried disease, and were a real threat and it was some two or three years before they were finally and completely eliminated.

The delouser was a new experience. It consisted of completely sealed iron non-absorbent walls giving a chamber about 30 foot square into which men were herded until they were jam-packed together standing up, all of course completely naked. Steam was then injected, and with the more superior models, followed by shower water sprayed from jets in the ceiling. Simultaneously our clothing was loaded on to racks and pushed into ovens for 'baking' – ultimately the baked clothing and cleansed individuals being re-united. This successfully dealt with the little brutes (the lice, that is) but of course as soon as you got back to the huts, those lice which had missed the performance by remaining secreted in mattresses, wood, etc, soon started up a new breeding campaign on the beautifully clean returning victims. The delouser had rather a lot in common with the terrible gas chambers subsequently found to have been used in the concentration camps and which were, of course, based on the same principle, and we were in fact never quite sure whether steam would be injected into the compartment, or maybe some gaseous medium which would have finally ended our misery once and for all.

Toilet facilities were not of the most up-to-date pattern. They were in fact just a pole supported at intervals over a vast pit and the user had to be careful how he tackled the daily (or hourly as it had necessarily become) performance. I was particularly careful since rumour then had it that at least one poor wretch, debilitated no doubt from diarrhoea, fell in and was too weak to clamber out of the cesspit, ultimately drowning, suffocating or being asphyxiated in the pit, and it would be difficult to imagine a more revolting death.

Men were now being continuously sent out to various working camps or *Arbeits Kommandos*, and it was generally understood that rations were greater in the working parties than in the base camp. At the *Stalag* the inmates received about one fifth of a loaf (the whole loaf of brown rye bread being usually about eight inches long) for a day's basic ration with the possibility of a mug of chicory in the morning, maybe a receptacle of potato or cabbage soup in the afternoon; it was just a receptacle, for no eating utensils or crockery were provided. One had to find an old tin or some such article from somewhere, and spoons were at a premium (there was no call for knives of course). Any appearance of a piece of meat in the soup was entirely accidental and indicated that it was a red-letter day or the cooks had missed it. However, we were told that if we worked, we would receive one-third of a loaf instead of one-fifth, and this was indeed a tremendous attraction and men were keen to get out to work for the additional meagre benefit.

It was extraordinary however, how many men, habitual smokers, would happily exchange even the meagre ration of food for tobacco or cigarettes and still keep themselves alive. It seems that to the committed smoker, tobacco is more important than food, and could even produce some nourishment or maybe relief to the nervous system which had an equivalent effect.

I was not slow to take account of the superior rations offered at the working camps, and also the better opportunities for escape. To get out of the camp at Schubin was obviously going to present considerable difficulty, but at a working camp the surrounding fortifications would not be so forbidding, and the contact with the civilian population may assist materially in providing those essentials for escape such as civilian clothing, compasses, etc, without which any serious escape attempt would be impossible.

In the headquarters base camp at Schubin there was also a continuous scramble for permanent cushy jobs within the camp itself, having no additional rations, just perks. Since the commencement of captivity I had used what little German I had learned at school to immediate personal benefit, mostly in the role of negotiator in complicated business deals between those few prisoners who still had something to sell and guards always on the look-out for a bargain. However, I had not sufficient confidence to apply for a post of interpreter, which posts were largely filled by soldiers who had some previous family connection with Germany or neighbouring countries, such as refugee families from World War I, Russian emigrées, etc. There were few others amongst the other ranks in the forces who were able to undertake the responsibility of interpreting which is, of course, a very exacting and precise art if executed correctly. It was a two-edged sword. On the one hand, the Germans had to have interpreters amongst the various departments and compounds of the camp of some 10,000 men or more, and therefore were prepared to give any qualified prisoners some inducements to take on the task, but against that, the interpreter suffered the criticism from his own people that (a) he was pro-German (b) he was fifth column (c) he must have had German sympathies to be able to speak the lingo (d) he was not really translating what was being said but was saying things to please the Germans for improvement of his own conditions. Diplomatically it presented quite considerable problems, as for instance, when the chap for whom you are interpreting says, 'Tell the German B...... he is a fat pig.' Of course the result is that the interpreter who may comply with such a feat of translation is clamped in jail and has his remaining teeth knocked out, whilst not being the originator of the quotation in any case. Anyway, I still kept my silence officially, and refrained from offering my services although in practice I did talk to the Germans and gradually gained some practical confidence to bolster up Matric-standard German.

I weighed up very carefully the pros and cons of getting on a working party and decided ultimately to get into one of the lines of hopefuls who were 'volunteering' before being compulsorily sent off somewhere unpleasant. On 29 July I was duly sent off to my first *Arbeits Kommando*. This was a forbidding thought since, whilst many of my colleagues were in fact manual workers in civvy life, I had been a clerk who seldom had had occasion to lift a spade in anger. I rather feared that the resultant effort might come very hard, at least at first. I need not, however, have worried.

I found it was quite a relief to get away eventually from the interminable masses of prisoners, counted in thousands, and to be in the smaller group of about 200 who were duly marched to the station and to the awaiting cattle trucks for the slow and painful journey (I imagined only in total about 50 miles, but we were hardly priority cargo) to a place called Hohensalza, which was located NE of Schubin and further into Poland. The Germans had re-named most Polish towns with German equivalent names following their occupation of the country, and in fact many changes were brought about in the boundaries of Poland in the east after Hitler's short-lived non-aggression pact with Stalin had resulted in a complete re-alignment of the eastern boundary of Poland and the extension of the Russian boundary to take account of the whole of the Ukraine. The result, of course, was that the area of Poland now occupied by the Germans was not the whole country over which Britain and France had gone to war in consequence of their mutual pact with the former Polish Government. The Russian boundary had advanced to the west by about 250 kilometres, which had thrown the internal communications into some confusion, apart from the very much more important fact of producing direct confrontation between Germans and Russians on borders passing through the former area overrun by the Germans. The Russians had, in fact, taken up their new line in time to show a front to the German Army which invaded Poland, and the areas around the new front were not all that far removed from the towns where the working parties were now situated. Hence one reason why the first thoughts of escape entered into my thinking and the thinking of many other like-minded prisoners, although what reception we may get if we did achieve an escape to the east and be able to cross the front into the Russian-occupied area, was not at all certain.

Hohensalza was a reasonable sized town, maybe 10,000 inhabitants, and from the station we were duly marched to our new home which was some three quarters of a mile from the town centre in a very deserted country area (of course!).

The camp was just an area of open field of about ten to fifteen acres sealed off with the customary barbed-wire fence, and with a purpose-built hut for the German guards separately fenced off, whilst the prisoners were given a barn to live in; the floor of the barn was completely covered with straw, so that we bedded down on the straw in lines just like cattle in stalls. In fact, the cattle would be probably more comfortable, since the straw is frequently renewed, which ours was not. The obvious immediate beneficiary of the system were our friends the lice, who now had great heaps of straw in which to find shelter when bored with consuming British beef. The barn and the straw, together with the meagre droppings from the prisoner's food table, served to attract a large supply of rats, and at night time we found we could listen to the dear little things scuttling about in the straw and coming up occasionally for a bite of good imported British flesh or an inadvertently discarded morsel. The little darlings had not, however, reckoned with the fact that even a small amount of rat meat is preferable to nothing in a weak potato soup, and eventually when one had scraped all the bits off, a goodly number put together could be thought of as nearly the equivalent of a rabbit stew.

Our work was to be on building sites, and I found myself demolishing walls of damaged buildings and buildings destroyed during the German attack on Poland, of which there were a considerable number in the town. The local inhabitants, the Poles, who of course absolutely detested the Germans, a feeling which was very manifestly and forcibly reciprocated by their captors, offered the British prisoners what sympathy they could. There was undisguised friendship from the majority of the Poles who realized that the British were only there because they had taken up the cudgels on the Poles' behalf after the German attack on their country and therefore they were prepared to do what they could to help, which unfortunately was not a lot. There was clandestine passing of the odd slice of bread which was a terrific sacrifice by the Poles who were near a starvation diet themselves, and also if apprehended was an offence literally punished by death – immediate shooting. We saw one elderly and frail Polish lady who tried to pass something to one of us as we were marching from work through the streets of the town, and was apprehended by the guards, thrown to the ground, whereupon the guards proceeded to kick her furiously whilst she lay on the ground. This well illustrated to my mind two apparent facts: that propaganda which insisted that Poles and Jews were sub-human and only animals had registered rather fully with the Germans; and/or that there is something in the make-up of the Germans which severely distinguishes them from most other civilized races. If it was the former, then I could not imagine any British soldiers actually performing in such a callous and brutal way especially to an animal, and if it was the latter I only hoped it was a temporary lapse. I found it difficult to imagine myself in the future even consorting on an equal basis with such a German on holiday or in business, having a drink at a bar and sitting talking in the train, but presumably if by any chance the Allies won the war and all returned to normal, such a situation could arise. It was with some regret that I realized I may have in fact to strike off the whole German race from amongst those with whom I could consort in the future, if and when I might regain my freedom, through some, at that time, apparently unattainable good fortune.

Another very sad example of our captors' evident nature was shown at one of the buildings we were led to, so that we could start demolition work. There was a ghastly smell in this particular quarter and eventually we were led off to another building to carry out our demolition duties, but we were reliably advised by several sources that the first building we had been taken to had been filled up by the Germans with Polish Jews when they advanced into the country and subsequently set fire to. It was clear from our brief observation of the building that it had suffered a severe conflagration internally and the smell did the rest; regrettably we soon found out this example of German treatment of Polish Jews was not unique, and it became very evident that many such atrocities were carried out in those Polish towns immediately after the Germans invaded. It seemed quite astonishing to me to think that any German soldier, presumably in execution of a direct order from a superior and theoretically better educated officer, could actually get round to pouring petrol on a building filled with human beings and apply a burning torch to it to start the inferno. What on earth had made them take leave of their presumably normal sense of decency and respect for their fellow creatures? I shuddered to think that I was now the defenceless prisoner of such people.

Today, I am able to consider such horrific events in retrospect. It may be argued that these were exceptional times and that there has been exaggeration in recording such events, that in fact they just could not have happened. That would be a reasonable view for a reasonable person today to take. However, there was just no exaggeration of the facts which I and my fellow prisoners observed with our own senses. I know that records compiled since the subsequent 'liberation' of Poland by the Russians have substantiated countless such gruesome occurrences perpetrated against Jews and Poles alike, and quite apart from the more widely known atrocities of the main concentration camps, this was simply an example of which I had personal experience and witnessed. It seems amazing to think that at that time in Hohensalza in 1940 I and my colleagues virtually accepted this behaviour by the Germans as par for the course, such was the horrific degree of cruelty and inhumanity with which the Germans conducted their treatment of the vanquished 'enemies' of the State.

Demolition work was rather fun, but very, very dusty and dirty. I found it was quite a relaxing pastime standing on top of a wall with a pick and knocking down bits at a time, a job in fact through which one could give some vent to pent-up passions, but less attractive to those on the receiving end on the ground. It was not a little dangerous, but at least I found it was a form of labour at which my more accustomed labouring colleagues did not seem to excel over me. I was in fact surprised to find that my own method of working which I had thought out for myself, was much more practical than that adopted by my more professional mates. My theory was to move very slowly but to keep moving the whole time. This way I did not attract the attention of the guard, who welcomed the sight of a prisoner standing motionless, spade in hand or being leant on, for he would very promptly take the opportunity to set about the recumbent one with the butt of his rifle which would be severely applied to buttocks, chest and even face. Bruises and blisters were many, but they were such an entirely trivial matter considering other far more serious problems that I soon learnt that everything was relevant in degrees of misery.

The working party seemed to settle down to a fairly regular pattern of marching to work, labouring for about 10 hours in all, marching back and exhaustedly sleeping and then repeating the whole dose again the next day. There was no break except on Sunday, when the day was spent delousing and further sleeping in preparation for the next week's ritual.

The camp was primitive in POW terms since it was early in the war and the Germans were still assured of prompt victory, so the Geneva Convention was of no consequence. An odd POW more or less was simply a matter of numbers to the Germans and the inconvenience of burial, or, to be more precise, digging a hole and dumping. The advent of Red Cross parcels was still just a twinkle in prisoners' very cloudy eyes and they were not to arrive for another eighteen months or so yet. Food was minimal, consisting still of the inevitable one third of a loaf per day, a watery soup and a mug of chicory or some *ersatz* beverage, with the possibility of a small piece of garlic sausage on special occasions.

There was also a quite remarkable cheese or so-called substance which we occasionally received. We were actually quite terrified to receive it, it had such an atrocious smell it was quite unbelievable. Anybody who ever handled it suffered from contamination for some while, and whilst we were only issued with a small piece of the revolting stuff and were very, very hungry, nobody ever had the courage actually to eat it. I actually saw one ration which had inadvertently not been thrown into the cesspit but had fallen on the floor sending forth its stench signals, being removed by some brave soul, and when he tried to scoop it up with a stick, the whole piece of so-called cheese just ran away – it was a pile of consolidated maggots. The cheese was called Quark, a name rather appropriately given to-day to a variety of sub-atomic particles renowned for its unreliability; some of the modern scientist's quarks, however, possess 'charm', but ours most certainly did not!

It was not as yet possible to start trading in earnest with the guards, since this could only be effective with the Red Cross parcel goods to barter with, coffee, chocolate, etc, for which the Germans who also suffered considerable shortages in most luxury goods would ultimately give all sorts of goodies such as radio crystals, valves and parts, compasses and even civilian clothing etc – but this was all in the future. We were now the lowest of the low, nearly on a par with such filth as Jews and Poles, although the extent of their agony had to be seen to be believed – and then you couldn't really believe it. Nevertheless many of the Jews and Poles in their utter distress never failed to show nobility and determination not to give in which was a great example for all of us. Both seemed to have a sufficiency of courage to show their captors their superior moral fibre, even if they had nothing else to show. At one workplace where the British prisoners were digging alongside Jews and Poles a vast hole – Lord knows what for – I was stationed next to a very tall, and obviously distinguished, Jew wearing his yellow star with great pride. He was to my young mind quite elderly, though possibly not more than 50 to 55, for people appear to age pretty quickly under those conditions. Very clearly he had no idea which end of the shovel to grasp, but he emanated a sense of distinction above all the guards and the rest of us. We were told he was a member of the Rothschild family in Poland. We had, of course, no means of checking this as a fact, but one thing was very certain: he was clearly an intellectual and a member of the 'Upper Class', and from his appearance one would immediately assume he belonged to some aristocratic family.He was suffering this enormous set-back in life with such obvious dignity that he became an example to us all – even I think to the guards who viewed him with some awe – and in his new distressing circumstances commanded admiration. He had had so much farther to fall than the rest of us.

It was extraordinary how the daily illnesses to which, in normal times we all seem to fall victim such as common colds, aches and pains, bad stomachs, flu, etc, seemed to recede into insignificance when faced with the vastly greater problems we became accustomed to dealing with and which came under the general heading of 'survival'. I do not, in all those months of living under the stars and in the rain and eating mouldy food from ditches etc, ever recollect catching a cold, flu or even a rheumatic pain (perhaps I was too young for that questionable delight and which would, in fact, come much later in life), and apart from the fairly continuous hazard of diarrhoea, stomach aches and pains as such were the least of our problems. I do, however, clearly remember on one occasion lying in our barn on the straw all night and alternately sweating and shivering, soaking my clothes through with perspiration and obviously running a very high temperature, no doubt well in the hundreds. Realizing that unless I went to work in the morning I would get nothing to eat all day, I forced myself to get up and march to work with the others, still steaming away with the very high temperature. After a day of the most abject misery spent digging holes, I returned in the evening as right as rain – no temperature, no flu and certainly no pneumonia. The only conclusion was that my mental approach to whatever the illness may have been was such that the overriding demand to work to get food overcame the illness that had taken hold of me and would normally have required nursing care. No doubt by forcing myself to carry on, I just sweated the whole thing out.

It was at this time that we received our first mail from England. We had been given cards to fill in with names, POW number and a brief statement to say we were well, doing fine and being treated excellently in a German holiday camp, but had up till then received no communication from home. I was at Hohensalza until the end of October 1940, so it must have been a good five to six months before I heard anything from my parents. I counted myself at all times during captivity, lucky to be young and single with no ties other than my parents, who both, I am quite sure, must have suffered immensely from that initial uncertainty as to my fate, not knowing whether I was alive or dead. But the men I was really sorry for were those older men who were married and maybe had children. Their suffering must have been so much greater, and the terrible agony they felt and the sense of helplessness when hearing from relatives or friends that their wives had been unfaithful and gone off with a Yank or the local pacifist was quite sufficient to very obviously unbalance their minds when added to their already miserable lot. As if they did not already have enough problems to cope with, for the other prisoners could always tell when someone had received such piteous news, as the victim would just close up and not care about anything; food, hygiene, etc. If only the women who caused their erstwhile lovers such agony could see the result of their shallow, despicable and impatient actions. It was at such times that the more usual grasping and selfish attitude of the inmates of the camp would suddenly change to one of compassion, and help would at once become available to the victim who would certainly not be ridiculed for his shortcomings but offered sympathy and practical assistance, even at immediate and great cost to his mates.

A further very worrying feature was the obvious joy with which the guards would daily inform us with great glee of the results of German bombing attacks on our homeland, and a casual comment by a guard to the effect that Coventry, for example, had been wiped off the face of the earth, supported by pictures in a local German newspaper, were quite sufficient to ensure that all those in the camp with relatives in Coventry would have something more to worry about. There was no doubt that in very many camps this imparting of bad news to the prisoners by the German guards was a move clearly calculated to cause additional distress. I was myself caused considerable worry when delighted guards informed me that so many thousands of houses in London had been destroyed in one particular night attack by German bombers. I believe they quoted 90,000. If we were to believe everything we were told about the progress of the war, we could have safely assumed that all our relations must have become the victims of explosions or conflagrations.

The distribution of mail was therefore an extremely important event in our otherwise humdrum lives. Upon the cry being issued 'Mail up' the most anxious group of individuals one could imagine would congregate with varying degrees of hope or fear in their hearts, and as the relatively small number of letters would be given out, quickly calculated by the anxious crowd as being far less than one to each man, tension mounted amongst those many prisoners who had received nothing, until the final passing of the last letter would leave many with the most agonizing fears: had German bombers extinguished that family which represented their last ties with civilization, and a long lost word called 'love'? Had the wife fallen for that bloke in the reserved occupation living up the road, or had the letters just been mislaid by an uncaring German postal organization? Many walked away from the gathering with tears forming in their eyes, many with hatred growing in their hearts as time passed by, and the whole traumatic performance would have done credit to an American soap opera.

During the stay at Hohensalza the scheme to escape was hatched by me and three of my closest friends. I am not sure now who thought of it first, but I think I should lay the blame, or credit whichever way you look at it, on one of the four of us who had teamed up together to form a sort of clique. Peter Andrews was a bit older than the rest of the bunch and probably that much more intelligent, but I think it was a pretty general decision between the four of us that nothing could be lost by having a go at breaking out of camp. This effort terminated in the unfortunate episode related earlier, climaxing with our lice-ridden appearance before the firing squad.

Escaping was really a pretty hopeless task since one just did not have anywhere to go. Europe was completely held by the Germans, and the only possible route for escape from where we were in Poland was to the east to Russia, which was very much an unknown quantity. If you got there, would they just send you back? Would they shoot you or send you to a camp in Siberia for a change of scenery? There was no established route via safe houses operating at that time and in any case such sophisticated an organization seemed impossible to reach for the ordinary soldier. It is understandable that the highly efficient escape mechanisms involving considerable outside assistance from the civilian population should eventually develop, but these were still very early days in the war and we were now located a very long way from the Western countries, France, Holland, Switzerland, etc., which ultimately specialized or participated in establishing escape routes.

Of the three escape attempts I personally made, if they merit that term, only the first, from this camp at Hohensalza, could be regarded as having any of the usual ingredients of reasonably careful premeditation and planning, and although we had no idea of how eventually to cross the border into Soviet Russia, or even what it may look like, or indeed where it was situated, we may well have been successful in reaching it, since the plains of Central Poland were pretty deserted and the majority of the populace clearly as helpful as they could be under the circumstances, and although we may not have been assured of safe houses en route, we reckoned that we could have got quite a distance over open fields, living off the raw vegetables grown in the area – mostly root vegetables, swedes, turnips, sugar beet, etc, all of which are quite sustaining carbohydrates if sucked raw or if circumstances allowed, cooked.

Peter Andrews, who was foremost amongst my most immediate friends, was from a White Russian family, and had joined up as I had as a Territorial. He spoke Russian well, although his family had been naturalized British subjects since arriving in Britain after the revolution in 1918, and he spoke better English than most of us. However, he did not speak any German, so for something to keep our minds occupied I offered to teach him German in return for him teaching me Russian. The latter was quite a task, involving as it did the learning of a complete new alphabet, but we had plenty of time since there was nothing else to do when not working, and we made rapid progress with our respective subjects. The aim then in our minds was to escape to the east, and my Russian-speaking friend Peter would do the talking when en route and at the border, and I would be able to at least play a supporting role; we would pass ourselves off as Ukrainian farm workers who, since the re-organization of the border, were to be found all over the place. It all may seem a bit crazy in retrospect, but there did not appear to be any realistic alternative open to us if we wished to discharge our first responsibility as prisoners of war and try and escape to cause disruption to the enemy, but there was also that very remote chance that we might get somewhere in the end, which of course we did, though not where we had hoped.

The working parties were much easier to escape from than the main *Stalags* for there was nothing like the amount of wire around the perimeter and usually no sentry towers, just patrolling guards. In the camp at Hohensalza, the inmates were locked in the barn at night and just a couple of guards were kept on duty patrolling the area between the barn and the perimeter wire which was not much more than a substantial barbed wire fence. The barn, however, formed the external wall to the compound at one point, and by getting through the wall on one side one could step into freedom, at least temporarily, and there was a convenient wood adjoining which would assist in enabling us to put distance between ourselves and the compound during the hours of darkness. There were no openings in the barn wall that side, no windows or doors, so the plan was to gradually hack away a hole at the base of the barn wall, which was much thicker than anticipated, carefully working on it during the night and covering it up during the day, and try and obtain a map and compass and other necessary equipment.

Peter and I agreed to taking on the two other close friends of ours in the barn to accompany us on the escape. Needless to say, it was pretty impossible to make a hole in a thick barn wall in the closed community in which we were housed with any degree of secrecy and the whole camp had of course to know what was happening. We had many requests for participation from the others and the ultimate choice of just two more to join Peter and me was difficult to make for fear of offending other would-be fugitives, but we managed in the end to convince the rest that too big a party would be impractical, and in any case many of the others upon reflection considered the proposition not to be very worthwhile.

We fixed a date rather at random, and as the day approached we began to wonder what we had taken on. I certainly became very apprehensive of the dangers inherent in the scheme and we discussed between us time and time again the chances of success or failure; in view of the clear statement which had been made by the camp commandant to the effect that any escapees would be shot when recaptured, the result of failure was a little off-putting. It was probably our mutual fear which served to keep up our spirits and ensure that no one backed out or dared to suggest giving up the attempt, combined with the fact that our present lives and future as German slaves did not represent very much to lose.

We had purposely chosen a Saturday night for the break-out, mainly for three reasons: there were fewer guards on duty on Saturday, on which day we only worked for half the day; we ourselves should be less tired not having worked a full day; and lastly with any luck the guards should be at least a bit drunk by around midnight. But by the Saturday morning we were beginning to get a bit edgy.

'It might be bloody well snowing by tonight,' observed the ever pessimistic Martin, who was a regular soldier and appeared to inherit a particularly melancholy outlook presumably as a result of his years in the army. None of the other three of us considered his happy remark worthy of a response, and he had to suffice with a couple of grunts, although the joyous possibility of trudging through thick snow was not lost on us any more than was the fact that our tracks in the snow would be available to the following guards and their dogs, unless the snow was continuous and obligingly new snow would cover up our tracks.

'What if the Jerries get wind of it and are waiting for us on the other side of the wall?' was Martin's next helpful remark. In fact he might well at that point have qualified as a top psychic, as results ultimately showed, but our ever ebullient leader, Peter, shot him down with a not-so-prophetic remark:

'The only people who know anything about this hole in the wall are inmates of this barn, our fellow prisoners, and I am quite sure they would neither have any desire to tell the Jerries, nor have any ruddy opportunity.'

Peter had been chosen as a sort of unofficial leader, probably because he was the oldest; not that that fact put him in a class of 'has-beens' since he was only about twenty-five at the time, but that put him way ahead of the rest of us. To be fair to him, it was probable that he was also appointed because he had more sense than the rest of us put together, and was of course fluent in Russian, which was going to be our native tongue once we were out of the camp; a printer in civvy life he certainly had more organizational ability than the rest of us, and since on these occasions a leader must be appointed, he was duly regarded as such.

'Now, have we got all the bits and pieces?' he demanded as the crucial hour for the break-out got close. The bits and pieces consisted of a few uninspiring pieces of rather dry bread, some sausage by courtesy of a noble Pole who had risked his all to get it to us, water bottles filled, a tin of condensed milk which may have been left behind from the Ark or World War I and a few other morsels which would keep us going until we could get into the fields and stock up with whatever crops or vegetables came our way; a compass, which was our prize piece of equipment purloined from somewhere, and some civilian clothing of a sort, at least trousers and shirt or jacket for each of us, by courtesy of friendly Polish allies.

'Have you got the map safe?' queried Thomas, sounding I thought just a little nervous. I replied that of course I had the ruddy thing safe, safely hidden somewhere in the region of my crotch in case any sudden inspections or roll calls which may have involved a more cursory search. We all realized that as the day wore slowly on, we were beginning to become irritated with each other and impatient for night to come. The adrenalin was beginning to flow.

Eventually darkness fell, and no amount of relentless playing of pontoon with the camp's only complete pack of cards could prevent the high pitch of nervous tension which we had by then reached. We listened carefully to all the usual guard movements outside, not of course being able to actually observe anything through the lack of windows, and assured ourselves, from the tramp of feet, that snow had not fallen. Had there been snow on the ground, we would of course have been in real trouble, as it would not have been difficult for the Germans to trace our movements from the footstep impressions in the snow. As it was, with no snow, we faced the other great terror of the escaper, the German guard dogs of which at least one was kept at the camp and no doubt others could be quickly rustled up. Dogs were the enemy we feared most for there was no shaking them off, and on dry ground our scent would be easy for them to follow; should they catch up with us, the confrontation with a well kept Doberman Pinscher was something an emaciated and not athletically fit prisoner should avoid at all costs.

All our mates in the barn went off to sleep in the usual way, and this in fact made things even worse for us. There we were, all geared up for the great event and at the peak of nervous tension, surrounded by a bunch of snoring bodies comfortably wrapped in greatcoats, brown paper wrappings and other old rags they had managed to pick up en route from France to Poland. A few kept one eye open to see what would happen to us and whether we would actually get away, but the majority were more concerned with their own fate and beauty sleep. The night dragged on and we ourselves began to feel so drowsy we were scared of going off to sleep before the break-out, and eventually wandering about outside half asleep, which would never do, so we just had to force ourselves to stay awake.

'Right lads, let's start removing the bricks,' came the final instruction from Peter, which sounded like a death knell to the rest of us. We had made a hole at the base of the wall just big enough to crawl through, and after working on it each day we had very carefully replaced all the bricks and hid the inside face with the straw and odd belongings we had in the hut. Outside we knew there was quite long grass and hoped that this would completely hide our work although we had not actually fully removed the outer bricks leaving this until the time of our departure.

We now set to knocking out the remaining outer bricks, and Martin was detailed to finish this job off. He had just started to bang out the first of the bricks when suddenly our world collapsed around us.

'Christ!' suddenly came from an ashen-faced, trembling Martin. 'There's a bloody Jerry boot out there.'

'Let me see,' broke in Peter, ever calm, at least outwardly, but it was too late for him to even get a chance to look.

Whistles suddenly blew in all sorts of places and the German boot outside dealt a number of vicious kicks at the hole. Simultaneously the barn door was flung open and half a dozen guards well armed with machine guns and rifles burst through the door, accompanied by the Camp Commandant and supported by the bloody Doberman Pinscher.

By now, the snoring had abruptly ceased and the whole barn was alive to the intense drama that was occurring in front of them, None more so than the four principal participants, who were of course the focal point of attention, standing there looking no doubt somewhat sheepish, apart from being absolutely terrified, dressed in makeshift civilian clothing and rather obviously equipped for a break-out. Without any hesitation, the commandant shouted out the names of the four offenders who then stumbled forward to receive whatever fate had in store for them, clearly remembering the commandant had on so many occasions stated that anyone caught attempting to escape would be shot. My personal reaction to being nominated as an escapee was not over-joyous but rather apprehensive in the extreme. I must say I did, however, wonder how the commandant knew so conclusively the names of the culprits before we had even got out of the hole.

We shuffled over to where the commandant stood with his merry men, and were immediately checked and searched for weapons. Nothing in that line was found on us, which was most fortunate for us, otherwise there would have been little doubt we would have died there and then. Satisfied that we were pretty harmless, the four of us were duly marched out of the barn to the accompaniment of numerous kicks and blows from the guards' rifle butts, and shoved across the quadrangle to the guardroom, where we

were made to sit on a bench in the middle of the room with three guards facing us and three behind, with our hands resting on our heads, and our subsequent fate, recorded earlier, of being led out to face a firing squad did little
to enhance my already withered desire for excitement in life.

6

The Punishment

Our dramatic appearance before the firing squad and subsequent reprieve and return to the guardroom had done nothing to improve my physical or mental condition or that of my three miserable comrades. All the dreams of getting back to Blighty, the remote thoughts of reunion with loved ones and even reunion with a pint of bitter and chunk of Cheddar cheese with crispy bread lavishly spread with butter had all vanished with the first sight of that jackboot outside the hole we had spent so many weeks preparing. In front of us now appeared a very uncertain future, at the best involving some substantial punishment from Germans who excelled at meting out such medicine, especially for dastardly crimes against the state such as escaping from a prison camp. We all three had an awesome regard for the ability of our new masters to punish anyone for any reason or for no reason, and we had to consider the immediate future with great anxiety.

In particular, I felt such disappointment that not only all the effort put in by my mates and I, but also that help afforded by Polish civilians at such risk to themselves had been so wasted, without our ever being able to savour, even for an hour or so, a little freedom on Polish soil. If we had got out and given the Germans a run for their money this would have been some compensation, but to have ignominiously to surrender without even getting out of the barn was not very satisfying. To be betrayed by one of our own compatriots was particularly galling, since it was quite clear that the Germans had complete chapter and verse on our escape proposals, and the subsequent removal from the camp of the little Welshman told its own tale.

We were never allowed back into the barn again after the escape, not even to collect our meagre possessions or uniforms which we had exchanged for an attempt at civilian clothing. Despite the weather being so cold, we had on only the civilian shirt and trousers purloined from the town or from allies amongst the Polish civilians. My trousers, which were very obviously civilian were now taken from me, leaving me clad only in shirt and army underpants, and so regaled I was eventually led from the guard room with my colleagues for a march to the station for the journey back to the *Straflager*, or intense punishment compound, in the headquarters camp at Schubin.

This may sound a somewhat embarrassing way of travelling in public, accompanied by a posse of guards complete with machine guns, but the civilian population seemed to accept it as part of the 'norm' in Nazi Germany and one could only feel a sense of intense sympathy emanating from the local Polish civilian onlookers, and not mockery. At that particular time in Poland there were a very large number of itinerant 'enemies of the state' to be found trudging about on the run or under armed guard, so there was nothing exceptional about a trouserless Englishman. Europe was, in fact, fast becoming one enormous internment camp consisting of those who wholeheartedly backed the governing regime and showed it in no uncertain way for immediate reward, those who gave it tacit but docile support and the vast army of slaves and unwilling supporters. The captured British soldier, not officer, had to classify himself as one of the slaves during the unhappy year of 1940, before the Germans had even questioned the obvious outcome of the war with England and completely ignored the provisions of the Geneva Convention regarding treatment of prisoners.

We were sent to different camps for obvious reasons and I ended up in the *Straflager* of Stalag XXI A and was unceremoniously dumped into a tent with other recalcitrants to commence an arduous period of German military punishment, at which the Germans certainly knew their stuff.

The *Straflager* was just a field at the highest point of the camp where the prevalent winds were most effective in producing continuous icy blasts, and was similar to the general compounds except that the inmates were housed in tents rather than huts, presumably so that the effect of the freezing winds would be felt more severely, thereby at all times serving to break down the will of the recalcitrants temporarily enjoying the benefit of the few weeks of rehabilitation.

German punishment tactics are very cleverly thought out to, at first, ensure that the criminal is psychologically broken down. You cannot really achieve a proper indoctrination unless all previous subversive views are completely knocked out of your system, and the way to do that is, first, to reduce the subject from a state of 'human being' with a conscious will and some dignity, to a state of being a grovelling animal with no will but just an urgent desire for food, water and peace. So to achieve that first victory, you have to make certain that the subject is restrained from having any access to water or food, which in Germany then was not a difficult thing to do, and give him no peace. This was most efficiently obtained by ensuring that the hand-picked guards, chosen solely upon the grounds of being utterly inhumane and completely devoid of any of the usual emotions of sympathy or mercy which are found in most human beings outside Germany, could practise their morbid art upon the captive audience by dragging them out of the tent at any time of night or day, marching them round and round the compound and forcing them to perform all sorts of trivial penances. These included dropping a piece of paper on the ground, and then obliging the chosen one to pick it up, at the same time chastising him in no uncertain manner with kicks and blows to all parts of the anatomy for having left litter on the ground, and other similar petty-minded acts designed to destroy the individual's willpower. The black and blue and bleeding inmate would be then kicked back into the tent and the German hero proceed on his way satisfied that he had made a significant contribution to the nation's war effort or to his own ego.

The offenders were made, of course, to work during the daylight hours. This work used to consist in the main of carrying out ridiculous tasks like digging a deep hole and then digging another similar hole and putting the proceeds into the first hole, therefore following yourself round the compound with continuous lines of dug and filled holes overshadowed the whole time by a guard who derived great enjoyment from urging the digger to greater effort with his rifle butt or jackboot. Another popular pastime was getting the victim to clean something meticulously - utensils, boots, equipment, etc, - and then purposely dirtying the same articles by covering them in mud and dirt and getting him to start all over again. This sort of pastime was interspersed with bouts of furious physical training such as running on the spot until you literally collapsed, with a German with fixed bayonet or with whips playing a supporting role. Press-ups and other such exercises were performed literally beyond the maximum point of endurance, which would all have been reasonably acceptable if I and the others suffering the displeasure of the German commandant had had food in our stomachs. As it was, we were restricted to the inevitable piece of rye-bread and water. Not even chicory or soup. After all, it was a *Straflager* and we had committed the greatest crime in the book - escaping - and had to be made an example of, so we could only consider ourselves to be very fortunate to be let off with our lives. At night we were only supplied with one blanket each, sleeping on the ground; it was now becoming very cold so we pooled the blankets and slept together five at a time with, say, two blankets under and three on top - fine for the chap in the middle but not so good for the outsiders.

The whole performance seemed to follow, to an extreme degree, the general German military disciplinary code as extended to prisoners and other vermin, namely that of reducing the subject to a state of physical weakness and moral degradation and depression, to render him incapable of raising any further resistance to the conquerors' demands. Any element of inhumane treatment meted out as a result was merely unfortunate and part of the process of correction.

My stay in the *Straflager* fortunately did not last long and after three weeks or so I was called before the under-officer in charge of the enclosure.

'Corporal Palmer, you have been punished because of your stupidity in trying to escape from your prison camp. This was a dumb thing to do. You thought you could get to Russia but you do not understand that our glorious Führer is the friend of the great Russian leader Stalin, and if you had succeeded in reaching the Russian border, which of course you could not possibly have done, our friends the Russians would simply have handed you back to our frontier guards. So there is no sense in trying to escape again. You will remain at your working party and work hard for the wonderful future the Führer has promised the people of Europe, and always remember that the penalty for escaping is death, so consider yourself very, very lucky.'

I had in fact already observed in Poland the wonderful future the glorious

Führer was handing out to his new subjects; I furthermore was very doubtful that the Russians and their devious master Stalin were really quite so overwhelmingly in love with the Germans, in which view I was very shortly to be proven most correct. As to whether I was really lucky in escaping the death penalty was a matter of debate, considering the sorry state to which I had now been reduced. With no present and no future, death may well have been a reasonable alternative.

No doubt the lecture was intended so that I could pass the commandant's views on to the other prisoners, thereby, it was hoped, deterring them from making any similar attempts to escape. However, for the moment, I gave the under-officer my most affectionate grin which did not amount to a lot, and shuffled, rather relieved, out of the guardroom, accompanied by the customary number of bashes in the posterior from the inevitable rifle butts. I was in fact only too delighted to get out of the punishment block, and no working party could be anywhere near as bad, or so I thought.

So having been duly equipped with a second-hand pair of Polish army officer's breeches to cover the, by now, revolting British army underpants, I was immediately sent off with a batch of workers to a coal mine at a place called Kattowitz in Upper Silesia. The coal mines were actually in some demand by POWs since they offered slightly better rations and, above all, warmth in the colder weather. However, there was a dispute apparently going on amongst the Powers That Be to the effect that work in the coal mines could be considered to be direct involvement in war effort, and at least the British understanding of the Geneva Convention (and some German local area commandants had by now actually found a copy) expressly excluded the employment of war prisoners on work of this category. We had, therefore barely time to get to the working party and down a mine before the camp was broken up and became manned and occupied by Polish and other foreign civilian internees and war prisoners less adequately protected by the Convention.

In the mine itself, the work each day led us on to reach new pinacles of discomfort and distress. We assembled at about 6 a.m. to be lowered to the coal face in terribly antiquated cages, which were always getting stuck and breaking down, with the result that we passed the day wondering if the wretched things would ever get back up again. There were ponies in the pits, and I had the utmost sympathy for those poor creatures who had to live a life down in the dark – animals which were meant to be free in the fields. However, the prisoners themselves were also used by the Germans as pit ponies, and a party was each day designated for 'pony' work, being harnessed to the coal trucks in teams and forced to haul the train of trucks – maybe three or four at a time, along the tunnels.

The whole set-up was so primitive by accepted modern standards that it would be difficult for a young Welsh miner today to even imagine coal mines had been like it. Not even showers were available to the workers at the pithead, and we did not get a wash until we arrived back at camp, after a march through the town, and then there was an unearthly scramble around very few cold water points located outside in the yard, and the word 'cold' in

Poland in mid-winter takes on a whole new significance. Instead of having hot soapy water to remove the coal dust from our bodies, we had freezing water which literally froze on us.

Picking at the coal face was a soul-destroying pastime, and although conditions today in mines must be vastly different, I developed great sympathy for those who work in mines as a profession and felt rather ashamed to think that I had sat cosily in front of blazing fires at home without giving any thought to the very hard, dirty and unpleasant work which many people had been involved in to provide such comforts. We seemed to spend the whole day cramped up double, facing a wall of coal at the end of a very ill-lit tunnel, hacking away at the coal face and pushing the proceeds backwards to be collected by the supporting team. There was, of course, the inevitable and continuous cloud of coal-dust over everything, and in one's eyes, mouth, ears – you name it – and I felt quite sure that such a performance continued over an extended period must have been eventually fatal. Facing that black wall and enveloped in carbon fumes for ten hours a day breathing methane gas with a pitifully small admixture of oxygen, and accompanied by the inevitable guards urging us to ever greater effort was the very depth of misery, and we could be forgiven for believing that we had reached the absolute ultimate in terms of human distress. Everything is relative in life, and I had not yet reached that point, by a long chalk!

The mine was very ill-equipped, and the lighting consisted of oil lamps not very prolific in quantity or effective, and there was just no efficient ventilation system to remove the ever-present clouds of coal-dust. I felt that I was just hacking away at my life, as I spent the time attacking the black wall in front of me and trying to gauge how many more hours of the shift work we still had before we could get out of the black hole and see blessed light, and maybe even the last rays of sun, again, for at that time in the winter we went to work in the dark and came back in the dark.

The actual mining operation was carried out under the supervision of civilians – good patriotic German bastards in charge and supported by apparently very pro-German Poles or locals who were in charge of the teams of slaves working at the various tunnel heads. There was a further team of workers at ground level, which was near a railway coal-yard, whose more pleasant occupation was the loading, all manually, of coal trucks. The whole establishment seemed to be manned by a variety of different nationalities and the British were certainly by far the smallest group. There were Polish civilians, Polish POWs, French, Belgians, Russian civilians and no doubt, later, Russian POWs, Jews of all races, and the whole place was operated on a slave labour basis. There must have been more seething hatred of Germans and Germany contained in those underground tunnels than anywhere else on earth. Each party was, of course, kept under individual control by its own guards, and it was pretty obvious that the guards themselves hated the whole atmosphere although they accepted that it was all for the good of a greater German Reich extending across the universe.

But fortunately for me it was only a little while after I arrived, that the whole British camp was broken up and we were all returned to Schubin.

Presumably the complaints which had been raised invoking the provisions of the Geneva Convention had had some effect, for it was only the British who were removed from the hell-hole. As we marched away, breathing very clear sighs of relief, I was shattered to think that so many human beings, no doubt good, honest creatures looking forward to a reasonable life involving the usual balancing mixture of good and bad fortune should remain incarcerated in those tunnels, to live and probably die there amidst the clouds of coal dust and awaiting nothing more than the temporary end of the long shift and a brief glance at the sun if time allowed before being forcibly returned to the continuing misery which would sap their whole individuality by wrecking both physical body and mind. Even if they survived, they would return to civilized life, be it in France, Russia or elsewhere, to live only a part of a life in the future; the rest would have been left down in the pits. Only the general aura of hatred against their oppressors would live on to be decimated over the four corners of the earth and remembered by at least a few minds until extinction would ultimately erase the crimes from earthly records, but not maybe from all records.

The young Polish lad who used to sometimes be engaged in acting the part of a pit pony, who could not have been any older than me: how came it that he had had his life's prospects terminated so suddenly and completely? 'At least,' I thought, 'my lot are still fighting and there is some remote chance I may one day get back to England, but this obviously intelligent lad, who did not look as though he were likely to harm a fly, no longer had a homeland and was just a German slave – in slavery of the twentieth century pattern. And why was he chosen for this singular honour?' I could think of plenty of my scrounging so-called mates at home who would tell any lies and do anything to avoid getting called up, and at the end of the day they would emerge victorious with pockets full and good positions, whilst I and my fellow prisoners were, at the best, destined to have to rely on the goodwill of such mates in the future to be able to acquire a pint of beer, let alone a job. Maybe the Polish lad and I had been chosen by an unseen Master because of our ability to withstand the pressures involved, but I soon put that idea to one side. I was not at all sure that I *was* withstanding them, although the Polish lad seemed able still to raise a weak smile on the very rare occasions a joke was anywhere in the offing. No, there must be some other reason behind it all, but I could bloody well do with that pint of beer that appeared in my reveries. And so the daily philosophizing would go on.

That was the only action that remained to us as we would spend day after day at the same monotonous and most unpleasant routine; at least our captors could not control our ability to pursue freedom of thought and to dream. We could be directed here, there and everywhere and be shoved about and belaboured with rifle butts, but no German could actually control our thought processes. Philosophizing and thinking over the past were the two mainstays of our existence, and no one could take that away. Perhaps that is the point of the whole thing – to make you think and try to understand through contemplation and examination of past events. One thing was very certain: we lived for the day, for the hour indeed, and our actions each minute would determine our future chances of survival. I suppose there must always have remained some lingering hope that we would some day see better times, but it was very hard, in that coal mine in Silesia in the winter of 1940/41 to see where any relief might come from.

Perhaps that was the whole point: the Polish lad who could summon up a smile when his whole life had been so unjustly concluded by the action of some mad German dictator, he had a message to pass on which he could still pass on despite the guards standing over him. The message was simply that he could still smile; it was not the dictator who was the great man, but the Polish boy who was able to say, without speaking, 'Don't give up, it's only a big joke, laugh your way through it.' He was able to smile in adversity. All the great dictator could do was scowl in prosperity and wreck millions of people's lives in the effort.

We had our ups and downs and the downs certainly outweighed the ups. More than often utter despair was the overriding condition, but it only needed one little incident like the smile from the face of one who had even less reason to smile than we did, that would enable us to muster up enough strength to soldier on, content, if you will, in the pitiable knowledge that there is always someone to be found who is worse off than you – small consolation indeed but under such conditions, it helped.

On 25 October I was sent off with many of the members of the former coal-mine camp to a town called Kalisch by the Germans, Kalisz by the Poles. It may seem surprising that I am able to quote the actual dates. When I eventually returned years later to England, I brought with me the yellowed notepad pages on which, at the time, I wrote the names of the various places I went to, since really the whole thing was such a terrific adventure for the 'starry-eyed one' travelling to unheard-of places, that I felt quite proud of my world travels and was careful to keep a proper record to tell the folks back home, if I ever saw them again and if there were any folks or home to go back to. Hence the reason I was able to quote the exact dates upon which the various transfers from camp to camp were effected.

Kalisz must have once been a very pleasant town and is situated in central south-west Poland and our camp was not far removed from the middle of the town – about a half hour's march – and a substantial improvement on our former billets. It was not a camp in the strict sense, but was a building previously used as institutional premises, a school perhaps, and was at least a solid building; which was just as well, since the winter was coming on and it gets a bit chilly in central Poland.

We were employed on the digging of a main town rainwater drainage system which was to be connected with the canal which ran through the centre of the town, and all the work was manual. I got an uplift in status, which was not however to last long. I had registered my trade upon arrival at the main camp as 'quantity surveyor' which had no real equivalent in German and someone had translated this as *Bauingeneur* or building engineer. Some wide-awake official at the camp at Kalisz had noticed this and promptly suggested that I should be engaged in the preparation of detail drawings and plans for a drainage system, rather than waste time digging;

after all, it was only a Polish town and it did not matter much what happened there and in any case all the German draughtsmen were otherwise engaged on much more important things so I was accordingly given paper and pencil and allotted various tasks. Since I had not progressed much farther in my profession in England before the war than tea-making, I was really completely fogged by the whole performance, especially since it was all in German of course, but in view of the fact that it was warmer in the office and far more comfortable than digging, I persisted for as long as I could to bluff my way through. This may well have accounted for the fact that, after we had completed the whole drainage scheme and were returned to the main camp, I learnt that, when the final connection was made by the Germans and Poles between the canal and the drainage system, the canal emptied itself into the drains instead of vice versa!

At this camp we all began to recover a sense of proportion and to become a bit more human. The chief enemy was the cold, since the temperature in this part of Poland fell very low in mid-winter and we were allowed to stop work outside only when the temperature fell under 26° below zero Centigrade. I had started to suck a pipe at the time only because some well-meaning soul en route had given me one and on special occasions I filled it with dried leaves, tea leaves, dry dung or anything which would burn, even tobacco if I could find a sympathetic and particularly courageous Pole. Whilst digging and having it stuck empty in my mouth to suck on, it used to freeze in position in my mouth and I had to break the ice around the edges of the mouth to get it out. One poor old chap (about thirty) who slept near me in our billet and who had false teeth and used to put them into a mug of water at night by his bed, found they froze solid by the morning; so he kept them in his boots instead, wrapped up in a sweaty sock. They must have been quite tasty to put into the mouth in the morning!

At this camp I enjoyed, if that could be considered the right word, my first Christmas in captivity. I could not say that anything particularly exciting or especially enjoyable occurred – though we received a half a loaf of bread instead of a third – but the experience itself seemed only to accentuate the misery which was being experienced by us all in captivity, and especially so for those with wives and children a long way away. I never failed in the future to be impressed by the fact that the occasion of Christmas, whilst being of joy in itself and for children generally, is also a terribly sad time for those who have suffered bereavements or are lonely or parted from loved ones, and the more that today's commercialism extols Christmas the harder that suffering, experienced by so many, is felt.

It was at Kalisz that we were witnesses to an incident which we all found almost unbelievable in itself. Whilst marching back from work one day, a young girl who was standing at the side of the road near us suddenly lunged forward and thrust a loaf of bread she was carrying into the arms of one of our party. Very unfortunately she was seen by one of the guards who immediately rushed forward and hit the girl furiously about the head and body with his rifle butt.

The girl, was, however, pregnant and well advanced, and when she fell on to the pavement we felt that enough was enough and that the guard would leave it at that. But no, when the guard too realized she was pregnant, he proceeded to jump up and down on the girl's stomach as she lay in the gutter. The girl's screams were with us for a long time after, as well as the memory of the satisfied leer of the guard who appeared to be well content with his afternoon's work.

To knock the girl over at all in that condition was a callous and evil act; to jump up and down on her afterwards in her helpless state, goes beyond any expression I can think up. The guard's action, stemmed, possibly, from the propaganda which had been instilled into him that Poles were not human beings, only animals. But who could ever perform like that to an animal? Maybe he was pleased to be able to terminate the birth of a Polish enemy before his or her actual birth, but has 'my friend' Hans to resort to slaughtering the enemy before they are even out of the womb to get his kicks or to obtain some satisfaction from discharging what he sees as his duty?

Friendship was very frequently shown to us by Polish civilians, but the risks were so great that we sometimes wished they would refrain from such acts of kindness, even though there may have been a very welcome loaf of bread at the end of it. They were sometimes unnecessarily courageous. I myself maintained a sort of 'pen pal' relationship with a girl and her mother, surreptitiously passing notes on the way to work, or on a building site, and to this day I have their photographs on the backs of which I had to heavily erase their names and addresses which they had very unwisely written on them and which, if they had been found on me by the Germans, would most surely have resulted in a concentration camp for them or even death.

Our task in digging holes, trenches, etc, for the drainage system of Kalisz came to an end in April 1941 and we were duly packed off, as a complete working party, to a place called Schildeberg. Schildeberg was located a little way north-west of Kalisz, still in Poland, but the camp was well outside the town so we did not have much opportunity for association with Polish civilians, which was unfortunate. The availability of civilians was always imperative to obtaining occasionally a little extra and in particular was an essential to the preparation of supplies and equipment for escape purposes.

The name of the town in which the camp was located was not really important and not always easy to discover except by noting the names on any remaining signboards many of which had, of course, been destroyed or damaged beyond recognition at the time the Germans overran Poland. We knew the name of the town we were in and that was about all and to fix the precise location required the acquisition of maps. In fact, when writing the odd letter home I devised what I thought was a rather brilliant wheeze to let my parents know where I was. I wrote several consecutive letters, and by several that meant the maximum allotted limit which was one per month, but each successive letter I addressed to my parents with wrong initials for the Christian names, i.e. in transmitting the name Kalisch I wrote to my parents instead of Mrs W.E. Palmer, Mr and Mrs K.A. Palmer and then Mr and Mrs L.I. Palmer etc. At the UK end my father obviously realized there was something afoot and since he had then moved to East Grinstead near a military hospital establishment, he drew the matter to the attention of some officers who investigated and eventually advised him that I was at a town in Poland named Kalisch; I considered this to be a successful piece of Secret Service work, but unfortunately pretty useless.

Schildeberg was only a transit camp but I was there for about two months before departing under my own steam. The camp was monotonous and nothing very exciting occurred during my stay there except for one ghastly incident. To get to our barrack room we had to ascend an external wooden staircase and one day when we were going up this staircase en-masse after parade there was some shouting below and suddenly came rifle shots with bullets whizzing past my ear; the soldier immediately in front of me fell on to me, shot dead, and the one above him fell down the stairs severely injured. In fact we all collapsed to the ground which was of no great consequence except to the poor chap who was killed and the one injured.

We learnt later that a guard had just received news that his mother had been killed in a British air raid on Berlin and as a retaliation he decided to shoot one or two of the prisoners. He must have missed me by inches, or more probably millimetres, since the guard was located somewhere behind us and the bullets travelled past my head to finish up with the unfortunate recipients immediately ahead of me. The incident was sufficient to start a mini-riot in the compound as men ran in all directions to escape from the shooting, which in fact ceased after the initial burst. However the chaos in the yard took some controlling and eventually the whole guard was brought in and the men lined up and shepherded back into the billets urged along by an impressive array of machine guns and much coarse Teutonic screaming. The senior British NCO complained vociferously of course to the Germans, who had little alternative but to admit the shooting for what it was; the German report, of course, merely stated that an 'incident' had occurred as a result of which one prisoner had been killed. But that did not bring back the dead man who had ascended the steps just before me. I have wondered, however, just what that guard must think about his action today if he is able to think at all; he was well aware that he had shot the prisoner dead, but would he really have enjoyed lasting satisfaction from such an action or maybe ultimate remorse at causing further unnecessary suffering?

The fact that towns and cities in Germany had now begun to be bombed by the RAF did present a problem to us in our relationship with the Germans guarding us. Whilst we found it often helpful to butter up our immediate guards in order to obtain some small concession to reasonable treatment, the result of a reported air raid on that guard's home town could rapidly undo all our effort and have unfortunate consequences for ourselves.

Then one day it suddenly happened again. 'I'm getting f— fed up with this dump,' remarked Harvey, a Geordie mate of mine, and an ex-member of the ill-fated 51st Highland Division from St Valéry. 'How about making a break, Graham.' This always seemed to be the fatal start to a conversation which usually ended in disaster. We duly discussed the pros and cons, the cons being obviously in the preponderance, but all the usual problems were explored. 'Where to?' 'How do we get any equipment in this hole?' 'Anybody got a map?' 'How do we come by civvy clothing?' and so on. To any more rational-thinking person, these objections would suffice to call a halt at that point.

Harvey, which was oddly enough his Christian name, not surname, came from that breed of northerners from the British Isles who were not deterred by the mere irrationalities of a situation. The remnants of the Scottish Division who seemed to infest the camps were made up, not surprisingly, of Scots of whom many came from the Glasgow area and were of the type who appeared, at least on the face of it, to be frightened of no one, especially Germans with machine guns, although it was soon made apparent to me who learned from experience that there was a definite point of return which could be rapidly reached by them in this philosophy. The Geordies, who seemed also to have heavily invaded the ranks of the 51st Highland Division, were, however, another matter altogether. Not so spontaneous in their threats and slower to rise to anger, they nevertheless seemed to possess a certain ultimate resilience and determination, which may have been lacking in their territorial neighbours across the border.

I liked Harvey, and trusted his determination, even though that did not answer any of the questions still outstanding.

So we embarked on further discussions leading to a plot to escape and the 'hows' and the 'where to's' had now to be answered somehow or another. The general direction in which we should travel seemed fairly obvious: there just was nowhere else to escape to, except one direction; the East. And this is what attracted our attention, for by now my continuous study of Russian on all possible occasions and growing fluency in German was bearing fruit and I could manage some limited conversation in Russian usually with Poles who did not particularly like speaking the language but were always prepared to help, as well as much improved German with the guards who were always pleased to have somebody who could interpret their screams. I had also earlier struck up a friendship with another offspring of an old Russian émigré family who had helped me enormously in my efforts to learn the language as we had worked together at Kalisch.

The question of equipment was pretty hopeless. We did find a map of the region, of sorts, and a compass which worked sometimes, but not reliably, but generally our preparations were exceedingly limited and after making these ridiculously brief and general plans – just some attempts at clothing to look more civilian and saving rations when possible and working out some general sense of direction – the two of us just decided to do a bunk and move east at night across the fields. A very vague and crazy scheme no doubt when compared with the more sophisticated and better prepared 'professional' efforts but nevertheless better than remaining cooped up doing nothing. After all, it was summer 1941, and surely it would not be too uncomfortable wandering across the plains of Poland, which looked pretty deserted, and living 'rough' off the land for a short while?

I did not personally feel very happy about the lack of planning behind this effort at escape; we had of course vaguely heard about highly planned brilliantly executed escapes by POWs through tunnels and so on, mainly by officers or RAF personnel; the casual 'do a bunk' performance we were now involved in seemed a rather pitiful and lack-lustre attempt. The truth was that whilst we knew we were under a moral obligation, as prisoners of war, to render ourselves as much of a nuisance to the enemy as we reasonably could without necessarily jeopardizing our own safety, and this included escaping, we really had no use for tunnels and no means, at this stage of our captivity, of getting any superior equipment, such as buying fake identity cards with Red Cross goods and so on, all of which later on in our confinement became possible. At least the result would tie up temporarily a few enemy military and civilian personnel in hunting us down and eventually recapturing us and this in fact seemed to be almost the main reason for undertaking the escape. The ultimate possibility of actually achieving freedom after reaching neutral territory was very much pie in the sky and, although we did of course dream of such an eventuality, we did not seriously consider there was much hope, starting from central Poland and with absolutely no outside assistance, addresses of 'safe' houses or even reliable or detailed maps. The maps we could get hold of were not really of very much use. The invasion of Poland by the Germans appeared to have set off a similar invasion or incursion by the Russians, and the old maps could no longer be relied upon to indicate even the correct location of any frontier, apart from which we did not, of course, have up-to-date information on the political relationship between the Germans and their new neighbours.

The whole thing was more a matter of complying with one's military obligations and hoping for a few days away from the relentless and monotonous daily existence as a prisoner. In fact, even to get away from one's own comrades and feel the resultant freedom of movement in the open fields was a tremendous temptation and any added bonus in the form of actual escape to freedom was almost unbearable to seriously contemplate. I actually had to close my mind to such a thought, writing the chance of success off from the first, to lessen the eventual disappointment as failure.

Since my previous escape attempt I was well aware that the Germans had changed their views about the war, just a little. Whilst previously they were fully confident of immediate invasion of England and a victory which would enable them to extend their empire over the whole of Europe, the intervening delay and a few air raids over Germany, coupled with some minor complications in negotiations with Americans and Russians, had undermined their confidence in an easy victory over Britain just a little, although they were quite sure of ultimate success and used still to take delight in reporting to us the massive air raids over London and the numbers of homes destroyed and people killed. However, the commandants had by now unearthed copies of the Geneva Convention referring to treatment of POWs and escapees had a little less to fear, in the event of being apprehended than was the case previously. So long as an escaping prisoner kept his Army Pay Book, did not carry arms or assault anyone, particularly civilians, or steal anything, he was unlikely now to be indiscriminately shot, and would only probably be committed to a spell in the *Straflager* which I had of course already experienced. However, once he had discarded his uniform, there was always a chance of being arrested as a spy and shot out-of-hand without further enquiries being made.

It all very much depended on how you were recaptured. Being confronted by a German soldier who had just heard that his girl friend had been killed back home in a British air raid would severely enhance the odds on him pumping a few bullets into a defenceless prisoner in sweet revenge, afterwards claiming he had shot the prisoner whilst attempting to escape. It was just too easy, and even if he had been in the company of some of his colleagues, no doubt they would have had little compunction in backing him up. On the other hand, being recaptured or giving yourself up to a civilian or to a group of people would improve the prisoner's chance of survival, and probably illicit nothing more serious than a few kicks in the crotch and blows to the head to reinforce the feeling in the civilians' minds that they had delivered a few blows in the sacred cause of victory for the Fatherland. After all, the prisoner was only an animal, devoid of physical feeling and, more importantly, had no means of returning the kicks.

Being a combatant national in enemy territory in war-time was never an entirely comfortable situation to be in, but when those around you were being relentlessly bombed by your nationals and the bombs were apparently particularly directed on to hospitals and schools, sympathy for your person evaporated and the chances of personal reprisals upon you severely increased, especially if there was little likelihood of any repercussions.

Anyway Harvey and I decided to do a bunk from one of the daily working parties which used to depart from the camp to different locations every day.

We both managed to join a party which we knew would be travelling to a work place, a railway coal yard, some quite considerable distance farther east than the camp, and after hiding our illicit equipment and civilian clothing under our uniforms we joined the work party as volunteers and travelled in a lorry, with about thirty others, for some one and a half to two hours before arriving at a bleak railway yard miles from anywhere. It could not have been a more suitable spot from which to make our break. Anyway, it would give us a very useful start in the easterly direction we were aiming for, and when the day's labour was over, we adopted the very simple ruse of having two of our mates counted twice before being loaded back into the lorry, which was not very difficult to arrange due to the remoteness of the place and the fact that no prisoner would be likely to escape to nowhere, which made the guards fairly confident and therefore less vigilant; the counting was done by a guard from the front and we were lined up in columns of five. After the first few columns had been counted, two mates at the back hopped round and joined the last column, effectively being counted twice and making up the correct number; we however, hid low in an empty coal truck until the party had departed in the lorry back for the camp.

This of course also served to give us a very useful head start, for our absence would not be noticed until the lorry got back to camp, some two hours later, and since we were in a very deserted location, we were able to make prompt headway and remove ourselves as far as possible from the coal yard in the twilight. So, after hearing the lorry depart, we cautiously peeped out from our filthy coal truck, saw not a soul in sight and, hey presto! the great escape was under way.

Off we went, with the object of travelling by night across fields and hiding during the daytime in woods, ditches or anywhere one could hide – all very crazy but exciting in its peculiar way. It was bound to come to nothing and that is what it did shortly come to for my colleague. Some three or four days after travelling in this way in the general direction to the east, and we may have moved some forty or fifty miles or so across fields, Harvey contracted the most ghastly stomach pains. Illness was something we had not really reckoned with when embarking on the escape, for it was just not something one seemed to think about any longer. A person really had to be pretty fit to start with to get ill, and that was not a condition we enjoyed. In our pretty dire straits, such ordinary complaints as colds, indigestion, 'flu, bugs, etc, were of absolutely no consequence and were just shrugged off as a mild irritant. But with Harvey now it was something quite different. He could hardly walk and seemed to be absolutely paralysed with pain from his stomach around the lower part of his body. We had, of course, been eating some pretty odd meals, for apart from the meagre provisions we had taken from the camp, we lived off odd vegetation met with during our tramp across the fields, and which consisted of various root vegetables, eaten raw and which probably required a fair amount of digesting, questionable mushrooms, doubtful water, etc.

'I'm going to have to pack it in,' Harvey had said, obviously very reluctantly. 'Just can't go on.' He had already spewed his guts up, and after I had made a cursory and unwelcome inspection of the rejected delicacies and had thought I espied blood, but it might have been the raw carrots or some over-ripe tomatoes we had recently come across and included in our last meal, I realized that there was obviously something radically wrong with the Harvey digestion.

'Come on, there's a farmhouse I can see in the distance ahead. We will take pot luck and give ourselves up in the hope we hit on a friendly farmer,' I suggested. But Harvey was not having any. At least, if he could not make it, he was going to make ruddy sure that at least fifty per cent of the partnership could continue with the expedition.

'No, you carry on. I'll take pot luck with whatever happens in the farmhouse.'

'Can't we both go in and hope for the best?' I suggested, but Harvey, whilst suffering the most excruciating pains, which we both suspected was some form of extreme diarrhoea or maybe a food poisoning, had quite definitely insisted on going on alone.

'I obviously can't carry on roughing it in this way any longer,' he had surmised, 'and I will only be a hindrance to you. You can do all the speaking, knowing the languages, and have a better chance, probably, on your own of getting through than with me. They can't do much to me, being sick, and will probably just return me to the camp. They will, no doubt, ask me what happened to you since they would know that the two of us had escaped together and I will say that you left me the first day after we escaped at the coal depot, since we thought we had better chances on our own, and I now have no idea where you may be. Go on, mate, and bloody good luck!'

A friendship founded in mutual trust and understanding and cemented over a short period by a relatively dangerous joint undertaking became shattered in so many moments. The last few days of co-operative understanding, heart to heart talks in the middle of woods occupied only by a few rabbits and birds, was ended by that feeble wave and courageous grin bidding of good luck.

I always retained a soft spot for Geordies since then. Good, solid rational thinking from a chap who was suffering in the extreme from continuous pains but as he struggled the two hundred yards or so from the copse we were hidden in, across open ground to the small stone farmhouse or maybe it was only a worker's cottage, I somehow felt that I had lost a limb. It seemed to me that two people's joint courage exceeds the sum total of two people's individual courage, and I felt like a cripple who had his crutches taken away. The further trouble with such separations was that I knew darn well that, in the complex organization of prison camps in Germany, I would probably never even see Harvey again, which was precisely the case. The weak little wave as he left seemed so final yet so insufficient.

We had agreed that when he eventually got to the farmhouse, if the farmer was friendly he would get him to go to the front door or go himself and give me a shout that all was well, but if not, it would be better for me to buzz off.

The farmhouse door opened to Harvey's knock but I could not see by whom. Harvey disappeared inside.

I waited a long time but no one came to the door, and eventually a man came out and got on a cycle and went off down the road. I suspected that he was going for the police, so decided to get out fast, which I did.

I was now on my own and not very happy about it either; it is one thing to share the burden of hardships with someone else, to be able to moan and curse and swear to someone who would at least make sympathetic noises in return, in fact just to know that there was someone else of your own breed available to talk to, but when completely on one's own it is a very different story. If the truth were known, I was not at all happy about my future prospects at that particular moment and would gladly have exchanged lots with almost anyone including those tucked up safely in their POW barracks.

However, it must be remembered that, from an entirely practical viewpoint, I was already a prisoner and if I was recaptured I would still be just a prisoner. So what would be the point of just giving oneself up? Furthermore, although it may sound sad for one so young, at that time, in the early years of captivity, lives were valued at a very low premium – it was odds against surviving the war so an early decease would not be of much inconvenience and could certainly spare me a considerable amount of present and probably future discomfort. When relating the event later to my fellow prisoners, the general opinion concerning my decision to carry on went something like 'More bloody fool you, cock' or something equally sanguine, but without doubt most realistic. The most serious problem with being a lone escapee was that when you were eventually apprehended it was very much easier for the Germans just to annihilate you, with no witnesses, than it would be if there were two or more persons involved. Furthermore, the very fact of the loneliness involved was exceedingly discomforting.

As to what happened eventually to Harvey I was not entirely clear. I was able to discover that he was returned to the *Stalag* but fortunately it appeared that his stomach problems were of not the great consequence we had feared. They could well have resulted from tension, or maybe drinking dirty water or eating polluted food. It may seem odd that I was not able to keep in contact but of course, once friends were separated in POW camps they tended or were forced to go their various ways, and it was not possible to phone up one's mates in other camps or communicate with them in any way (although later on it became possible to write a letter to a close relative in another camp). Since I was not even in the same regiment as Harvey, once we were parted there was no further likelihood, over the next four years at least, that we would be liable to meet other than by pure accident; after repatriation it was of course an entirely different story, since we were by then all anxious to get on with the future and forget the past.

So whereas my life was intimately involved with Harvey over a short period of traumatic experiences this all very quickly became erased from the mind in the greater cause of immediate survival and ultimate living; in fact, after the war we would just not wish to be reminded of these episodes for rather obvious reasons, and very few prisoners who were captured in the early days of the war ever eventually went out of their way upon release to meet up with their fellow sufferers. I did, in fact, once meet in England one of the three colleagues I was involved with in the abortive escape attempt from Hohensalza. Peter seemed so very, very different as a prosperous business man, and he in turn could hardly recognize me without the stars in my eyes!

So off I plodded in general direction east – the original Lone Ranger – and found no shortage of convenient woods and fields to hide up in during the day. I did not see a soul and repeated the operation for several days, still going I hoped, east.

The whole question of navigation was one of pot luck. I had a compass, which I tried to follow, but I think I relied more on lining up the occasional buildings, woods, etc, that I could see in what I hoped was a straight line; a very primitive method which usually leads to disaster, but it must be remembered that central Poland is very flat, uncluttered by towns or even houses, and the occasional wood or clump of trees becomes a landmark which, together with the compass, enabled me, I hoped, to proceed in the general direction of a border with the Ukraine although I had no idea where exactly it may lay.

There was still a remarkable absence of people about, and as I progressed farther to the east the absence of people seemed almost uncanny; I did not see more than two or three people each day. This part of Poland, which was in the general neighbourhood of Krakow, was flat and interspersed with the occasional clump of farm buildings or a small village, and so travelling without detection was not really very difficult. I felt I could have continued in this way for some time. There were crops in the fields and with as little exposure as necessary I seemed to be able to find enough of something to eat, and the odd pond was never far away from which to fill a water bottle, or clandestinely from a stand-pipe or water butt in a farm at night. Before Harvey left, he had generously left me his remaining rations, which probably made him sick to look at in any case, so I was able to keep going for several days more on our prepared rations. I was heading in the general direction of Krakow, or so I thought, but might have gone past it; I did not really have very much hope of eventual success, and in any case I really had no idea where the Russian border was to be found. However I did not have many alternatives other than to plod on. The map I had was an old one, and in fact it must have been almost impossible to find a map showing the new boundaries following the Russian incursion into Poland, so I was really 'flying blind'.

There was a plentiful supply of root vegetables in the fields, but I was never sure I could distinguish between sugar beet and turnips, swedes or what have you, not being a farmer's boy. They were difficult to eat being exceedingly hard raw, and I sometimes had to resort to the very dangerous process of cooking them up in a dixie, usually carried out at night-time because of the tell-tale smoke or otherwise just sucking at chunks. Once or twice I came upon market gardens with supplies of lettuce, carrots, onions etc, which was terrific. I even found some tomatoes on the rare occasion and duly stocked up with a supply to last a few meals. The weather was generally kind, being fairly warm during the day, when I did not move far and only when it was very clear that there was shelter ahead in the form of woods, and obviously in sparsely populated areas; it was cooler at night when I was chiefly on the move, and a helpful moon and clear nights provided sufficient light to enable fairly rapid negotiation of any obstacles although I frequently came across unexpected ditches, morasses or some similar unexpected trap. I heard all sorts of weird and wonderful sounds, sometimes quite frightening, when I may have disturbed an animal in the course of its nocturnal slumbers.

Loneliness was, of course, the greatest problem. There was absolutely no one to speak to except the occasional rabbit, and then the exchange was brief and one-sided. I realized that I was not really happy with this solitary existence and to have had someone around to whom I could have at least kept up a running repartee of moans would have been a great help. On my own I had too much time to think, something which seemed strange after living in camps and even in the army where most of the thinking is done for you.

When you are stuck in a camp behind barbed wire, you yearn to get out. When you are out, and have nowhere to go, amazingly enough you begin to feel the loss of the company and the result is an increase in nervous tension.

Lying in a wood in eastern Poland, even in daytime, with not a sound anywhere except an occasional animal scuttling around, became rather unnerving and even made me prone to hallucinations. I began to imagine people were moving about, probably as a result of the permanent demand upon my senses to avoid confrontation with anyone at any time. At night-time, on those days when the moon got a little tired and was unable to provide very much light for me to proceed by, the strain of peering into the semi-darkness ahead was, to say the least, tiring and did nothing to help my flagging spirits.

I began to wonder whether it was all worth it, 'Why not go over to that farm cottage, and give yourself up? They would probably give you a nice hot cup of coffee at least, before getting the police.' Such temptations did continually arise in my thinking, but only to be knocked out by the more rational view – 'Well, at least you are not a prisoner at the moment – you can go and do what you will, within very definite limitations, but then there are always limitations to your free will even in normal civvy life, so what's the difference? You are now, to all appearances anyway, a free man, you can speak the local language at least to some extent, you are probably amongst friends as far as the local population are concerned anyway, so why lose it all and give yourself up.' This reasoning won out in the end, and I just plodded on. It seemed to be the most deserted part of the world, although once or twice, during day-time in particular, the drone of motor vehicles and sometimes planes could be heard in the distance, presumably on the roads connecting the few cities or big towns. I suspected, and rightly so as it transpired, that the rumbling was of a military character, best avoided at all costs.

There was a nasty fright for me in one outhouse I had secreted myself into, which was not far from a farm. During the daytime a woman suddenly came to the door when I was trying to sleep and looked in straight at me. I spoke a word or two in English, being half asleep and not thinking too clearly, then explained in half Russian half Polish my nationality and business, and she went away. I was terrified she had gone for the police, so got ready to evacuate, but a moment or two later she came back laden with sandwiches, sausages and a bottle of milk. Good old Polish women! You can't beat 'em! She said nothing whatsoever, just put them down on the ground by the door and disappeared completely.

On another occasion I espied, miles from anywhere, a bicycle and thought to myself, 'Ah – that's better than walking.' But I also was well aware that escaping prisoners could get into serious trouble if found stealing from the civil population, so I left it severely alone. Good job too, for a minute or two later a farm worker appeared. He had obviously been having a leak behind an adjoining clump of bushes, took one hard look at me but made no sign of recognition. Again, I started up with a 'Good morning' in English clearly indicating I was not 'one of them' which I am sure he instantly recognized. He fiddled about with the bike for a moment then got on and dropped, and I am quite sure it was on purpose, a packet of sandwiches and sausage off the back of the bike which I retrieved with grateful alacrity whilst he silently but rapidly pedalled off on his way.

It must be remembered that the local population were sympathetic in the extreme towards us, but absolutely terrified of being caught helping us. Also, there were a considerable number of itinerant persons around, resulting from the holocausts produced in the central European countries, and there were refugees from the law wandering about all over the place.

The Poles showed the utmost courage when doing anything for the British, even some little act quite trivial in itself. In this particular case, the Pole obviously assessed that I was an enemy of the Reich but there was always the possibility I was a decoy. Although there was no one else anywhere near us, subversive activities had always to be clandestinely executed. If the Pole had been discovered helping me, death may well have been his punishment or maybe at best a concentration camp, which was effectively the same thing. On the other hand, it must be remembered that had he gone straight to the local constabulary and alerted them to my presence, being in fact an accessory to my recapture, he would most certainly have been suitably rewarded, although any such reward would have taken a lot of living down as far as his neighbours would be concerned. So he was on a hiding to nothing, in terms of personal benefit either way, but to me the consumption of a delicious sandwich was a very considerable reward. Unlike the Pole, however, I would have faced little additional discomfort had the action been intercepted by the authorities. So sympathy could most safely be displayed by the Pole by accidentally on purpose dropping some food, but any attempt at conversation or obvious assistance may ultimately have been disclosed to the authorities and would have had for him the most dire results. I can only hope he received his reward somewhere on earth or maybe he has had to wait until Judgement Day, but I am quite sure that his 'thinking box' was of a higher calibre than that possessed by the German soldier who took delight in jumping on the pregnant girl's stomach.

However, the day following this episode, and indeed any episode involving the arrival of sandwiches was then an important event in my life, when trying to sleep in a shed I had come across one day in a fairly remote field, or so I had thought, I heard a tremendous amount of noise coming from vehicles on a road some hundred yards or so away and quite a lot of shouting in German and some occasional shots. This activity gradually increased, and there seemed to be a growing rumble and noise of engines of heavy vehicles; I could not avoid getting extremely curious to know what was happening but was much too scared to leave my hiding place, and hoped it would just go away, which it did not.

Eventually the noise got too continuous and close for comfort and I heard the odd bursts of machine guns, the continuous rumble of what seemed to be tanks or at least caterpillar tracks and groups of marching soldiers, and quite a lot of aerial activity. Not being able to stay put for ever, at early nightfall I ventured forth to see what was happening and walked into what appeared to be a full-scale war going on. There was a red glow in the sky in the general direction of what I had imagined was Krakow and where I thought the border was with Russia which I was aiming for and to which I must have been much nearer than I had previously thought, or had even gone past and that red glow struck me as being exceedingly ominous. All this activity in the middle of the night combined with what appeared to be the reflection of some vast inferno, did not seem to me to add up to anything advantageous to my personal cause.

Right *A sombre me in 1939 anticipating the worst.*

Below *A photograph taken since the war of the stretch of beach at St Valéry-en-Caux in France which we had to run along to escape from St Valéry in an attempt to get on a boat at neighbouring Veules-les-Roses, in 1940, where I was taken prisoner.*

Left *Two obvious members of the 51st Highland Division carrying an all-important tub of steaming potato water to a barrack of about 250 inhabitants eagerly awaiting its arrival.*

Below left *Two prisoners urinating in a hole between barrack blocks. Not a picture the Germans would have liked to have seen published generally. The overall air of depression and unhygienic quarters were factual and are well portrayed in this illicitly taken photograph.*

Right *A young Polish girl and her mother. At the Arbeits Kommando (working party) at Kalisz they tried to befriend me and pass me bread whilst we marched through the streets to work. They slipped me the photos and wrote their address on the back which was extremely unwise. Had these photos been found on me, they would have been shot, so I tried to obliterate the addresses with ink.*

Right *A colleague and me (on the right) in front of a barrack hut at Lamsdorf Stalag 344. Our hands are in chains. The picture is poor but for someone to be caught photographing in the camp, let alone possessing a camera, would have led to very dire consequences. I don't know how we even managed to get the films developed — also quite a feat!*

Far right *A clearer photo of a prisoner in chains at Lamsdorf. The tying or manacling of prisoners' hands was of course strictly in contravention of the Geneva Convention on treatment of war prisoners.*

Left *Myself and the British sergeant in charge of the camp at Adelsdorf (wood wool factory). We were not really so closely attached! It was for an effort at a play with which we tried to break the monotony. My 'plus fours' were French army officer issue. I think the skirt was a curtain.*

Below *Old photograph of Adelsdorf.*

Right *Old photos of Lamsdorf (top) and Freiwaldau, through which I was led to the camp in the mountains where my third and ill-fated escape attempt was made.*

Adelsdorf

valdau – Adolf-Hitler-Platz   (Die Perle der Sude

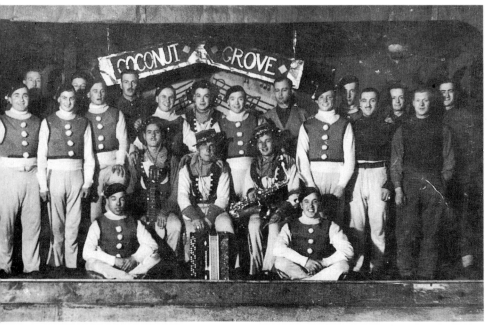

Left *Photograph (official) of the pathetic football team at Adelsdorf. We played a team of six since the pitch was not big enough for 22 players. I am on the extreme left.*

Below left *The concert party at Stalag 344 in the later days of captivity (1943, I think). This is an authorized photo taken by the Germans for the prisoners to send home, as propaganda to illustrate what a good time we were having in the nice German holiday camps! Not very comparable with the illicitly taken photos in the camps.*

Above right *The knife I carried whilst a PoW. It was made in the shape of a Russian hunting knife by a Russian PoW who officially had no tools. The materials were titanium and steel taken from a crashed American bomber, and Perspex from the glazed observation panels of the aircraft. The penalty for a prisoner found by the Germans to be carrying a lethal weapon would be instantaneous death, so I was always at risk in carrying such a knife which, during searches, was carried in the most unlikely positions on my person.*

Right *A photograph I picked up off the ground when, after release at Nuremberg in 1945, I ventured out of the camp and came across a bombed-out German artillery unit. I imagine the owner was blasted away with everything else. What a waste it all was.*

Above *The main hospital at Gross Strehlitz in Upper Silesia where I acted as official interpreter for Russian and other nationals who were prisoners and hospital staff. The prisoners' quarters were, of course, huts in the former car park of the hospital.*

Below *A more humane photo after repatriation to an English hospital. I and my personal nurse are on the right! A vast improvement on prison camps!*

I first assumed that I had fallen into organized German manoeuvres of some sort, but they looked rather too realistic to me from the red glow and the obvious sense of urgency in the whole thing, and I became rather full of apprehension. After seeing so little for so long, this sudden display of furious activity completely upset my plans, and seemed quite out of keeping with the placid Polish countryside I had grown acclimatized to. I had, as I say, seen the occasional aeroplane earlier, and heard the sounds of heavy traffic in the distance, but I had put all that down to army manoeuvres or the like, but seeing that red glow was quite a different thing.

My curiosity was my undoing. I was spotted by some German soldiers moving along the side of the road and bullets came my way with a vengeance. There was no 'halt, who goes there?' or any of that nonsense. As soon as a soldier had espied me, he fired a sub-machine gun in my general direction, at the same time shouting to other soldiers around him. It was quite obvious to me there was no possibility of escape. To run back into the wood would only attract a hail of bullets, which were already spasmodically coming my way. Luckily all missed as I sheltered behind a broad tree trunk and I shot my hands up over my head with amazing alacrity and stepped perilously forward. Surely all this could not be going on for the recapture of one miserable escaped prisoner? Anyway, I stood there in great trepidation, hands very high above my head and awaited the final bullet; I was very happy and relieved when the soldiers unexpectedly accepted my sole surrender. Then came the real shocks. I tried to explain to one gormless creature who I was and what I was doing there; the conversation was, however, very brief and much to the point.

'Comrade, I am English. I am a prisoner of war escaped from Stalag XXI A.' The German, completely unimpressed by the explanation, could only scream, 'You bloody Russian swine, come out here. You think we are all dumb, we Germans?'

I was beginning to think the Germans suffered from some national defect or inferiority complex for they were always imagining other people thought they were dumb, but what really struck me was why on earth did he think I was a Russian? Surely the Russians were supposed to be allies of the Germans or something? Why on earth should he think a Russian would be hiding in a wood in Poland and masquerading as a British prisoner of war? Things did not seem to add up at all, and obviously something had gone horribly wrong with my calculations or I was just having a nightmare. The vicious swipe I got from the German was definite assurance that it was no nightmare. So I lowered one hand to get out a paybook to show the German, but was immediately struck again.

'*Hände hoch, hände hoch*' repeated the German apparently getting agitated so I complied without further question.

I was then very roughly shoved over to where an officer was standing, surrounded by a group of twenty or so Germans of various ranks. The German who had taken charge of me pushed me roughly in front of the officer and saluted.

'I found this one in the wood over there, *Herr Leutnant*,' reported my captor with a few heel clicks and obviously expecting an iron cross or two for his efforts. 'Says he's an English prisoner of war,' he went on, breaking into a derisory laugh. I thanked God for my knowledge of German. I duly explained to the officer, who seemed very pre-occupied with other problems and really did not have much time for me, who I was and why I was there. The officer seemed pretty unimpressed and was only interested to know whether I had been alone or was part of a group, and did not pay much attention to my pleas, and eventually ordered one of his men to take me and another pitiful-looking soul he had there, by truck back the general way I had come. The pitiful one appeared to me to be a very ordinary Polish farm labourer of about fifty years of age and looked absolutely terrified, even of me.

In five minutes we were in a village and in the centre, guarded by a strong German force well supplied with machine guns, were a number of soldiers and civilians of various types towards which the weapons were threateningly pointed and amongst whom I was duly thrown. To my utter astonishment the soldiers whom I did not recognize from their uniforms I found out were Russian, and it was then that I discovered after a brief exchange of grunts in my best Russian with a somewhat surprised young man next to whom I was wedged and who was dressed in one of those strange uniforms well covered with red stars, the unbelievable and ironic fact, that the Germans had just decided to attack Russia during my recent perambulations and the area I was picked up in was right on the border where they had mounted one of their first devastating attacks against the Russians on the Ukrainian frontier. The captured Russian soldiers amongst whom I now found myself were outpost troops or border sentries who had been unlucky enough to be amongst the first of the very many Russian troops captured by the Germans in their initial onslaught to the east.

My whole world had once again collapsed and to say the future looked bleak was just an enormous understatement. I could hardly credit my fantastic bad luck and roundly cursed both Hitler and Stalin for upsetting my plans so peremptorily. No one was the least impressed by my British Army Pay book, which I had resolutely held on to, and my knowledge of Russian then completely and finally sank me. A German soldier acting as interpreter between the Russians and Germans briefly questioned me in Russian, which, like a prize twerp I cleverly answered in Russian – the result was obvious – the interpreter immediately told his superior that I spoke Russian and therefore must be a Russian. It just goes to show how easy it is to get too clever for your own good! In fact, I even looked like a Russian, or at least like a fairly typical central Asian. Whilst the average European considers the average Englishman to be tall, thin and fair, I could only boast of being short, stocky (not fat!) and dark. In no way could I resemble an Englishman to an already disbelieving German, especially when I could apparently speak Russian. Once again the German trait of the inferiority complex had shown up.

'You think we Germans are idiots?' the interpreter had said. 'You dress up in civilian clothes and try and tell us, in Russian, that you are British. You are a dangerous Russian spy.'

I had to admit it sounded a bit of a tall order. But then, the Germans and the Russians both seemed to believe that any stranger was automatically a spy.

It would be difficult to do justice to a description of my thoughts at the particular moment when the stark realization of my predicament sank in. It took time to sink in, for there were a lot of incidental activities going on the whole while which effectively prevented me from sitting down and taking stock of the situation. Shots were occasionally fired, people were struck for no apparent reason, there was a considerable amount of German shouting and screaming, and those unfortunates, including me, in the pen were terrified and dumbfounded.

Clearly I was in a holding cage, surrounded this time not by barbed wire, but by German soldiers every few yards forming a cordon around the caged victims situated as far as I could make out on some sort of village green, with machine guns trained upon us from every angle. The machine guns were used, with relentless regularity, to subjugate any actual or imagined attempt at disobedience to the raucous commands issued continuously by our masters or just fired in order to subdue any lingering element of defiance or even individuality which may remain to the captives, or to mow down anyone who may have tried to move out of line just to observe the call of nature.

We were left for what seemed to be a very long time in this compound, some few hours I suppose, awaiting further groups of Russian soldiers who were continually added to our numbers, so that we were eventually tightly jammed up against each other; so much so that we were obliged to carry out urgent toilet requirements where we stood, and in view of the very nervous psychological state we were in such natural events were exceptionally frequent. The result was, as can be imagined, a disgusting mess which led me to realize the extent of the crass inhumanity of the Germans towards their captives who they obviously and sincerely regarded as cattle. Given similar circumstances with guards of my own nationality, I am quite sure officers would soon have established some toilet arrangements, however crude, and even at the risk of losing the odd escapee or two. Such an obvious requirement never occurred to the Germans whose only instructions from their superiors were not to let the prisoners escape and to hell with their bodily requirements!

I was very obviously surrounded by people not of my race, both as guards and as prisoners, and there was probably no Britisher within many scores of miles with whom I could converse in my native tongue. This is a surprisingly distressing fact and the extent of despair it produces can only really be assessed by someone who has been unfortunate enough to experience the predicament. We all take it very much for granted that there is always someone around us with whom we can exchange views, sympathize with or moan at or even invoke the assistance of a national consulate in a foreign land, and the fact that people are available to whom one can talk presents a sense of reassurance that all is not lost. Even when I was first taken prisoner in France and herded into pens, I was amongst my own kith and kin and could at least discuss the disaster with others, even though the comments from my Scottish comrades in the 51st Highland Division were at times completely undecipherable to me.

Now, however, I was entirely amongst foreigners, mostly enemies and a few curious but disinterested fellow-sufferers who all looked very strange to me, and on a grey dawn morning somewhere in eastern Poland, with incessant shouting in a variety of foreign tongues, indiscriminate firing and an utter disillusionment of the past and despair for the future, I was afraid. The word does, as I say, no justice to the condition I found myself in, probably because I was rather benumbed about the whole thing; there was an air of unreality in what was going on around me, and a nightmarelike quality which I hoped would all suddenly vanish when I awoke, but regrettably I was only too aware that I was already horribly awake and I had suddenly been transformed into a Russian prisoner of war of the Germans. At an age just short of nineteen, for one who rather wanted to live the sort of life that people usually did live, this sobering fact represented a shattering blow.

The next few days were just a continuation of the nightmare; we were led as a dejected group of creatures from one place to another, at each being joined by more dejected ones, almost all Russian soldiers though there may have been some Russian and Polish civilians amongst them. This went on for a period which seemed to last about three or four days although all idea of time had disappeared. As far as I could make out, I had been picked up some way to the north of Krakow, and there was a small town called Vovgorod somewhere in the region. The general opinion, so far as I could gather from my new colleagues, seemed to be that the German forces I had encountered were making a spearhead attack towards Lutsk. Whatever they thought they were doing, I could personally have done without them. In fact had this crazy idiot Hitler not have decided to attack the Russians just at that particular moment, but had left it for a day or two, I would have passed over the border and reached freedom, or at least reached Russia. Whether that would have equated with reaching freedom was another matter, and today in studying the result of the rapid collapse of the Russian forces in the Ukraine area, I must arrive at the conclusion that I may well have been wasting my time and energy anyway in making for the eastern borders. Had I passed into the Soviet territory, which for all I know I may already have done, I could well have finished up with the same result – to be scooped up in the vast pincer movements, which the German panzer units were so efficient at producing.

The several days of marching with long lines of defeated Soviet troops took me back to my days following the surrender at St Valéry, but this time, instead of being at least with my own kind and being acclimatized to the general behaviour of my fellow sufferers, I was one of very many disillusioned and despairing soldiers of Papa Stalin, and that was a very different matter. Whilst the behaviour of my own kith and kin under such debilitating circumstances had been pretty horrible, it was as nothing when compared with the conduct of the captured Russian troops.

The general evaluation of life to those farther east than Germany seemed to be far lower and lacking the importance attached to our terrestrial stay by those in the more western regions of Europe and particularly so since many of my new comrades-at-arms emanated from beyond the Urals where life was not rated at a high premium. It was from the very start abundantly clear to me that I was now consorting with a bunch of wild animals as fellow prisoners, and that was how the German guards seemed to see it too. There was no pretence at order or discipline, just rows of fierce animals kept in line by guards on foot or in trucks, armed to the teeth with machine guns which they used at every possible opportunity, not to wound but to kill as many as they conveniently could at any excuse and with one apparently enjoyable burst of fire. If you fell out of line or even blew you nose you risked instant death, and so did all those around you.

On the rare occasions that soup or even water appeared, there was just a wild rush, some got it and many did not, and I soon realized that survival could only be achieved at the expense of one's fellow men. There were no queues, no discipline and of course as far as I was concerned, no friends, only wild hungry men who looked at me realizing I was not as they, and regarding me as even fairer game than their motley fellow countrymen. My situation was not at all comfortable.

This traumatic method of existence lasted during several days of being herded down one Polish country lane after another, all the time being savagely shoved and forced off the road into ditches and fields to allow for the passage of German troops and armour travelling up to the front in the opposite direction. We were continually forced off the roads by wildly screaming guards to allow a few mighty generals to travel past, and then re-assembled only to be pushed aside again for a fleet of troop carriers or artillery convoys. No wonder progress was painfully slow and tiring and we certainly seemed to have been reduced to the lowest possible level of humanity, nay, even animal existence. A herd of cows would have fared better; they would represent valuable steaks for the conquering Germans to fill their already oversize paunches on. We were clearly just a confounded nuisance. The whole long line of dejected ones seemed to just stumble its miserable way along without much interest by the participants in what was happening, which was probably to my good fortune. Whilst in the main I was surrounded by soldiers sporting a red star somewhere on a uniform or on a cap, I was distinguished by wearing my mixture of civilian clothing and ex-army pieces of some European uniform, French cavalry trousers or maybe Polish, a battle-dress type blouse, civilian shirt and British army boots, the most valuable item of all. Most of the civilian foreign workers to be found trudging around Central Europe were similarly clad, as there were no Marks & Spencers type stores then open to anybody other than to the affluent party members in the more prosperous cities in Germany and most of the clothing available at the itinerant workers' level was from captured army stores, or literally 'army surplus'. One thing I did not sport anywhere was, of course, a red star. The other prisoners did give me the odd look, although there were quite a few others in civilian dress or odd army uniforms, and together with the fact that I could not yet understand some of the more colloquial and less attractive Russian phrases which were directed at me, my position was definitely not a happy one.

Fortunately I managed to find a couple of well-built allies obviously from the European side of Russia who were sympathetic and accepted with great interest my story of how I got there, and I stuck very close to them. They in turn had to fend off, on my behalf, several attempts by other prisoners to suggest that I was some sort of German spy and not one of them and that I should be disposed of. I already rather suspected that such disposal could well be in the direction of their stomachs, for although my new colleagues had only been in captivity for presumably a few days, they did not appear to me to have been very well fed prior to being captured, and food of any sort or to be precise anything that appeared to have any chance of being digested by the human stomach, and I am not too sure that those of my colleagues emanating from Siberia and beyond had human stomachs, was likely to be consumed by the ravenous mob, and I estimated I think fairly accurately that that included me. Subsequently I was given evidence that cannibalism was well on the cards.

However, as time progressed, I felt my position a little more secure, so long as I had my 'minders' around, but that clearly could not be for long, for amongst that highly disorganized array of foraging creatures, it was not easy to stay together and I did not greatly fancy the looks I received from some of the other wild-eyed half starved animals from beyond the Urals. Many still had retained vicious looking knives which could clearly be used to kill, and they would no doubt not hesitate just because I maintained I was English. The meat could still be tasty despite the foreign import, and the boots looked sound, so I had to remain permanently on my guard.

It was a very unsatisfactory position to be in, and I wished many times that I was behind barbed wire and safely tucked up in a British prison camp, something I would never have earlier imagined I could wish for. Everything is relative, especially in terms of misery.

I made many attempts to try and convince the accompanying guards of my real identity, but this was quite hopeless. I could hardly get close enough to a guard to be within shouting range, let alone to try and explain to them I was English. The guards kept their distance, probably being scared of catching some disease like typhus or inheriting some of the disease-carrying lice with which the Russians were infested, or were afraid of being set upon by the prisoners who did not seem to mind the fact that they would probably be shot dead as a consequence of such action. Therefore the guards stood well back always with machine guns trained on the groups of prisoners, so there was absolutely no hope of having a cosy chat with one.

There was one very frightening episode when I happened to be, purely by accident, near the compound gate when some bread was brought in. Being accidentally near the centre of distribution I was the fortunate recipient of a chunk of bread thrown in by the Germans and left for those who could get there first. As was the custom, I pushed the bread at once into my mouth, which was the only way one could ensure of retaining it, but I was attacked by a bunch of asiatic-looking gentlemen from, probably, Mongolia or some region not very remote from China, who seemed to think they could extract the bread from my stomach. I was thrown to the ground and even my mouth was wrenched wide open whilst struggling hands and fingers tried to retrieve the bread which was then on its way down the gullet. Fortunately, one of my burly mates appeared and the attackers eventually gave the task up as hopeless.

My two new-found friends, who both emanated from the Leningrad district and were regular soldiers, despised the rest of the rabble and showed that Russian soldiers, at least the regular ones, could maintain the same standards of discipline and cleanliness as any other race. They were, not surprisingly, as regular soldiers avid supporters of the Soviet regime, but did not appear to uphold their support by vilifying other political systems, such as those that existed in the West. In fact they were true patriotic soldiers, upholding their nation and their leader at a time when it was more popular amongst the captured Russian troops to turn the blame for their predicament against their government and against Stalin.

They were both giants in their way, well over six feet and with body frames to support their height, and were no doubt well capable of looking after themselves in any scrap confined to muscular prowess. Pjotr, or Peter, to give him his English equivalent, was somewhat older than his colleague Igor, but both came from the same home town and regiment. It appeared that their regiment had been despatched to the German Russian border in Ukraine, ostensibly as part of a defence force for Kiev some six or eight weeks earlier and they had had no idea that they would be embroiled so quickly in a fight with the Germans with whom they had been told their nation had a non-aggression pact. When they were attacked they had been simply overrun by German panzers and were surrounded by a German tank force before they really got ready to defend themselves. It all reminded me very much of the pattern I had experienced in France.

Still, I was thankful to have at least someone who believed me and who was prepared to stick with me, and we marched or struggled together along the Polish by-ways making the best of a very unpleasant situation. What a tremendous difference there was between the disciplined, intelligent Russians from the West and the barbarians who apparently came from the other side of the Urals. No doubt the latter have their strong points, but when the chips are down and they were very much down then, discipline proves its worth.

Eventually we were all thrown into a huge camp with many thousands in it, but where it was I then had no idea. It was just a huge POW camp in the middle of a very open space miles from anywhere and to me it was just the end of the world. The starry-eyed one had now met the punishment he no doubt had well earned in his short life, a punishment meted out presumably to those who drank too much beer, since I could not really think of any other past crime which actually merited being passed straight into that mythical, but now very realistic, place called Hell.

7

Hell

There it was, stretched out over an area about half a square mile, the shattering actuality of that place one could read about in theological books or hear about from the pulpit: Hell itself, complete with demons and miserable downcast sinners, a real live furnace and no doubt somewhere around, Satan himself. For no other synonym can realistically and adequately compare with the inside of the camp I ended up in after that most gruelling march, if it could be given such a title, for some four or five days down roads littered with, at first, the wrecks of Russian army debris and later an assortment of Russian and Polish army trucks, private vans, cars, etc, and endless streams of the human and material flotsam left behind by conquerors who by now were probably some way into Russia.

The march itself for me was probably even more distressing than for the other captives. At least they were amongst their own flesh and blood – neither of which ingredients was particularly conspicuous amongst them – and they were at least used to each other's customs and smell, and there was no shortage of the latter. I myself had been living rough for some days and the finer points of hygiene such as hot showers had long been relegated to just a memory from the past, but the people I was now intimately involved with did not appear to have ever discovered baths in their past lives, let alone under the present extenuating circumstances. The smell of unclean and disease infested humanity was ghastly and the behaviour of my new neighbours would have not gone down too well at the London Zoo.

Every time food of any sort appeared, there was just a wild rush and resultant fighting to get at it. Nobody had ever heard of a queue, and once you got your hands on a piece of bread or a potato you had to put it straight into your mouth and swallow, or else a gang of twenty ravenous animals would attack and seize it. The toilets were wherever the needy one happened to be standing and the improvised formal toilet accommodation hastily erected by the Germans was just a quagmire and could not be safely approached, even with a gas mask.

The Germans had just given up the unequal battle. Obviously they had captured an enormous number of Russian soldiers in the first few days after crossing the border, and were now completely unable to cope. They did not even care, for they referred to the Russians as 'animals' and treated them as such. There was no orderly dishing out of food as there had been in the British camps; the Germans just opened the barbed wire enclosures and threw in what little food there was and retreated as quickly as they could.

The four days' march under these conditions was pretty shattering for me especially since I had not anticipated such a disastrous turn of events. I was not far behind in the battle for rations once I had learned the technique, but the dirt and stink really took a lot of acclimatizing to. The march in France in the early days had been pretty rough, but at least you could lie down at night and retain your clothes if you did not take them off, which of course you did not. Amongst my new inmates, however, if you lay down to sleep even with your boots on there was a fifty-fifty chance some miserable soul would come along and knock you over the head to steal them and probably pinch your trousers at the same time. There did not seem to be a very advanced state of camaraderie amongst the Russian soldiers, and many of them looked as though they had been prisoners even before they were captured by the Germans; they were pretty thin and gaunt and many were bootless and generally ill-kempt. So was I, I suppose, at St Valéry, but somehow this seemed even worse. I lived now in continual fear of being slaughtered, not only by the enemy, but also by my own fellow prisoners. I think the lack of comradeship may have resulted partly from the violently differing political views held by the Russian soldiers as well as from the vast territorial distances and environmental variations they were used to at home.

It was very clear to me from the start that the Uzbeks, Tadjiks, Turkmens and even the Azerbaijanis to name just a few, let alone the Mongolians and races from farther east, really had nothing in common with the Soviet regime as administered from Moscow, and were Russian in name only. Many of them took the opportunity afforded by capture to be most explicit in their condemnation of anything and everything Russian or Soviet, whilst the former loyal Party members did their best to uphold their belief in the unified Soviet Empire. With such continuous internal differences existing in the camp, usually resulting in violence, who needed enemies?

The most noticeable difference between this Russian camp and the British *Stalags* I had been in was definitely the complete lack of discipline in the Russian camps. Even in the early days of captivity in France, the mass of ordinary soldiers, who had been carefully separated from their officers, re-aligned themselves with an element of instinctive discipline, behind the senior warrant officer around, sergeant-majors of various grades and even took some notice of their NCOs at the level of sergeant, and therefore the latter were able to produce some sort of control which ultimately enabled the Germans to provide for some element of equal distribution of supplies to their captives. In the main, the ordinary British soldier was still, at least subconsciously, aware of his military responsibilities and a regimental sergeant-major was still a creature of awesome power with a terrifying ability to mete out punishment to those who disobeyed him and therefore fell foul of the Army Code of Conduct, despite the obvious fact that that same sergeant-major had absolutely no means of implementing any threat of punishment. This sense of discipline continued into the *Stalags* and even into working camps, overseen by warrant officers and NCOs who assumed the usual responsibilities of officers.

However in the Russian camp it was an entirely different story. The percentage of non-Western Russians seemed to be very high, and these gentlemen did not care two figs for their military superiors, or even for their government and indeed nation they had ostensibly been fighting for. In fact, if anything, they showed definite hostility towards the regular army troops and party cadre, upon whom they blamed the responsibility for their present plight. The result was not only lack of any discipline, it was in fact pure chaos. To add to all this, it was clearly apparent that the Russians had been half starved before they were even captured, and pathetic diet, poor quality clothing and equipment, poor pay inhibiting their ability to acquire smokes and the smaller luxuries available to their civilian counterparts all combined to produce a very different end product to the average British Tommy.

When we eventually arrived at this new camp, I hoped that things might improve, and most important of all, I hoped that I would be able to convince the Germans as to my true identity, though how I expected to be given any such opportunity I could not easily foresee. It seemed astonishing to me that the Germans, who were supposed to be civilized creatures, could condone the state of affairs which existed in this camp. Admittedly they had been inundated with prisoners, but it was the very callous attitude to the whole thing which I found so contrary to the picture of the typical German I had imagined for myself in the past. The German must have been rather like a Britisher really, fairly civilized, but how on earth could he think of another race, the Russians, as animals and then actually treat them as such? They screamed at the poor Russians and then prodded them with fixed bayonets, all just as though they were cattle in a field. Every prod produced a wound which festered very rapidly under such conditions. And everyone seemed to be the same – young, old, private soldier or educated high-ranking officer – they all displayed the same behaviour towards their captives and, worst of all, they seemed to thoroughly enjoy dishing out this inhumane behaviour. The word 'compassion' presumably did not appear in the German vocabulary.

The inmates of the camp were, as far as I could make out, in the main captured Russian soldiers, Russian and Polish Jews and some male civilians, probably Russian, Polish and Jewish. They were, without any exception, the most dejected, filthy and hopeless group of humans you could expect to see congregated together anywhere. Dejected, because their dreams of a life had come to an immediate end, filthy because water was non-existent, they teemed with lice and all manner of vermin and every known disease was present including typhus, and hopeless because they knew, as I knew, and as the Germans and even their Maker knew, there was absolutely no hope of any recovery from this depth to which they had sunk, through no fault of their own. Many were ill from the rigours of enforced captivity, many wounded and most diseased but it was probably the mental effects which were the most devastating. People can keep going whilst there is hope, but take that away and you get just a mass of helpless zombies, vacant in expression and deed and with no spark of interest in the subject of living.

The rations were almost non-existent. In fact in attempting any description of life in that camp, one would soon run out of superlatives. In any case, in today's more civilized world, it would be difficult to credit any detailed descriptions except to those who had had the great misfortune to be themselves incarcerated in a concentration camp and no doubt they would not wish to be reminded of the whole ghastly business; nor would those who may have had loved ones who died in such camps, and there must be today many relatives about of those who died, for there were very many who died. Sufficient to say that the existence was utterly subhuman and represents a lasting disgrace and smear upon those who perpetrated such conditions for their fellow humans to experience.

There was no medical provision and men just died, many every night. I have since learned that in 1942 about thirty-seven per cent of all inmates of concentration camps died. The figure seems low to me, from observation at the time. When they died, their nearest comrades would fight for the remains for consumption as food and the body would not be disclosed to the Germans for as long as possible. At roll-calls, the corpse would be taken out and held up to be counted and then returned to be hidden in the hut. By this means, the edible carcass could be preserved and the body counted for the purpose of obtaining whatever rations may have been available. Not surprisingly, I found myself unable to participate in cannibalism or in this whole macabre performance even though it was happening around me all the time. I suppose in fact the word 'cannibalism' is very unfair. These people were driven to dire extremes by their circumstances; they did not eat human flesh because they enjoyed it. Hunger and thirst are in any case only too capable of deranging the mind. Furthermore, many of the prisoners came from remote parts of Siberia, Mongolia and other areas beyond the Urals, where customs even at that time were rather different from Western European ideals.

What is the crime involved in holding up a corpse to be counted for a piece of bread and then taking it away to be stored for re-use? I am sure the deceased would not be concerned, probably very much to the contrary, bearing in mind the fact that he would not have received a decent burial in any case, only slung into a pit with hundreds of others and covered with lime to aid decomposition. The only crime involved is that of producing a situation where such a macabre performance is warranted by circumstances invoked by the real criminals: the Germans.

We were housed in single-storey huts of concrete block walling and corrugated iron roofing, and with wooden three tier bunks with wire netting to take the mattress which did not exist. In each hut there were about three to four hundred men, and I was in a hut, about in the centre, where one of the inmates near my bunk died the first day we got there. In fact many others died later all around me but the first one who died was unfortunately not very far removed from me. Adjoining me were a number of dark, swarthy-looking gentlemen who I imagined were from the East, Mongols, Cossacks, Kazaks or some such breed; they had round faces and slit eyes and were dark, short and hairy. Not the sort of people you could trust with a dead body.

I noticed that they had showed a rather too great an interest in the death of this unfortunate young soldier, clearly from a European part of Russia, but I was most surprised when one of them climbed up to the bunk and started examining the body. I assumed that he was inspecting the corpse with a view to possibly purloining some article of clothing, not that anything the poor chap had in the way of vermin-infested rags was very inviting. After he had returned to his motley group, there was some discussion between them, and I next noticed that about four of them had gone up to the bunk and were removing the body from the top layer, unceremoniously dragging it over to their own quarters. Others amongst the prisoners watched idly and very uninterestedly, and no one seemed particularly surprised or took any action to intervene.

They then proceeded to strip or rather tear away parts of the clothing from the deceased one, exposing the buttocks, or what was left of that part of the emaciated anatomy.

The Germans had not searched the prisoners very well when first captured – they probably did not want to get too close to them and were content to see that they were not carrying any rifles or other weapons, but many of the Russians appeared to have retained knives hidden in all sorts of unlikely places. They now used the knives to good effect upon their erstwhile comrade who was duly but secretly cut up. They appeared in fact, from what I could see, to slice layers of flesh from the corpse, mainly in the region of thigh and buttocks. My view was interrupted by their backs and other impedimenta, and I certainly did not relish the idea of getting up and taking too close a look. I felt somewhat nauseated by the whole performance, but it is surprising how one can become acclimatized to such horrific scenes without actually remonstrating or even indicating disgust at least to one's immediate neighbours. I suppose fear, lethargy and an utter feeling of hopelessness all took their inevitable toll.

The corpse was kept well hidden most of the time, but had to be uncovered occasionally. Needless to say, the stink eventually was revolting and even managed to surpass the normal vile scent of unwashed, diseased and incontinent human beings to which I suppose we became acclimatized, and this alone put a limit on the length of time it could be kept hidden. There was also a fair amount of blood floating around which required continual mopping up.

The guards never came into the huts so would not be aware of what was happening. Presumably they either thought it was too dangerous to mix with the wild animals, or more likely, they were scared of catching typhus or some similar disease.

There were central heating stoves in each of the huts, the sort of thing you could burn any old rubbish in and so popular in Poland and it was here that the dark-skinned ones did their 'frys' – cooking the flesh at least partially to enable it to be consumed. Here again the smell was absolutely atrocious, since the smell of burning human flesh is acrid and nauseating, blending, or maybe one should say complementing, the already extensive stink of stale sweat and body dirt. No one seemed to complain and I felt myself to be in a pretty trickly position to raise my feeble voice, being in a minority of one. Anyway, I figured that should I raise any complaint based on moral grounds, I might well be the next to be cooked for supper, so in order to retain my rump in a whole state I maintained an incredulous but very appalled silence. I excused myself with the view that there are different customs throughout the world, and this particular custom may be normal in outer Siberia or somewhere, even though it was hardly acceptable in Kingston-upon-Thames. Eventually not even the Russians could stomach the smell and the remains of the corpse had to be dumped outside the hut for collection by the corpse collectors, or deposited in the latrine pit. I am quite sure that there were very many other Russians who were witnesses to the performance and who may have been equally stunned by the enormity of what was happening, but they seemed to pass it off as though it had nothing to do with them. It was just a quaint custom from the farther East. To be fair to the participants, they in their turn probably regarded me as some sort of feeble white-skinned sissy who jibbed at having his mate's left thigh for high tea.

I hope it is not thought that I am being unjustly flippant about an occurrence which was, of course, absolutely horrific. It was at all times quite essential during captivity to attempt to maintain some element of humour. Without such humour it was that much more difficult to remain sane. When it comes to an event as dramatic as that which was then performed before my astonished young eyes, human nature must have an outlet in the obverse direction, that is, try to make as light as possible of something which may otherwise have introduced a painful new dimension to my whole concept of life. It was, of course, in no way funny. It was not, I regret to say, an uncommon or isolated incident in that particular camp and I suppose that in other camps containing hordes of Russian troops, many Asiatic by birth and nature, starved almost to the point of death and awaiting a painful death from forced labour and the brutality meted out to them by their captors. With no ultimate ray of hope anywhere, some less squeamish inmates with unusual tastes may have resorted to such ultimate behaviour which, when the fact is penned many years later, may seem incredible in the extreme. The ghastly truth was that our minds had been gradually conditioned to accept such behaviour as 'the norm', however horrific it may now seem in retrospect.

I have no experience of life in the well-documented Jewish concentration camps and nothing more needs to be said in expression of the horror of those camps. However, the inmates were almost entirely civilians united by a strong mutual religious creed. In this camp for Russian prisoners of war, there was vast internal political and racial dissension amongst the inmates to add to the horrors meted out by the Germans, and little depth of communal religious feeling.

Every day, at dawn or shortly thereafter, the bodies of those who had died during the night, together with the bodies of those who had suffered in the gas chambers located in the adjoining civilian section, were loaded on to carts and the carts could be seen leaving the camp, drawn by horses and laden with their grisly cargo going off to a vast dumping ground some way off from the camp which many of the prisoners had been engaged upon digging and were continually employed in extending. It is very probable the carts sometimes contained bodies of some unlucky souls who had not yet finally expired, but were just helpless to assist themselves further, but these, together with the other remains, were all dumped into the pits, sprayed with lime to limit the further spread of disease and assist in decomposition and then covered with a layer of earth by other prisoners to await the next load to be dumped on top, German practicality at its most efficient, with extraordinary little regard for human dignity.

In the camp itself there was no life as such, no effort and little communication between the inmates. There were frequent rows and fights between the younger more militant communists and the older soldiers who blamed Stalin openly for their predicament. Many seized the opportunity, long denied to them, of giving freedom of speech an airing after so many years of enforced silence under a regime which did not take kindly to criticism.

They did, of course, eventually recognize me as an Englishman but not at once, because my limited Russian which had every opportunity to improve at a vast rate of knots, could be passed off amongst Russians who came from all over the Soviet Republic and indeed from some areas where Russian was not even spoken – Azerbaijan, Turkestan, Kazakstan, Uzbekstan, etc, all of which areas have dual languages and local dialects. So, being by stature dark, short and swarthy, I could look like any other good horse-riding Cossack, although the only time I had sat on a horse I fell off! The Russians I got to know better were as helpful as they could be and were of course of tremendous assistance in polishing up my knowledge of the language so much that I began to forget English, having no one to speak to in my native tongue, and I even started to dream, or rather have nightmares in Russian.

Amongst the thousands of Russians newly captured there were some who had Russian books they lent or gave to me, even Pushkin, Tolstoy, and a tattered and much used copy of *War and Peace*. Taking on Dostoievsky under such conditions was hardly a simple task and I soon found that I spent so much effort at translating the words in those books that the contents of such great literature did not impress itself upon me, although I certainly managed to understand the background nature of those great writers by studying their fellow men all around me, of all different types and sizes, both European and Asiatic in appearance and very varied in character and their rather naive and suspicious, but in the main honest, manner of conducting themselves (except maybe in the matter of their dietary habits!). Concentration on learning, however, became more difficult as the physical body weakened, but there was a lot of available time and I think that the stimulus to the brain only did good.

I had, of course, not been acquainted with Russians before and now I realized that the national type called Russian does not really exist. They came from over such an enormous area that the word Russian had to cover everything from the more cultured West European to the primitive tribes almost Chinese in appearance. I decided, on balance and despite the atrocious conditions under which I saw them, they were not a bad lot. Admittedly they had their share of bully boys, usually younger party members who tried to maintain their authority, and they all seemed to always be slightly afraid of something and highly suspicious of their fellow creatures, which maybe was the result of their political education, and it seemed to result in everyone looking over their shoulders at everyone else and no one trusting their neighbour, despite the fact that they had very little to trust them with.

I could easily appreciate that the central government in Russia would experience great difficulty in keeping control over such vast areas and over such greatly differing types of peoples and I could understand that there must be many districts which still today are not entirely overjoyed at the idea of being controlled from Moscow. When the foundations are not secure, the whole building is at risk and I rather thought that maybe the aggressive stance taken by the Russians in international politics may be necessary to divert attention from internal problems which may arise from the central control of such a widely diversified and polyglot nation.

The depth of degradation which was reached in this camp could only be seen to be believed; and the word 'sub-human' to describe the treatment and resultant behaviour in the camp may suffice but I felt incensed with the German Command for allowing such conditions to exist, not, I suppose, that the Germans themselves were very distressed. I was, nevertheless, equally surprised that amongst the soldiers of the much vaunted Soviet army there appeared to be very little element of discipline to counteract the animalistic tendencies of most of their colleagues. That such a camp should exist at all was an utter disgrace and the Germans were, in my view, to blame for not putting a greater effort into preserving life, hygiene and humane treatment for the many thousands who suddenly fell into their hands. They just produced compounds into which the captives were put, guarded them at a safe distance with machine guns to prevent escape and that was that. Food was thrown in and from that point on, let the prisoners get on with it, and let them bury their dead as they succumbed.

Of course the Germans had a difficult job and their own rations were not exactly plentiful. But I rather felt they gave up without really trying and were content to call the Russians 'animals' and treat them accordingly. But I was also very shocked at the inability of the Russian soldiers to keep any sense of order and discipline within the compounds, despite the impossible conditions. In 1940 the British prisoners had suffered conditions not so very much less horrific, but there always seemed to be some sense of discipline, loyalty or at least humanity around. Even in the camp for British non-commissioned officers and men where no officers were allowed, the authority of a sergeant-major always persisted, and that fact produced an element of discipline even under the roughest conditions. The authority was passed down the ranks to sergeant, corporal, etc, and despite the perpetual grumbling, some order was maintained. But in the Russian camp there was absolutely no evidence of internal discipline or order.

I lost all track of time in this camp and calculating from the notes which I still retained this all occurred in May and June 1941. Many times I tried to approach guards to establish my true nationality but none were the slightest bit interested and it was, in any case, very difficult even to approach a guard. Their fear of their captives and of their captives' vermin, and readiness to protect themselves by immediate assault with a weapon by firing or otherwise meant that the prisoners were always in groups; the individual had ceased to exist.

But one day a remarkable and as it happened, exceedingly fortunate 'accident' occurred. Whilst I was rendering assistance on a working party emptying latrines the under officer in charge of us, amidst furious shouting in German at us to urge us on to greater activity as was the custom, suddenly resorted to shouting *in English*. The words he did in fact emit were not very good English and cannot be fully repeated here for fear of causing offence but they were to the effect of 'Come on, you f— b—'. The accent was not too bad, and after I had recovered from my astonishment I said to the guard something like, 'Matey, we are not f— b—.' This made the guard curious and after a preliminary encounter conducted in English from a great distance and from which I learned that the guard had once lived in London I again related my tale and showed him my British army paybook. Instead of ignoring the matter this time the guard told his superior, a *Feldwebel* or sergeant, who also interrogated me, this time in German, and finally I was led to a camp official who noted my comments and made no further statement other than that the matter may be looked into. My English paybook was taken from me and kept by the guards, which fact worried me a lot since this was my final tie with my homeland and the only way of ever establishing my true nationality for, maybe, all time and last hope of ultimate reunion with my family and with my nationals.

Handing over that paybook was probably the most important and exacting gamble I have ever taken in my life. On the one hand, once the paybook had gone, to a German camp officer whose identity I had no knowledge of, the only primary means I had of identifying myself as a British soldier went with it. Without it, I was just one of the millions of Central European, Polish or Russian slaves of the Germans, and eventually, if I had survived the German camps, which was pretty unlikely, when the Russians eventually recaptured the territories in 1944 I would most likely have been shipped off to Siberia with countless other ex-prisoners, still unable to officially identify myself, and in an environment which would not have been concerned to distinguish me from the other millions of wretches confined in the Russian labour camps in the East. In other words, I doubt if even the Russians after the war would have listened to my story, and at best I might well have been shot as a British spy, so that side of the gamble was a lingering and painful death in obscurity in lands far remote from Kingston. On the other hand, the very existence of the paybook amongst an efficient breed like the Germans might well prompt some enquiries to be made. Such was the gamble.

It should, however, be also realized that at that stage of the German onslaught into Russia there was little or no order amongst the enormous number of captives, both military and civilian, who were rounded up and confined within the barbed wire. Nobody had interrogated the great mass of prisoners (they may have interrogated the captured Russian officers) and nobody had even taken the usual name, army number and rank. We had just been counted and allocated into compounds. I presume that eventually the Germans must have produced records of their captives, and maybe at that time I might have been able to establish my nationality. It would have seemed a bit ridiculous to record me as 'Russian POW No..., from Kingston-upon-Thames, Surrey'!

Nevertheless, some hope re-entered my life and I awaited for a couple more harrowing days but there was no further reaction so I began to fear that nothing would come of it and that I had lost the all important paybook for ever. However, on the third day a guard came to the hut and from a reasonable distance from the door shouted my name and told me to get my kit together (what kit I don't know!) and follow him out into the compound and across to where the delousing plant was situated and a washroom. The delouser was, I believe, only used at that stage by the guards. All the time I was in the camp I never saw any of the prisoners being deloused, nor heard of any enjoying such delights, but certainly the guards were always scared of coming too near us and kept their distance and probably deloused themselves every day. Here I was not deloused; that would have cost too much in fuel for one person, but told to strip and given a warm shower. My clothes were put in a bag and presumably consigned to the flames somewhere, and I was duly kitted up with a new set of clothes consisting of a Polish army jacket and French or Belgian cavalry trousers. What a sketch I must have looked, but at least the sudden effort by the Germans to smarten me up or at least make me look clean, gave me some sort of hope that salvation from hell may be on the way. I have never gone out of my way then or since to be even remotely optimistic, having learned the hard way always to anticipate the worst, but I must say that at that time the fact of the individual treatment to a shower and new clothes raised at least a flutter of hope in my heart. To take it further than that was tempting providence.

I was then led to the camp commandant's office where I was shown into a room where the commandant was sitting with another man, a very well dressed and prosperous looking civilian (one of the very few).

The commandant was the first to address me in German. 'Are you POW No 6909, an English prisoner of war and former English soldier No. –' He hesitated while consulting the paybook. 'No 6144002 of the "aist sooray regiment" ' he enquired, in a surprisingly friendly tone.

'Yes, sir,' I replied trying to emulate a soldier worthy of the East Surrey Regiment.

The commandant then turned to the civilian who then addressed me in faultless English. 'Corporal Palmer, I am told you have been kept in this camp because the German commandant thought that you were a Russian soldier. You were apparently captured – I should say recaptured – on the

Russian border and it transpires that you had escaped from your working party at Schildeberg and were attempting an escape over the frontier to the East.'

My heart went through the ceiling. They at last believed me, and my joy was unbounded at that fact, but also it was exciting even to be addressed in English. 'That is correct, sir.' I lost no time in agreeing the statement.

'We have checked your statement with the German officials at the camp at Schildeberg and they have confirmed that you did escape from that camp, and that you have not as yet been reported as recaptured. Fortunately for you your Army paybook identifies you sufficiently, and you will therefore be released from this camp and transferred to Stalag 344, a British camp. The German guard commander does not propose any further punishment to be given to you for escaping,' he added, magnanimously.

I restrained myself from going over and kissing the dear old chap, who, I probably erroneously thought, was Swiss and who may not have appreciated the action, but with those few well chosen words I had been born again, rehabilitated to the land of the living and spared from existence amongst the dead and dying; I was almost overcome with joy, but maintained every effort to observe true English traditions in so far as emotions were concerned acting as though people were spared from hell every day of the week. Maybe they are, but not so obviously. I sufficed myself with, 'Thank you very much, sir' to the civilian and then turned back to the German Commandant.

I have no idea who the civilian was. The Swiss, who generally acted as intermediary through the Red Cross had no dealings as far as I knew with the Germans in respect of Russian prisoners whose country were not signatories to the Geneva Convention and I feel quite sure they would not have allowed a Swiss representative anywhere near the Russian camp, despite the fact that the administration buildings were quite separately located some distance away from the prisoners' compound. On the other hand, being a British prisoner and theoretically at least protected by the Convention, had my paybook found its way to a British POW organization somewhere, a *Stalag* for instance, maybe Swiss intervention could have been arranged. Whoever he was, as far as I was concerned he was an Angel of Mercy, Swiss or Chinese. To this day I have no idea where he came from – he spoke German of course with the commandant fluently – and maybe he was from some German governmental department, but I very much doubt whether the Germans would bother about one miserable British prisoner, especially an ordinary soldier.

I was then given a lecture by the commandant upon the inadvisability of trying to escape from prison camps – he need not have bothered for in no way was I ever going to embark on any more futile and exceedingly uncomfortable escape attempts – and I hastened to assure all present, with great conviction and little truth, that I would be a good boy in the future. The commandant made some very appropriate excuses to the neutral for detaining me in the Russian camp. Anyone who speaks English, German, Russian could only, of course, be an English spy and that is why I had not been released earlier. What an English spy would be doing in the Ukraine which is apparently where I was when first picked up, I could not imagine, though presumably the tale was sufficient for the neutral to have as an excuse to cover the inefficiency of the German mix-up, although to be quite fair about it, I felt I really only had myself to blame for embarking on the escape in the first place – but how was I to know the Germans were going to invade Russia at that precise moment? I do not think, however, that I can justifiably blame the Germans for my unpleasant stay amongst their Russian prisoners.

Anyway I was then left alone with the commandant and a guard whilst the civilian went out with the camp second-in-command. I asked the commandant what would now happen and he explained that I would be provided with an escort and returned to the English *Stalag*. He once again repeated that, despite the heinous crime of escaping in which I had been apprehended by the brave German soldiers and which would always be futile, I would not be punished any further, and in view of my undertaking not to escape, and the fact that I might not have had a very enjoyable time mixing with the Russian animals, the commandant felt that I had experienced enough punishment already. You can say that again, I thought but in fact I thanked the commandant profusely for his graciousness. In fact, I would have gladly licked his stinking Bosch feet if it had been necessary to further my departure from Hell.

I did, however, take the opportunity of complaining in a very meek and mild manner, so as not to jeopardize anything, about the conditions in the camp and the commandant in reply made an explanation which quite shattered me with its ice-cold Teutonic logic. 'It is quite simple,' the commandant replied, 'I have a camp with maximum capacity of 25,000, and rations for 25,000, Every month I get a further intake of 10,000 so I have to get rid of 10,000.' Q.E.D. Anyway, he went on to explain that Russians, Poles and Jews were not like 'us' – I particularly noted the 'us' and wondered if the Germans were still winning the war! They were only animals – '*verbläde Tiere; Untermenschen*' – bloody animals; sub-human, so they only needed to be treated as animals. And there you are, what more can one say and under the circumstances I felt I had better maintain a dignified silence without actually offering wholehearted agreement.

Ultimately, the civilian returned and I was led out of the commandant's office with a modicum of respect from the commandant. He even said, '*Auf Wiedersehen, Englander*'. 'Not if I see you first mate,' I thought. I attempted as smart a salute as I could muster in my weakened state, and clicked what heels I had left, turned about and demonstrated some attempt at marching out of the office with a heart that was floating some hundred feet above me with joy.

I was put into the back of a lorry with a guard and the civilian sat in the front with the driver and off we went, out through the gates of hell but leaving, much to my chagrin, 25,000 Russians behind reducing by 10,000 each month to allow for replacements.

As we passed a little way from the camp, I could see the prisoners working at the pit where the corpses were dumped, and I longed to be able to draw the attention of the Swiss civilian to it if indeed he was Swiss. I was not allowed, of course, to talk to him, and anyway the very intelligent-looking gent probably knew already what the situation was.

From the Russian camp it had been possible to see a little distance away another camp, which rumour had it was an internee camp; rumour was, however, wrong, for it so happened that the other camp was in fact a British POW camp at a place called Lamsdorf and situated only about one and a half miles from the Russian camp, and that is where I was now taken to.

Looking back out of the lorry I could see retreating into the distance the hell-hole I had just left. I wondered to myself who they were having for lunch today – the old chap in the lower bunk of the three I had just vacated looked pretty terrible – if he failed to survive, I had a horrible vision of the voracious far-eastern looking gentlemen smacking their lips at the thought of another stew. Was there no way in which anyone could help those poor wretched creatures I had left behind? The answer was obviously in the negative. Short of winning a war and annihilating the callous German High Command, the organization the Führer and his merry men had built up over a considerable number of years would persist, and that organization ensured that the German race were to regard themselves as superior to all other races, and other peoples unfortunate enough not to be born German, could be treated and ultimately disposed of as if they were not a part of the human race and which did not therefore deserve continuity of existence. Of course, the far-eastern gentlemen were involved in a battle for survival which relegated human beings to the lowest possible level, but would they have sunk so far if the Germans had conjured up at least a bowl of soup every day for their famished captives? Can the blame for the appalling or almost non-existent level of sanitation which existed in the camp be put on the inmates, or perhaps it should be reserved for the Germans who provided insufficient water and vastly overcrowded conditions as a specially designed ploy to ensure that their captives' will and individuality would be crushed? It will surely take many decades for the very existence of such a prison camp, and of course, for the many probably far worse civilian concentration camps to be effaced from human memory and even longer from human records, but let us hope that those who suffered and perished did not die in vain, let us hope civilization has learned some lesson from it all.

No one can imagine my relief at seeing the orderly, clean and respectable camp in which my fellow countrymen were kept, and I almost shouted for joy at the first prisoners I saw, much to their astonishment.

On arrival at the camp, I was duly deloused and given further new clothing, this time British, and then taken before a sergeant-major in charge I think in some part of the camp who heard my story and just laughed. 'That will teach you to escape again, Corporal, except in organized escapes!'

His remark was two-edged: the British authorities in the camp, whilst supporting escapes for obvious patriotic reasons only lent their official blessing and material support to escapes which were thoroughly planned and set up with their own knowledge and assistance. The trouble with such a procedure as far as I was concerned was firstly that I had already once been involved in an escape attempt, at Hohensalza, which was known to the NCO in charge and all his colleagues and the result, as has been seen, was that someone 'sold' the whole tale to the Jerries for a bun, so I was very certain I would keep quiet about any attempt thereafter. Secondly, the official escape attempts made from the *Stalags* seemed to be only in favour of the repatriation of those individuals – preferably airmen, naval or marine personnel or high-ranking NCOs or technicians who could serve some useful purpose if fortunate enough to get home. I did not of course come into any of these valuable categories, so I did not suppose I would have been able to qualify. Of course the authorities were very right to insist upon control of escapes from the *Stalags*. Indiscriminate attempts by all and sundry could seriously jeopardize the serious mass escape efforts which were very carefully planned and equipped and which frequently involved a number of participants. But from the working parties it was quite another matter, and such heavily organized attempts were not essential.

At the time, the impression I got of that sergeant-major was that he was some sort of high-ranking god who was addressing a miserable piece of vermin who had had the temerity to creep about on his planet. It did not worry me particularly because I was so elevated in spirit to be 'home' again that I accepted it all as perfectly normal. Upon reflection, however, it raised one of the great anomalies of the whole POW scene.

The sergeant-major was, I believe, a company sergeant-major. He was in charge of a compound which may have contained about 1,000 men, and his superior would be the regimental sergeant-major in charge of the whole camp, which I think numbered about 20,000 prisoners, He was a clean-shaven, youngish man, well-built and obviously well-nourished, and was immaculately turned out. He looked to me fitter and considerably smarter than the German soldiers who were my escorts. He offered me as much sympathy and help as the oriental looking gentlemen in the Russian camp I had just vacated, whilst obviously having no need of my left buttock for lunch. He was, however, a prisoner, as was I. The moral support for his immaculate turn-out and well being lay in the attempt to show the Germans what good soldiers the British were. With it went a very comfortable life-style supported by a vast amount of 'perks' obtained at the expense of the great mass of the prison inmates, and I feel it is only fair to say that the result was the discipline so missing in the Russian camp.

I suppose it would, therefore, be incorrect to suggest that such a front should not be maintained by senior military hierarchy in the camps, and with it the whole paraphernalia and principle of a degree of co-operation with the national enemy – our guards – but to combine those privileges with derision and disdain for the ordinary sufferer who had experienced an overdose of suffering in pursuing the task of making himself a nuisance to the enemy, went a bit too far. It touched upon one of the major areas of dispute in prison life; should one go along with the Germans at least to some extent to allow for a reasonable degree of comfort for all most of the time, or should one make oneself, and in fact the whole camp, a confounded nuisance to the enemy and represent a continual thorn in their side? I did not really care a lot about the sergeant-major's reaction, but it would have been nicer to hear something a little more appreciative and sympathetic from my superior. To combine his very formal status with an element of humanity would have been a welcome bonus.

So I accordingly agreed with the sergeant-major wholeheartedly that it had taught me a lesson. I was in fact in a mood for agreeing with anybody about anything, so long as it allowed me to get back to sanity and for once it was even nice to hear a sergeant-major speaking in a language reasonably like English. To hear my own tongue spoken again was indeed a pleasure, no matter what was said. After the very cursory meeting with the sergeant-major and a brief medical examination by a duty medical officer, which did not seem to elicit much more that a few septic sores and cuts and a rather obvious state of under-nourishment, I was allowed back into one of the many compounds.

One thing I did notice, however, when being ultimately allocated back into a hut, was that I was treated with a not inconsiderable amount of suspicion by my fellow captives who could not quite credit my story and since there were none of my former camp mates in this new camp at Lamsdorf there was no one to corroborate it. I was questioned many times about Sussex, which I had given as my home county and various things to do with Blighty, but it was not until some back mail caught up with me at Lamsdorf that I started to become accepted. I was, however, able to give a verbatim report on the Russian camp which could be seen by the inmates of the British camp in the distance, and the guards, with whom we were now able to communicate, were able to confirm my general comments, but not, of course, the more intimate and horrendous details. However, I was not permitted to remain long in the camp; maybe the Germans were not keen to allow me to spread too much information about the camp in the distance.

This camp at Lamsdorf, Stalag 344, had been used in the 1914–18 war as a prisoner of war camp, and when I had been brought by road I noticed large cemeteries adjoining the main entrance. The camp was situated near the station of Annaberg and the guard in the back of the lorry with me had taken great delight in explaining to me the past history of the camp and in particular in pointing out the two cemeteries. There were literally thousands of graves marked with crosses in the cemeteries, and it transpired that there was a deadly outbreak of typhus in the camp when it had been used as a prisoner of war camp in the previous World War I and the inmates had fallen ill and died in their thousands and been buried just outside the main gate. They were nearly all British, Canadian and Australian prisoners who had come to the camp never to return to their native homes. This was a very sobering thought that was left in my mind but as I surveyed my new home – rows and rows of single storey barracks of timber and corrugated iron construction, each holding about 200 men – I considered just how beautiful it looked compared with the hell-hole I had just left.

I arrived in Lamsdorf on 16 September 1941, and most of the stars in my eyes had by now become severely dulled or completely extinguished.

8

The Jam Factory

On 8 September I was sent off once again on a working party to a place called Zuckmantel, a small town in Upper Silesia which possessed a main road with a row of shops and houses and workplaces either side, and little else other than some quite good class residences and a less pleasant stone quarry. It was the latter, of course, to which my attention was forcibly directed. The town was situated quite near the former Czechoslovakian border, a point which also immediately attracted my attention.

The building in which we were housed consisted of one large brick-built hut which may have been a warehouse or store previously, completely enclosed by quite forbidding-looking wire fencing, and equipped with two-tier bunk spaces to accommodate about thirty prisoners, and a kitchen and wash-house. All in all a very cosy little establishment, compared with the former residences I had experienced, almost in fact verging on 'homely'.

The work at Zuckmantel at first was in the stone quarry, and not at all attractive. It was not only wet, cold and thoroughly uninteresting work cutting up slabs of stone and moving them around, loading on to lorries etc, but also very dangerous and much more skilled than I had ever imagined. I was astonished at the enormous weights of stone which could be relatively simply moved by skilled positioning of wedges etc, but also found to my cost that there was a continual and very real threat of getting one's toes and fingers crushed in the effort.

In fact, the arrangement of such 'accidents', on purpose, became an effective means adopted by some of the prisoners, to crush the odd finger in order to benefit from a few days or weeks of light duties in the camp instead of passing miserable days in the quarry. It always seemed to be wet and cold in the quarry situated a little way out of the town, and standing there for ten hours or so each day in a cold wind often clearing the snow off the stones first and manhandling icy cold levers etc, could not be considered the height of enjoyment. I am glad to say I did not fall for the temptation of smashing a finger or two, as I valued my body too highly. Some of those who did resort to such a ploy finished up with permanent injury from crushed bones and even gangrene from frozen untreated wounds.

Still, there was considerable improvement ahead, and I was shortly, again in view of my designation as an engineer, to be transferred to a carpenter's shop. This was much more interesting and I actually began to enjoy the work, supervised by a sympathetic elderly German or former Silesian who was prepared to treat everyone as a human being – a pleasant change. The work was interesting, in as much as we were actually allowed to work with tools, which of course could be lethal and were strictly controlled as to issue and return, but having quite sympathetic civilians in charge of us who were as helpful as could be expected made the otherwise monotonous construction of timber boxes etc, less tedious. It seemed to me that many of the inhabitants of Silesia – a territory that seems to have changed hands many times in the course of history – although now calling themselves German did not have their hearts entirely behind the German cause.

However, I had only worked in the carpenter's shop for a few weeks before I was sent – amazing to relate – to work in a jam factory. This was of course, the closest thing to Utopia, although we were not, in fact, the recipients of the finished product. Our job was to load and unload tins of jam on to huge lorries destined for army supply centres, and cart great barrels of fruit around the town, from railway station and stores to the factory etc. The loading operations were mostly boring and quite heavy work since the tins were very large.

I became, however, very impressed with the size and power of the German lorries. On one occasion, after our team had loaded fifteen tons of jam on to a lorry and ten tons on to a trailer, the lorry would not start so another lorry was loaded with a further fifteen tons and that lorry was then hitched to the first and together with the trailer pulled the whole lot, all 40 tons of jam and three vehicles! In Britain, it would not have been allowed on the road, but I wondered whether our vehicles would in any case have had the same power under the bonnet.

Pulling quite heavy farm carts loaded with barrels of fruit was the more attractive pastime for the prisoner since we could at least see the town and some civilian life. We must have looked a lot of charlies, since two of us were literally harnessed to the front of the cart just like oxen and pulled the cart along whilst two more held the enormous barrels steady at the back and did a little pushing. All that was needed to complete the picture was a guard sitting at the front on the barrels with a whip, but two of those in fact would accompany us on foot with rifles at the ready. We then had to pull the cart from the station to the factory through the town, which must have presented an amusing and humiliating spectacle for the German inhabitants.

The manufacture of the jam lent itself to some suitable acts of sabotage. Apart from regrettably letting a barrel or two of fruit accidentally drop thereby splitting the framework and spilling rotten fruit all over the place, which occurrence was always heavily rewarded with a few blows from a rifle butt, we enjoyed clandestinely 'doctoring' the jam being mixed and cooked in the vats after we had learned that the jam was destined for the troops at the Front. The vats were very high and to get to the top one ascended ladders fixed to the sides and one of the prisoners' jobs was to hand up the barrels of fruit and empty them into the vat. When we learned that the contents were destined for brave German soldiers we started to assist odd quantities of dirt and mud to creep into the vat but as we grew bolder, the operation was stepped up until everyone of us deposited our daily toilet proceeds, carefully saved in bottles and tins etc, into the vat.

There was, fortunately, very little supervision, and it was surprising the guards did not wonder why we so frequently asked to be excused to visit the toilet whilst working there. Presumably the Germans enjoyed their jam, but what the eye does not see . . . etc. However, we really were foxed when, at Christmas that year, the factory owner, whose name was Friedl, kindly presented each of us with a tin of jam; some very hungry ones ate their jam, but an enormous quantity of jam, no doubt well impregnated by good British lavatory droppings, found its proper home in our own toilets for many of us could not face our own medicine!

Christmas 1941 was a great improvement over the previous year, and the factory owner did at least show some signs of humanity in trying to make the lives of his unwilling foreign labourers a little less unpleasant. We conjured up – and 'conjure' is about the only word that could be used – quite a cosy atmosphere in the billet and life seemed a little more tolerable. We succeeded in stealing a little holly, and the kindly Mr Friedl even provided us with a bottle of beer each, which received the treatment a bottle of champagne would normally receive, but unfortunately tasted like coloured soda water.

After Christmas I was, once again, given the opportunity to use my undoubted talents as an 'engineer' by being removed from the highly technical post of chief carthorse and put into the design office for a local building company. Whilst this again proved the most comfortable of activities in mid-winter, I could not hold down the job because really, as a student quantity surveyor, I knew remarkably little about constructional drawing, and also because I felt it was not really 'proper' for a POW to be engaged in such skilled work.

The latter was my excuse for leaving the job, but the former was probably the more realistic reason. However, I was not immediately sent back to my post as a carthorse, but was engaged by the factory owner as a gardener in his own private garden. This was, of course, the pinnacle of occupations for a POW and I gave the digging and planting my most careful attention, and especially the occasional removal of anything edible which resulted. I came under the direct supervision of the owner's wife and began to wonder whether, perhaps, the wife may have taken a fancy to me for some strange reason (and it must have been strange, bearing in mind our somewhat unpresentable condition!) for although when I started working the garden I got my instructions from the boss via a guard, it was not long before the boss stopped appearing and his wife started taking such an interest in things and gardening generally that she seemed to spend the whole day there, and the guard was told to go and amuse himself elsewhere. She was, actually, very kind and surprisingly enough seemed to be rather pro-British and I did very well for dinners and even got the odd small bottle of schnapps given to me (not for services rendered to the enemy!). This was a most enjoyable job but unfortunately did not last long as a new working party was assembled from the members of this *Arbeits Kommando* to go and form a contingent to work in a town called Adelsdorf near Freiwaldau which was not a long way away.

The new camp, about 200-strong, was a purpose built camp for foreign labourers consisting of wooden huts surrounded by a galaxy of barbed wire added for our particular benefit and was rather more of a pukkah POW camp than the cosy little establishment we had previously been in. When we were assembled for the first roll call, it transpired that none of the German guards knew any English, and none of the English knew any German, so not much progress was made and as I had earlier been chatting quite freely to one of the guards in my now much improved German, I was duly picked out and appointed camp *Dolmetscher* – interpreter.

I was not at all sure that I was entirely happy with this undoubted honour, since up till then I had always regarded the British sergeant in charge of a camp and his henchmen, including of course the interpreter and the cooks, as nearly as bad as the Germans themselves, so I was a little unwilling to join the 'Establishment'. I had to admit that whilst my view of the British NCO commanders in the camps was probably rather unjustified, for there was no doubt that the sergeants who were placed in complete command of a party of, say, 200 men, and who were used to having an officer to turn to and on whose shoulders they could offload ultimate responsibility, did have an exceedingly difficult job to do and had to combine administrative duties with a high degree of diplomacy to keep the peace between the Germans and their mutinous captives. The currently popular word 'militant' was a very suitable word to describe the permanent general behaviour of the inmates of the camp, and it never took much for trouble to flare up between the various groups of individuals and the senior NCO was always in demand to sort out the problem. Anyway, someone had to keep order and report daily to the German camp commandant, and the latter had to have someone to shout at. There was a permanent cloud of 'aggro' around everything in the camp, so to be fair, the British camp leaders had their work cut out to keep order and did a difficult job pretty well at the same time receiving their reward in terms of wealth (extra rations) and power, as well as being excused some of the less rewarding camp duties such as latrine cleaning, snow shovelling etc.

So now I had to join them and at the tender age of nineteen I felt my responsibilities quite heavily. Men were always getting into trouble – smashing things (called sabotage), striking guards (called assault or attempting escape), stealing (called stealing) etc, and really I eventually became camp lawyer rather than camp interpreter. I was left with the task of thinking up 'mitigating circumstances' as excuses of one sort or another at the same time as doing the interpreting, and if I succeeded, that was my job, and if I failed I was considered at the least to be a 'fraud', if not something worse. It was impossible to please all the people all the time, and some of my charges were so darned ignorant they were continually a source of embarrassment as well as being a potential danger not only to themselves but, more importantly, to their own colleagues.

The job had its comic acts very occasionally. On one assignment, a very serious case of assault by one of the prisoners against the guard and a civilian manager, the case was tried in a local army barracks by an army colonel and civilian magistrate. During the proceedings, the colonel asked the guard who was giving evidence of the assault upon him, what the prisoner had then said to him, the guard replied, 'Sir, he called me a "f...... b...ard"', whereupon the colonel turned to me as interpreter and said, 'Interpreter, what is a "f...... b...ard?' This left me on a spot, so I gave an absolutely literal translation of the two words, much to the amazement of the court. The colonel thereupon questioned the guard, perhaps a little humorously, asking him why he was indulging in sexual intercourse whilst guarding prisoners and for information as to his parentage, and I had to come to the rescue by explaining to an incredulous court the true significance of the expression, which is not easy and defies logic. It was eventually determined by a grim and stony-faced bunch of Teutonic warriors that the expression was derogatory and not a term of endearment or a statement of fact admissible as evidence.

I received no privileges for my interpreting duties, no extra rations, and was obliged to work the eight hour shift in the factory along with the others. We were producing wood wool which was used for packing and spent our time feeding logs into mechanical saws for shredding. There were three shifts round the clock, and, needless to say, many accidents and fingers getting chopped off, as well as machines getting mysteriously damaged. I discovered that the wood wool packing was used by neighbouring armaments works for packing shells and ammunition for the front, and as a result there were many unpleasant confrontations with the Germans when the prisoners tried to invoke the Geneva Convention condition which precluded British war prisoners from being directly engaged on military works etc but to no avail.

This made the unwilling workers a bit peeved and there is no more formidable object than a member of the 51st Highland Division from downtown Glasgow feeling peeved, so we decided to burn the place down. This would not have been difficult, since there were enormous stacks of dry wood wool all over the place, but the Germans seemed to cotton on to the possibility too. It was tried once or twice in a fairly small way but unfortunately vigilant guards extinguished the small fires and on one occasion the prisoners themselves were called upon in the middle of the night, being rousted out of bed and marched up and formed into queues in the factory to pass along buckets of water with which to douse out a fire deliberately started by their colleagues on the night shift.

This was a fairly civilized camp and a reasonable amount of sport and leisure facilities were enjoyed. For me, however, the end was clearly in sight when the normal roll call was demanded at about seven o'clock one particular cold grey Saturday morning. On Saturday there was only one shift worked, which was the stint from eight o'clock until 2 p.m., the factory then closing for the weekend. Since the night shift had returned to the camp at six o'clock, all the inmates were, theoretically at least, in the camp at seven o'clock, hence the reason why a roll call was held then to ensure that the whole camp would be present and the guards could get off for the weekend; at least some of them.

'Good morning, interpreter,' came the quite jovial greeting from the second senior German NCO, an *Unter-offizier* or corporal, who had above him a *Feldwebel*, or sergeant, and of course the officer who was commandant with the rank of lieutenant.

All seemed quite normal on this chilly early winter morning, and the British sergeant in charge of the camp, Sergeant George Willis, I think of the Royal Engineers, was duly instructed to line the camp up in the usual lines five deep for counting. A lot of weary and bleary-eyed creatures stumbled around the parade ground and eventually came to rest more or less in lines of five. The counting commenced, carried out by German guards, bits of paper were scribbled on by the Germans for the four different sections of the camp (we were divided into four groups for ease of administration and to line up with the four separate barrack huts) and the bits of paper taken to the corporal for comparison with the records. A pause, which gradually became a long pause and then a recount of each section.

'What's wrong?' whispered Sergeant Willis to me, as the two of us stood out in front of the assembly, just apart from the German sergeant so that I, as interpreter, was sufficiently close to him to hear his instructions which I could then transmit in English to the assembly, but not so close that the German sergeant might catch something from me! 'Do you know anything?' Willis followed up to me. I did know something, but there was no opportunity to disclose anything now to the sergeant who had not been made party to the terrible secret. The recount had elicited the same result as the first count, and the look of beneficient happiness on the German corporal's face very gradually was replaced by a rather obvious look of thunder.

'Two of the swine are still in the huts,' he thundered. Then to the German corporal, 'Go through the huts and force them out with a bayonet, the lazy swine.'

In went the guards and an uncomfortable twenty minutes was spent standing in the cold. Most of the camp tried to get a little extra sleep on a Saturday morning, those not on the work shift, and consequently came on parade wearing trousers and jacket and little else. They were usually back in the hut within five minutes, since the Germans too wanted to get back inside, so this unwarranted delay was not welcomed. When the guards reappeared from the huts and reported negatively to the sergeant, the look on the German sergeant's face was even less joyous. 'Interpreter,' he screamed at me. 'Where are they, the two men?'

I was well aware of the location of the two men – they were somewhere, I hoped, en route on a train from Freiwaldau to Breslau, on a crazy expedition to get to a town near to the Baltic ports and a boat to neutral Sweden. And the best of British luck to them, but when I received the first crack from a very hard German ex-labourer's fist across my face, I was not so sure that I fully appreciated the honours that went with being camp interpreter. The British commander, Sergeant Willis, just stood there and looked on because it was no use the Jerry sergeant screaming at him – he didn't understand. There was only one sensible course for the German bastard to take – scream at the interpreter because he understood and in any case he was fairly small and easy to hit. So the interpreter duly stood his ground and received several vicious swipes from the German which did not improve my looks, now severely impaired with blood coursing all over the place from a nose which always did tend to bleed profusely if struck in anger.

After further recounts, by which time everyone, including the guards, was beginning to freeze, it became obvious, even to the dim German creatures masquerading as soldiers that the unbelievable had occurred and that two men were actually missing from the camp. It was then that the German sergeant played his ace card. He walked over to the guard hut and set in motion the escape alarm, a rather piteous wail not unlike an air raid siren. The fact that the escaped prisoners were probably some hundred miles or so away from the camp did not seem to register with him. What did very clearly register with him was that the fact of losing two of the prisoners under his command could well mean the loss of a cosy job and an unpleasant visit to the even more chilly Russian front.

'How are you feeling?' queried Willis in a whisper and as soothingly as possible after the German corporal had finished lambasting his already bloody interpreter. 'Oh, great,' I muttered through heavily swollen lips. Then of course the camp commandant arrived on the scene, no doubt from a comfortable bed in a local home with a local *Hausfrau* whose husband was probably defending the fatherland on some Front or another, and his mood was not exactly joyous either.

'*Was ist los?*' (What is wrong?) he queried in a thick deep guttural half croak heavily laced with Schnapps and stale cigars. He was advised and after the information had been with him for several minutes of intense digesting, was no more amused than were the other guards. Once again, and with true German efficiency, he ordered a repeat re-count of the assembled shivering prisoners, not apparently believing that his own men had reached the giddy heights of intellectual capacity to themselves be capable of adding up to 200. And, having got the same inevitable result, he marched imperiously round the huts ordering the guards to go in and bayonet all the beds and anything that looked as though it could contain a body, all producing the same negative result.

And then the poor old interpreter went through it again. It appears that punishment in German military terms should not be too fairly meted out, but concentrated on one fairly small and defenceless creature. This time I was confronted with an even less handsome face in the person of the lieutenant himself, placed some foot away from me and stinking of garlic sausage and stale Schnapps and a repeat of the previous conversation with the sergeant was duly carried through.

'Interpreter, there are apparently two men missing from this camp,' he blasted at me. 'You will tell me where they are now and how they have escaped.'

I wished they would turn that bloody siren off. I could hardly hear what the old twerp was screaming about, although I could well imagine and the high-pitched noise was not doing much for my already whirling head. However, I maintained as dignified a silence as my dejected bleeding state and rapidly swelling lips would allow.

'You must know that it is forbidden to escape from the custody of the

Wehrmacht, and you who are responsible for the men missing will now tell me where they are and how they got out.' The officer repeated his demands at the top of his not inconsiderable vocal capacity six inches from my ears. I thought he should have clearly seen that I could barely talk already, thanks to the lambasting I had received from the brave sergeant and a mouthful of blood and loose teeth, but he went on: 'And unless you tell me at once, I shall ensure you will suffer on behalf of your whole rotten camp.' That was a threat I had not anticipated until then, and I was not overjoyed to hear it. Still, respond I just could not unless I bubbled forth a blurry croak through a mouthful of blood, so I just stood there and glared pretty dumbly and probably insolently at the officer, which probably did nothing to improve the state of the latter's liver.

The idiots could easily have found how they got out, anyway, because there was a damn great gap in the perimeter wire behind one of the huts, very cleverly cut by one of the escapees over a period, and loosely re-assembled during the day, and cut with a pair of wire cutters obtained from one of the more sympathetic civilian workers at the factory. It had, however, been hastily and roughly replaced by mates when they came out on roll call under a pre-arranged agreement.

Then it all started again, but worse. Bang, crash came the no doubt more educated and polished gloved fists of the lieutenant alternately to each side of my head and then, hardly playing to Queensberry rules, a vicious assault on the genitals with his jackboot which finally felled me. I thought it wiser to stay down, and received another kick in the ribs for luck.

Eventually, after a lot more swearing and screaming, the parade was eventually dismissed, by which time the guards had actually thought up the idea of checking the perimeter wire and found the exit, thereby establishing an escape. I did not actually feel very well, but was aided and escorted by a group of my more sympathetic mates and others and stumbled back into my hut, whilst the remaining prisoners did their very restricted best to indicate to the Jerry bastards their displeasure at the whole morning's episode.

So that was that. Back in the hut a medical orderly did his best on me, and there was actually nothing that would not mend with time. I even became a little hero, at least for a few hours, but lost my job as interpreter, thank God! In future, dialogue between the Germans and their prisoners would have to be restricted to pidgin German and a multitude of signs, many quite rude! I myself was immediately put under sentence of deportation to another camp or back to the base *Stalag*, and only remained a further day or two whilst the Commandant awaited instructions.

I did later discover, however, that shortly after I left the camp in disgrace for having allegedly co-operated in setting up the escape and under suspicion for various other nefarious subversive activities including attempted arson, the factory was ultimately completely burned down by a mysterious fire. Well done, the 51st!

It was all rather a shame really for I had got quite acclimatized to this working camp and could have remained very happily for a longer period. It was situated in a more pleasant part of the countryside and the inmates were allowed on Sundays to go for walks which were in fact marches, well accompanied of course by guards, and permitted to spend their wages in a local small shop, which naturally did not have anything to sell, but the idea was at least civilized. We had to be paid some minimum wages, according to the Geneva Convention provisions, but this was not paid in current German banknotes – we received '*Kriegsgefangenengeld*' – a long word meaning very little but translated as 'POW' money which could only be used in the camps and was not legal tender outside. In fact, we spent it mainly by gambling amongst ourselves, but one could obtain some pretty useless goods for it from outside the camp in the village store by arrangement between the store-keeper and camp authorities; we kept an internal canteen stocked with German goods, but nothing that could be used to assist an escape – which covers most things – and virtually nothing to eat or drink except very gassy coloured soda water. Still, it was an attempt at civilization, and the camp had been one of the more pleasant resorts I had visited during this conducted tour of eastern Europe.

9

The Mountain

I was not, however, returned to 'base' – the *Stalag* at Lamsdorf – but taken direct to another working commando. This was not far from Freiwaldau in Upper Silesia but no name can be given to it as it was located half the way up the side of a mountain; it must have rightly been, in fact, a mountain being at the tail end of the Austrian Alps, and there was no village anywhere near, so after saying my farewells to my mates in the camp who were I think sorry to see me take the brunt of the Germans' fury over the escape I set out with my solitary guard for the station to take a train to Freiwaldau. The journey by train was always a novel experience for a prisoner, to sit in a compartment of a train with an armed guard in attendance and very obviously the centre of attraction for the civilian and uniformed passengers who necessarily crowded on to every one of the trains now operating very restricted services. I was very much the centre of attention, some locals being sympathetic but the majority probably viewing me as a member of a nation which had started dropping bombs mercilessly on German hospitals and schools all over the country, according to their national press reports. As a result one could never be quite sure whether to expect the sympathetic look or a glare of hatred from one who may have lost a relative or friend in the bombing affrays which were beginning to penetrate into Germany, and who probably enjoyed the sight of a young English soldier all battered and bruised, which I still was, and which must have satisfactorily fuelled the egotism of the 'Master Race'.

At Freiwaldau I was duly marched through the streets being the object of anxious glances from the locals and we eventually struck out of the town and embarked on a road which led off, almost immediately behind the town, to the foothills of a mountain range where we reported at what appeared to be a small army post. Eventually my friendly guard and I were taken by truck up and up a mountain track until we arrived at a small hutted camp in the woods which was the billet for the working party.

It was now getting on for late 1942 and unfortuately the notes I made at the time peter out at this point for reasons which will shortly become obvious, so for the following episodes precise dates are no longer available. However, there was snow on the ground and it was mid-winter when I arrived at the very spartan-looking establishment.

I was not greeted with any enthusiasm by the residents who, probably quite naturally, looked upon me with the greatest suspicion. There were about twenty-five prisoners in the camp and all was snug and cosy. Obviously the work was healthy and the rations reasonably rewarding because of the heavy physical labour involved in tree felling and logging, so the arrival of a new face late in the evening, being one who allegedly was British but chatted to the guards quite fluently in German was clearly a subject for considerable suspicion, despite the fact that the newcomer sported a variety of hues from bruises around the face.

I was initially given a wide berth by the occupants who occasionally threw out a 'telling' question about some army custom or civilian custom to test whether I really knew anything about the British army and had ever been to England, despite the fact that the Germans would hardly have bothered to plant a fifth columnist in a camp twenty-five-strong, miles from anywhere.

However, the problem ultimately resolved itself by an odd coincidence. One member of the camp, a territorial from a sister regiment to mine had a very unusual surname. I had in fact only heard the name once before in my life, and this was at work before the war. It was the name of a firm of quantity surveyors in the West End with offices not far from the office I worked in. I mentioned to this chap where I had previously heard the name, and it immediately transpired that his uncle was the boss and founder of that very firm. This, of course, lent considerable credence to my whole story and it was not long after that I became accepted in the camp by my suspicious fellow-prisoners.

The work was not unpleasant: we assisted in the felling of trees on the mountain slopes, general forestry duties, lopping branches, burning scrub etc, and loading whole trees on to sledges for transport down to a staging post lower down where the trees were loaded on road transport for the short journey to the railway station (some probably going back to the wood wool factory I had just left). The work was hard but healthy, and we had fun on the sledges accompanying the trees down the purpose-built slipway for a mile or so to the lower staging post. In fact I got my greatest kicks by 'arranging' for the trees to fail to negotiate a bend in the track, and they would then go plunging down the side of the mountain, which we all considered to be time well spent, though our guards did not always appreciate the joke.

About this time a great change occurred in our lives as POWs. The first food parcels from the Red Cross appeared; at least they got as far as those on working parties at about this time. They may well have reached the *Stalags* and bigger camps earlier but there was at first a prevalent view, no doubt a personally attractive one taken by the British camp commandants in the *Stalags*, that the parcels should be for distribution only internally in the *Stalags* and not sent out to the working parties, since the latter theoretically received better rations anyway. There may also have been a distribution problem, as the Germans did not relish the idea of using up their limited supply of petrol and transport taking food around the place for prisoners, when they could have done with the food themselves. No doubt the senior German officials concerned with the distribution throughout the camps did, in any case, obtain substantial 'commission' in terms of parcels, from the many they had available for sending out to the camps.

The difference these parcels made to the prisoners' lives cannot be adequately described. Apart from the obvious fact that we were able to get a greater amount of nourishment, although the arrival and distribution of the parcels in the early days was very intermittent, maybe one in six to eight weeks, they were instrumental in giving the prisoners additional, sorely needed hope because we could tell that, from the type of contents and even the manner of packaging, the old country could not be in quite the dire straits the Germans made the case out to be. At the time it did, of course, have the effect of making the Germans themselves wonder whether the war was going all their way. How come a country which was being blasted out of existence by the all-conquering Luftwaffe and had had most of its merchant fleet sunk by U-boats still managed to send its prisoners in Germany real coffee from Brazil? The other great effect the parcels had was that they provided the prisoners with invaluable bartering means externally – and that means with the Germans themselves be it guards or civilians on working parties with whom we may come in contact, as well as providing some collective wealth within the camp. During the war years, in Germany and therefore in most of Europe, food was wealth; money as a bartering agent lost most of its glamour, and direct or indirect barter with foodstuffs and precious metals, jewellery etc, replaced worthless Deutschmarks.

In the prison camps food and drink, and strangely enough tobacco, were the only essentials in life. No other commodity was of any value at all. This experience led me to feel for all time in the future that I should in life concentrate only in storing food and ensuring that vast supplies of food would always be available to me. This was not a matter of greed; it was purely a question of survival. Food is the only ultimate currency and at the end of the day, when all the metaphoric chips are down, a loaf of bread is worth more than a ton of diamonds – you just can't digest the wretched diamonds. In a society such as the Germans had produced in Central Europe since 1939, food had become the single most important currency even in the country areas. Eggs and bacon had become worth nearly their weight in gold and silver, and such luxuries as chocolate, coffee and even soap could command a very high price on the black market.

Anyway, the parcels which now started to appear, altered our lives very considerably. Although I would imagine that the German army officials, who themselves were so very hard up for most basic foods and certainly for luxuries, may have stolen vast quantities of the parcels destined for the prison camps and to be fair this is only an assumption but the temptation must have been there, the guards were always very ready and willing to do business with the prisoners. A tin of coffee could produce various parts for a radio, a compass or other essential equipment for escaping, and this made some minds turn, once again, to that particular sport.

However, the German commander of our small camp, who was a particularly nasty bit of work, also realizing the possibilities which may have jeopardized the security of the camp or maybe acting from pure jealousy, insisted that all the receptacles in the Red Cross parcels be opened and the prisoners received only the contents. The result was that when each prisoner went up to receive his parcel, every packet and tin was duly opened and the contents poured into the cardboard lid of the container, so one received soup, condensed milk, tea, soap, tobacco, beef stew, etc., all in one unholy mess. This was a trifle disappointing although from a nourishment point of view the problem could be coped with, but the goods were, of course, unsaleable to the outside world. The commandant maintained that, since the packing had been done in England, machine guns, knives, bombs, messages or something may have been put in the tins with the proper contents. Maybe he had a point although I very much doubt whether anything could be concealed in a tin of baked beans which would seriously jeopardize German security. Fortunately he did not remain long with us (with luck, he made his way ultimately to the Eastern Front) and he was replaced by an older and rather more humane type of German. He was however right up to a point, and often a tin of biscuits could be found to contain a brief message like 'Keep smiling – we're winning' or some similar pretty innocuous message, but certainly no machine guns!

Another very noticeable change which was now occurring in our lives was that most of the able-bodied younger guards were being replaced by older and, in some cases, even disabled guards. There was also a new approach adopted by the guards who, above all, were terrified now of losing their jobs. No doubt guarding POWs was a cushy number, but the great threat rife amongst all corners of the Wehrmacht was the ever-present disaster of being despatched to the Eastern Front. The danger inherent on being sent to battle with the British or Americans in Africa or later in Italy were as nothing compared with the tremendous fear the ordinary soldiers felt at being sent to the Russian Front. From stories gathered from the guards, it transpired that life was not entirely enjoyable bogged down in the snow around Stalingrad and conditions for the German troops in the intense cold fighting an army with apparently infinite numbers of troops to throw into battle, was both exceedingly uncomfortable and very frustrating and something to be avoided at all costs.

In talking confidentially to the guards, of course always alone and with no other German present, I could learn something of the real horrors of being sent to the Eastern Front. Climatically it must have been quite ghastly to stand on guard for hours on end in temperatures reaching 40° below zero centigrade, and the enormous guard boots worn by those stationed in such areas was testimony to the rigours to be experienced by the Germans. These boots were about 24–30 inches long and about 12 inches wide and were completely insulated with fur apart from being of thick leather uppers and soles about two inches thick. It was nearly impossible to move in the boots but they well illustrated the terrific cold to be experienced in Russia in midwinter. They were also equipped with enormous fur greatcoats and caps. They told tales also of the thousands of Russian troops sent into battle against the German troops, wave after wave attacking a German machine gun post and being relentlessly mown down by the Germans until the latter ran out of ammunition in the end and the Russians would eventually overrun the position by sheer weight of numbers. Desertion was apparently very rife amongst the Germans, and the German officers apparently spent quite a considerable amount of ammunition shooting their own men who had fled, and making examples of them. Supplies to the German forces were evidently very short as a result of the extreme difficulties encountered in distribution, especially to the more isolated and remote advance positions in Russian territory, and all in all it was quite obvious that, following in the wake of Napoleon, no German soldiers who were sent to the Eastern Front, if they ever returned, came back in the same state as they went.

They also knew they were fighting a ruthless enemy. There were no prisoners of war taken if it could be avoided and in the smaller patrol actions on the Front, any captives would be shot on sight, and probably first mutilated. Tales were told of the wounded and captured being stripped of their clothes in the freezing temperatures, for the German equipment, which was not a patch on the British or American equipment for quality, was nevertheless much better than the Russian. The captives left to freeze to death in the cold, probably after being mutilated and having vital organs cut off as souvenirs. Clearly the war in the East was nowhere near as civilized as that being conducted against the Western enemies of the Reich.

It could therefore be well understood that the guards were not now anxious to change places with the brave young patriotic German youth who at first had found the advance to the East through Poland such enormous fun, especially since it did not now appear that victory was going to be quite so easy.

All this made me start, once again, to consider the question of escaping. Obviously, it would be no great hassle to get out of the compound or even to run away during the day from where we were working. The guards did not really guard us at all in the mountains, since we were miles from anywhere in unhospitable terrain and nowhere to go anyway. However, escape from the camp compound was the better alternative since this would allow the escapees a greater period of time before they were found to be missing. If they got out after being shut in for the night, about 7 p.m., their escape would probably not be noticed until the following morning at roll call.

Where to escape to? Well, the answer to this was very clear. We could, from the place on the mountain where we were working see what appeared to us to be the top of the mountain on whose side our camp was perched. We were told that the valley on the other side of the mountain was Czechoslovakia and we knew that, despite or maybe because of German occupation of Czechoslovakia the local people might well be sympathetic to the Allied cause and might help us. We were also given to understand, through the grapevine, that there were established lines of escape or safe houses in Czechoslovakia leading through to Switzerland. This all seemed very attractive and rather too tempting to miss, so despite my previous unfortunate experiences, I fell for it, and started discussion seriously with two other lads, leading to the gradual assembling of provisions, the purchase of the inevitable compass, civilian rags, etc, and finally an agreed date. Most of these acquisitions could now be made by careful negotiation with civilian workers who were with us during the day, and even from the guards themselves. Coffee and chocolate from the parcels were the inducements.

We were of course quite crazy. The basic simple mistake was that just to look up the slope of a mountain and see what you think is the top is so ridiculously naive; when you got to that plateau, only then do you see the next and so on. The mountain was actually very high and only well-equipped and experienced mountaineers could have successfully tackled it, and we were really at a relatively low level.

Still, I made a few journeys up the hill from where we were working to prospect the terrain above, on the pretext of going for a leak, so much so that the guards began to wonder at and suspect the capacity of my bladder. However, I made the usual pathetic excuses based on extreme constipation intermittently varied by problems at the other end of the scale, and probably allayed their fears, and my forays up the hill did nothing to upset my view that if we could just get up to the top, a few hundred metres, we would all come tumbling down the other side to Czechoslovakia and freedom.

We ultimately arranged a date which was to be a Saturday evening after we were returned to the billet, so as to give us maximum time before the escape would be discovered. Getting out was absolutely no problem; the guards' hut was at the front of the little camp with a fence of double wire, but at the rear was only single wire fencing and since we were now in mid-winter again, there was an abundance of snow and odd boards etc, lying about to enable us to get through the window, which was not even locked, and clamber over the wire by placing boards, logs, etc, against it. It was quite clear the Germans never really assumed anyone would be crazy enough to try to escape from a warm hut on to a frozen mountain slope, but they forgot that there is one born every day – or in this case three.

The Saturday evening arrived and the three of us started on the course of pre-event nerves which I had already twice experienced. It would in fact be more accurate to say I had experienced pre-event nerves only once, in the case of the exit from the barn at Hohensalza where the preparation had lasted for some while prior to the actual event, thereby increasing anxiety and getting the adrenalin flowing. In the case of the departure from the coal yard, the whole matter was much more spontaneous with very little previous build-up, and I do not think it had any great effect on the activities of the nervous system.

The two going with me, Jock Ramsey and Bill Hughes, were both a little older than me, but had had no previous experience in the escape line. They were both from army regiments in the North and full of enthusiasm for the feel of freedom again, which the previous disasters suffered by me had done little to impair as far as I was concerned. It all seemed so simple, just to climb a couple of hundred metres or so up the mountainside and the rest must be pretty plain sailing.

The weather was not marvellous – there had been a considerable amount of snow but it was not actually snowing heavily on that fateful evening we had decided upon to make our break, so we should be able to get some distance away and allow the light snow to cover our initial steps away from the camp before the escape would be discovered the next morning.

'I can hardly bloody well move in all this garb,' moaned Jock standing up in the billet fully dressed for the fray and loaded down with several pairs of socks, underclothes, shorts, two old pullovers, two shirts, ex-Polish army tunic, heavy cloth trousers, balaclava, an old army greatcoat from some army long overrun, and you name it. We all three looked a bit comic, but the other inhabitants of the hut did not particularly appreciate the joke. When the escapees had gone and the flight had been discovered, it was always those who were left who took the brunt of the Germans' displeasure, as I had found out to my personal discomfort at the last camp. So whilst they gave lip service to supporting their comrades – 'Jolly good luck, chaps.' 'Give my love to my bird in Newcastle when you get there, but mind her left hook!' and other ribald comments to bolster up our courage, those who were left were pretty apprehensive as to what the morning might bring.

'Up you go, Bill,' I urged my mate through the window which presented no complications and once out in the night air our wits were soon sharpened to the task in hand of negotiating the wire fence which originally was about six feet high but had been reduced to no more than four feet or so above the ground by the snow. A couple of logs set up against the barbed wire and a plank and as the first one scrambled across it, the fence virtually gave way, leaving the remaining two a very simple passage over the remains to attain freedom, of a sort. The guards were no doubt well tucked up in their own hut playing cards and drinking Schnapps, and they seldom, if ever, patrolled the compound after dark.

Having successfully negotiated the wire fence, we were once again our own masters and free to take our own course through a white, wet, cold and generally inhospitable terrain and commenced our rather stumbling plod along a path up the mountain; of course there was no need for caution since there was not a soul around – not even a bear, and after walking for some little while beyond our usual work place we arrived at the plateau to realize that there was an enormous black hump behind it rising up into the darkness and, with not a small amount of growing disappointment in our hearts, we commenced upon the assault of the next plateau or ridge line which we could just make out ahead, through conditions which were becoming very, very much more uncomfortable. The moon was most helpful and the reflection of the light against the white snow made it quite light enough to see our way ahead, and even in the thick forest we were easily able to follow the foresters' track without having recourse to the torch we had equipped ourselves with. But if I had at that time had the remotest idea as to how our little expedition was going to end up, I would have gone straight back to the door of the guard room and asked to be let back into the camp.

The cold was absolutely intense and we all soon began to have an initial foreboding that things were not going too well. As we plodded on, we began to literally be numbed with the cold which we could feel coursing down through our lungs and through our nostrils and physically and mentally we began to weaken and succumb to the freezing conditions. We were now, in fact, progressing rather like a bunch of zombies, unable and unwilling to coherently communicate with each other and becoming seriously affected, not only by the extreme climatic conditions, but also by the moral disillusionment which was beginning to dawn upon us, that our escapade was not only ill-conceived and not going to be successful, but could result in considerable personal discomfort and danger. At first, it had all seemed so simple, but when we started experiencing difficulty in breathing at the higher altitude, and felt that our limbs and even our brains were not continuing to receive the right intake of oxygen and blood, we began to get very alarmed. None of us had, incidentally, been up a mountain before.

However, we stumbled on through the thick soft layers of snow, which became thicker and more difficult to traverse with every step, on and on up the mountainside encountering ever increasing difficulties and worsening conditions. Where it had been very cold at the camp level, it was now absolutely freezing – not just literally for it was freezing at the lower level so by now we were encountering a temperature of 25 degrees below Centigrade or worse. There was also much more wind higher up, where the forest thinned out, and it blew the snow into our eyes making it difficult to keep them open. Of course although we wore several layers of clothing, it was pretty primitive clothing being largely *ersatz* (artificial) and not of warm wool, and old boots which were worn and with very thin and in places incomplete soles, and the extreme conditions soon began to take their toll. We realized, all too late, that the whole thing just was not on; we did not have the equipment or stamina to tackle a mountain at night which probably many experienced and well-equipped climbers may have jibbed at. Besides which Bill was now more than blue with cold, in fact he was having difficulty in walking at all because of severe stomach pains and Jock was complaining as vociferously as he could in his weakened state about his leg which apparently felt paralysed; he kept saying he could not feel it at all and just could not get it warm. Finally he was unable to continue walking and had to come out with the unutterable statement, 'I can't make it any further.' He stuttered the words out as he slithered down against a snow covered rock enjoying the sudden cessation of having to drag his legs along any further. We were beginning to become confronted with an impossible situation. You can't make a man walk if his legs won't move; the other two of us certainly did not have the strength nor stamina to carry him or even to support him further since it was all we could do to propel ourselves forward, so where do we go from here?

The party stopped its tortuous progress and we tried to concentrate our minds upon the next move, although it was almost too cold to think straight. 'How much farther do we have to go on like this?' came the inevitable and unanswerable question. The mountain still seemed to loom up ahead of us with no apparent summit visible. However the most vital and telling comment came from Jock with the bad leg: 'I can't feel the bloody thing, let alone move it, and the pain is unbearable . . . terrific pain – it's thumping like mad – can't think properly . . .' The voice had trailed off to an indecipherable murmur and it was very, very clear that nobody was going anyway further towards ultimate freedom that night, and the major requirement for the expedition was to get help to Jock before whatever had immobilized his leg got around to immobilizing the rest of him.

Bill's position was little better. He had some sort of stomach cramp and was blue from cold and stuttering instead of speaking. He seemed actually unable to push the words out of his mouth and was bent double with agony and seemed to be frothing a bit at the mouth. I, in the meantime, was faring possibly slightly better, but suffering from great difficulty in breathing, and when I did get air into my lungs it felt like a draught of ice and I seemed to experience difficulty in expelling it again. I could not stop myself from shivering and violent pains were racking my chest from the efforts of breathing. The whole situation was obviously calamitous, and nothing short of a miracle was now going to save us all from an exceedingly unpleasant death in the snow up the top of a mountain a long, long way from Richmond, Surrey. The whole adventure had very rapidly become a nightmare and we would certainly have turned round and re-traced our steps if we had known where our steps were, but alas, the steps were by now well covered by snow and we could only guess in what direction to head for; it would not be difficult to make a very disastrous guess in conditions and in a place like that and finish up tumbling over a precipice. Anyway, we would not even be able to get downhill without leaving Jock, and that was clearly not on. So we decided to try to hole up for the rest of the night and found a minimum of shelter to support the three of us huddled together behind some rocks and shrubbery of a sort.

The night dragged by and became the night of ever-increasing horror and agony as the elements persisted in continuing to torture us, a torture that only the natural elements in the end seem to have the greatest efficiency to produce and to keep producing, relentlessly, to effect a rapidly deteriorating state in the three bodies tightly wedged together in an effort to generate some exchange of heat through the frozen and soaking wet clothing which failed to withstand the snow and icy temperatures. The hours until the first glimmering of dawn appeared through the trees passed so slowly that each minute was carefully weighed and the passing of each minute, whilst diminishing the available remaining strength, was in fact a victory to savour fleetingly before the next ghastly minute arrived and had to be endured. And so it went on, minute following minute to greater agony until the arrival of the early light enabled us to try and take stock of our horrible situation and forced us into some action for the sake of self-preservation.

That dawn presented a very dismal state of affairs as we viewed the ravages of a night which had surpassed any I had ever previously experienced in sheer horror. My colleague with the bad stomach, Bill, seemed to be barely alive; he was deathly white and blue and not able to speak at all and breathing irregularly whilst emitting a froth from the mouth and unable to move and his eyes did not seem to move normally; they seemed to fix in an unnatural stare, it was very frightening. Jock was suffering excruciating pains in his legs and side and seemed unable to have any feeling on one side of his body. I was hardly in the best of shape myself, but was probably better off although I felt so literally numb with cold that I found great difficulty in actually thinking properly and the greatest difficulty in breathing, with severe pains in the upper part of the body. Numb is really such an entirely inadequate word. I really could only wish myself dead, not having any real wish to do anything to preserve my own life and not having any energy or ability to do anything to assist my colleagues. In fact the actual thought of moving from our huddled positions maintained throughout the long hours of the night now seemed unacceptable although something of course had to be done. We could, however, see that not far from us was a mountain track of sorts, possibly under another sledge track for timber but discernible only as a wedge of clearing through the rocks and trees.

After holding a council of war, if it could be called such, consisting of a few incoherent mumblings and weak nodding of the head, it was agreed that I should make off down this track and see if I could rustle up any help, though from whom in this deserted hell no one could imagine. It was not actually still snowing, so it was suggested that I should mark the route as best I could; so off I set at a slow stagger, every now and then building a little cairn of sticks, stones or branches or whatever I could find, but I just followed really the track blindly in the hope that I would encounter some form of help from somewhere. Every step was agony, I felt absolutely numb with cold and my breathing had become very laboured and irregular and I suffered a permanent shiver throughout my body.

However, thanks be to a merciful God, I did not have to go too far before I came across three civilians coming up the track, who must have been most astonished to see such an extraordinary sight coming down from the top of the mountain at that hour of the day. I stammered out in my best German who and what I was and explained to them as best I could our plight and I gathered they were local forest workers on their way to an early start on the mountain.

They were very sympathetic and did what they could to help me including giving me a swig of hot coffee which was the greatest libation I had ever tasted; one continued down the track supporting me and the other two went on up the track to where I had indicated my mates were located. They were extremely helpful and immediately understood the situation despite the fact that they were presumably German or Silesian, more likely the latter. There was absolutely no point in trying to continue any escape and they telephoned down from a forest hut a little way down the track to the village to advise the local police who presumably told the military for within a matter of an hour or so, and a very welcome further mug of hot something and a sandwich, two German soldiers arrived in a tracked vehicle to escort me and my colleagues off somewhere. However, one stayed and went off with the remaining civilian up the mountain to see the other two, whilst I was carted off down the track in the jeep. I was still feeling frozen and shivering all over despite the coffee and felt very ill and barely able to get my breath, and this was interspersed with severe coughing fits and what with one thing and another, I really could not have cared less whether I was alive or dead. Come to think of it, probably the preference would have been for 'dead'.

Looking back on it now, it must be pretty obvious that I was barely conscious at the time, for I can recollect very few details of precisely what happened or the order in which things happened. The mug of chicory was something that remained in my memory, the fact that the jeep or whatever it was, was on snow tracks, which I had not seen before, but beyond that all that remains clear was an immense and intolerable physical and mental numbing which seemed completely to rack the senses, combined with incessant shivering and teeth chattering and agonized breathing. No doubt the medical profession have a word for it, but when I was taken to a small Wehrmacht post of some sort where I was given blankets and allowed to wait near a fire, the heat from the fire had the immediate effect of rendering me finally unconscious. I soon revived within a short time and tried to make enquiries as to the fate of my two colleagues, although the German soldiers present in the billet, although being as helpful as they could be, appeared to have no information regarding Bill and Jock, which caused more worry for me to cope with. I am sure it surprised me even in my semi-conscious state to receive any sympathetic treatment from German soldiers at this time, and the blankets and hot drink I was given may have saved my life.

However I was soon back into the rear of another truck, shivering the whole time, and driven off with the same guard and a new driver. Eventually we arrived at a town at the foot of the mountain and stopped at what appeared to be another working party camp and we were joined by two other prisoners who were also put on to the back of a lorry which was full of empty crates and cartons and presumably was used as a camp supply truck. I was not allowed to speak to the other two, which was something I probably could not have done anyway,and they looked at me as though I had just landed from the skies and were quite unable of course to understand my very distressed state; eventually, after what seemed an interminable journey but was probably not more than about an hour or so, the three of us were brought back to the *Stalag* at Lamsdorf.

I did not see my other two colleagues with whom I had undertaken the ill-fated escape again, although I did learn later that, very sadly, Bill Hughes who had the severe stomach cramp died from exposure and the results of that foolhardy escapade. I was also to learn that Jock Ramsey, with the bad leg, had a foot amputated, having contracted severe frost bite and an eventual gangrene from a frozen, septic leg. Altogether, a very terrible result and no doubt a far too severe punishment for what might well be considered no more than a very ill-conceived escape attempt. My own condition left me a very, very short distance removed from the Golden Gates.

10

The Main Camp

A t Stalag 344 Lamsdorf, to give it the correct title, I was immediately taken to the camp hospital. I was put into a ward locally known as the 'Death Cell' and was duly informed by the other inmates that the ward had only one exit - immediately leading to the burial ground. The hospital was a single storey building away from the main camp and a prisoner had to be half dead before being admitted into what was, of course, by far the most comfortable establishment in the whole camp - and very rightly so too. It was manned in the main by army medical officers and RAMC orderlies although there was one RAF orderly, I am not quite sure why. I was not, however, half dead - probably nearer three quarters. After admission and examination by the senior British medical officer, a Scots captain and former rugby player who pronounced me as still living, but only just, I was duly parked in this ward for the most severe cases. My condition was very poor or nearer critical, as a result of the episode on the mountain, and it was very much touch and go whether survival was on. I apparently had severe pneumonia, pleurisy and anything else worthwhile and to do with the chest that one can get from frozen bronchial tubes and exposure, and for some days I believe I was only spasmodically conscious. The Scots medical officer, a Captain McCloud, brought me back into existence but only after I had experienced many days with a temperature continuously knocking at the top end of the thermometer accompanied by beds drenched in perspiration and continuous intake of liquids and drugs. For some part of the time, I understand I was delirious and my consciousness seemed to float about all over the place, from public houses in Richmond - now a far distant memory - to the more immediate horrors of snow and my two colleagues' staring agonized faces peering through the snow at me on the mountain.

Anyway, the expert attention of the medical officers and orderlies ultimately ensured that I had no need to use the dreaded 'exit' but was able to come out the way I went in which was quite an event in that particular ward and a great tribute to the skill and the treatment afforded me under conditions which were far from ideal by hospital standards. The trouble, of course, with medical attention was the extreme shortage or lack of availability of drugs and medicines and the complete impossibility of any proper 'after care'. The hospital beds were in such short supply that one was barely able to stand and breathe before you got slung out and back in the survival battle in the camp proper. There was a *Revier* which was a sort of half-way recuperation centre, but with the type of problems I had – bronchial pneumonia etc – as soon as the patient could breathe fairly satisfactorily he was sent packing into freezing cold billets and to rations which could not be considered as conducive to rapid recuperation. All credit to the chaps who worked under terribly difficult conditions in the hospital, and in the matter of repair of limbs and surgery generally they did some terrific work, but for less tangible matters such as asthma and the like, the problems started as soon as you got evicted and were back in the main thrust of things.My breathing was not satisfactory when I was discharged and in fact I never breathed again really satisfactory for the rest of my life, but discharge was inevitable.Another permanent victim of that accursed mountain and its invitation to escapees, but still very much better off than my two colleagues; in any case a grateful government and nation would pay me a not too generous compensation in the future, so it had to be reckoned with as just another of life's little adventures which was to be coped with as best one could. There were always so many others I left behind in the camp hospital who were so much worse off, and who eventually used the door leading to the burial ground.

Whilst in the hospital I anxiously awaited the arrival of my two fellow sufferers, but neither was admitted. This caused me additional hardship in worrying and I had ghastly recurring thoughts that they had not been found. There was no real way of getting information about events occurring outside the main gate of the *Stalag*, and despite my repeated requests to all and sundry, no one was able to discover any news about the other two. I eventually was given to understand that Jock Ramsey had been taken to a local civilian hospital in Freiwaldau since his leg required immediate surgical treatment, but I was unable, for obvious reasons, to elicit any information on the fate of Bill Hughes. It was quite impossible in the *Stalags* at that time, to trace the activities of mates in other camps, although later on during captivity a system of internal correspondence between related prisoners in certain camps was organized.

The worst part of discharge from hospital was, of course, the immediate change of circumstances which faced the ex-patient. Nowhere in prison camps did one receive any real signs of sympathy or help from colleagues and from other prisoners. In the hospital itself there existed this extraordinary situation where people, well trained in the noble art of looking after other helpless people, actually did things for you and appeared to suffer the pains you experienced almost as though they were their own; the doctors and orderlies all gave of their best under extremely difficult circumstances and in conditions which they were certainly not used to working in, but despite all that, and despite the fact that they themselves were prisoners suffering many of the hardships experienced by prisoners generally, they still managed to project sympathy and hope and care to their patients which, whether there was a shortage of drugs or not, still succeeded in providing at least a sound basis for healing if not an ability to complete the cure. Such care and attention from my fellow creatures was simply something I had long learned to do without, therefore a concentrated course of such treatment by itself produced powerful remedial results whilst I was in the hospital.

The trouble, of course, was that the fact of being discharged, knowing a date in advance for discharge, conjured up all the old worries of survival in the difficult conditions of the camp proper, and the medical officer's order of a date for discharge was like a virtual sentence of death. It had to happen, of course, but it was with little relish that I eventually departed from the hospital, still very weak and wheezing away, but at least grateful for my life.

I remained at Lamsdorf until about mid-1943 and found a camp in which enormous changes for the better had occurred, largely resulting from the more regular flow of Red Cross parcels and Red Cross supplies generally. By now of course the fortunes of war had turned the corner in favour of the Allies and the victories in North Africa and potential landings in Italy were sufficient to provide some boost in morale to the 'old stagers' amongst the prisoners, those who had already been in captivity nearly three years, who would never have dreamed earlier that life in a prison camp could be so acceptable. The newcomers, from Crete at first and subsequently Africa, were able to bring the latest news with them, not only from the front, but also from home and those who had already been in captivity for many years were interested listeners for the new boys to practise their descriptive eloquence upon. There were camp libraries, theatres, schools, etc, and adequate opportunity for me to study in a more academic fashion Russian as well as Italian and Spanish which I also embarked upon learning. The principal objects behind the avid learning of languages, voluntarily at that and something I would never in my fairly recent school days have ever imagined I would undertake without compulsion, were, firstly, a persistent interest in people, and communication is the key to that interest; secondly, and probably much more important, one just had to have something mentally challenging to do to keep oneself reasonably sane, so learning some fifty or so words of vocabulary every night before going to sleep at least made the brain tick a bit and gave a small purpose of a sort to a life which, without such an interest, would have been aimless in the extreme. One also never knew when such knowledge may come in useful, and I had long ago learned the all-important lesson that any knowledge is never a waste. Somewhere along the line the usually torpid mind would benefit from the effort of learning and the material learned would somewhere at some time have a use.

It was now possible to get a supply of books, not only Russian but in the other two languages, and I ploughed methodically through *i miei Prigione* of Silvio Pellico and the inevitable *Don Quixote*, although not so much understanding the text as carefully noting the grammar and vocabulary. Of course, there were in those mixed camps always plenty of people kicking about who spoke just about every language you could think of. I found Spanish Blue Division prisoners to talk to and Italian dissidents of various types. It was at Lamsdorf eventually that I even, again quite voluntarily, took the Royal Society of Arts exams in Russian, Italian and Spanish on successive days and by a miracle passed all three. That was something else I would never have believed – that I would take exams for fun. Maybe the examiners in England were being sympathetic, but anyone taking examinations in Italian and Spanish on successive days had to be asking for trouble, but this did not deter me. The similarity in the two languages makes it extremely easy to confuse them, and it would be surprising if the examiner marking my Italian paper did not find more than one word of Spanish in it.

However, the real tribute goes to the Red Cross, who could now manage to arrange for prisoners to take professional examinations in a prisoner of war camp during hostilities, which exams would be of great assistance at the end of the war in providing skills for future jobs. The exams were held under perfectly normal examination conditions with padres acting as invigilators, the papers then being sealed and returned to England for marking – altogether a most admirable effort by the Red Cross into whose collecting boxes today I am always happy to insert as many coins as can reasonably be afforded. It also showed a willingness by the Germans to act in a refreshingly civilized manner for once by co-operating in this effort and this indicated maybe a more realistic view by them of the possible final outcome of the war, and no longer bore any resemblance to the earlier treatment of prisoners which was based very much upon the assumption that no other power in the future would be enabled to question the hideous activities of those in power in Nazi Germany, at that time when Europe was all but conquered – the little exception being Britain.

Camp life generally in the main camp could only be described as utterly boring and it was everyone's principal concern to find something to occupy themselves with in order to prevent this boredom from producing ultimate psychological disorders which would eventually be carried away after release, if one dare think of that word and as far as I was concerned it had long been banished from my vocabulary. A typical day would consist of rising, or to be more precise, being yanked out of bed at about 6.30 a.m. The bed was a network of wires suspended across a wooden frame usually in two tiers but occasionally three and maybe a straw mattress of some sort, although most of the straw disappeared into fires for cooking or keeping warm. There was an issue of two exceedingly thin ex-German army blankets which were made of some very ersatz (substitute) material guaranteed to allow a free circulation of cold air and that was the bedding. No pillow, the head had to be rested on any clothing that one may safely discard during the night hours without fear of having it pinched, or the head would be rested on one arm, a practice I continued to indulge in for many years after release.

Washing was performed in very crude timber-framed rows of 'basins' which in fact was a sort of large wooden drain running the length of the ablution lined with zinc and here one also tried to shave if things were good and conditions right; but a shave was seldom taken more often than maybe once a week or less except amongst the more prosperous inmates such as cooks etc, who had to keep up appearances to prove their superiority over the ordinary rabble. However, I always felt very embarrassed about the matter of shaving. As a result of my youthful years, I hardly needed to shave at all and felt severely handicapped by the light fur which was all I could produce for a long time whilst all around me were real adults with bristly growths.

The toilet still consisted of the usual pole suspended over a cesspit, so one had to hang on literally for grim life to avoid a very messy decease. One of my mates had indeed met an unfortunate death in this most unsavoury manner; being so very weak, especially from prevalent diarrhoea and other debilitating illnesses, some prisoners were just unable to prevent themselves from falling off the pole to meet a disgusting death by asphyxiation and suffocation in the pit of excreta from which they were too weak to extract themselves.

Breakfast was usually dished out after roll-call, and took place about 7.15 a.m., consisting of a tin of chicory, and the day's ration of bread was then distributed. This amounted to one fifth of a loaf of dark rye bread; a loaf was some 9 inches long, and the cutting up of a loaf into five portions was a work of art. The loaf, of course, had two ends or crusts, and it had, therefore, to be so cut that nobody suffered undue hardship by receiving an entirely crust end. This meant cutting the load both longitudinally and across, and the whole performance was watched by the participants and interested parties with the most acute attention; so much so that at times the crumbs were almost counted individually. This portion of bread was, of course, the ration for the day and was all the prisoners could expect to receive for the day except for a dish, or to be more precise, tin of hot water in which vegetables had been cooked and apparently hurriedly removed, in case they got irretrievably lost. This sumptuous banquet was usually served around midday and was awaited with great anticipation by the guests who first carefully inspected ladles etc to ensure no cheating, and demanded continual stirring of the tureen to make sure that first served had some chance of receiving a morsel of potato or swede and not all were left stranded at the bottom of the receptacle for the wise old hands, who amazingly enough took last place in the queue, to come along and get all the solids, if any. This was, in fact, one of the great gambles of the day – whether to get at the head of the queue to make certain you get a portion at all, and got it reasonably warm by then but consisting of little more than unpleasantly flavoured hot water, or whether to bide your time and wait to the end and get chunks with cold offering, or maybe risk getting nothing at all; life is always so full of crucial decisions but on balance I soon found that some I won and some I lost, which seemed to me to be the general principle with all such momentous decisions in life.

In between the 7.15 breakfast and roll-call and the midday distribution of victuals there was nothing to relieve the monotony, unless one was detailed for some camp fatigues such as emptying cesspits, cleansing ablutions, etc, cleaning out the guard's quarters or, if Lady Luck was really smiling on you, detailed for cookhouse duties and spud-bashing (potato peeling for the uninitiated); the latter of course offered the enormous opportunity of purloining maybe two or three whole potatoes, and if one had then been able to read those ridiculous horoscopes which the newspapers today proudly present, a good day would run something like: 'The moon is excellently

aspected with Saturn, and Leo in your sign is doing a tango so three raw
potatoes may come your way!' Unfortunately I found that the moon was
only seldom so excellently aspected.

The period in the morning was the real bore, and the prisoners would walk
round and round the confines of the camp with a mate and exchange life
histories, which was not really very much since most of us were not all that
aged and had not much to relate, and it was not difficult to exhaust a life's
experiences after one week of walking relentlessly round and round. Still, the
exercise was good even in the snow with a fierce wind blowing across the
plains from Siberia, but that did not help the grey matter keep in condition so
it can be readily understood why I embarked on learning languages to stop
the boredom. The afternoon would find us back on the wire mattress with
thoughts, dreams and occasional snores and there really was not much more
to the day. The inevitable card games were pursued, especially in inclement
weather which was the most usual, but the day was really just a great drag
until lights out about 9 p.m. It was rather extraordinary that, when bored to
tears with doing nothing, if the guards came to the door of the hut to require
a dozen men, volunteers, for some job of another, nobody but just nobody
moved and most tried furiously to hide. Never volunteer seemed to be the
invariable rule, but doing something, even if it involved work, was actually
preferable to doing nothing at all. It was really quite a relief to get out on to a
working party, for although one had to work, and work hard for the
Germans knew no other kind of work, at least the time went a bit faster. In
the *Stalags*, boredom was the key word unless you could get involved in the
various intellectual activities, theatrical jobs or something a bit creative to
stop yourself going barmy. In fact, every prisoner below the rank of sergeant
was obliged to work, and the sergeants were usually put in charge of the
working parties by the Germans, to keep up military discipline. They did not,
however, have to actually work.

The peace and tranquillity of this idyllic existence in the *Stalags* was
regularly interrupted by various unfortunate disturbances resulting from the
actions of the inmates or influenced by something quite outside the
prisoners' control. As an example of the former, the various escape attempts
and subsequent discovery of tunnels etc did nothing to improve
relationships with the Germans, who personally lived now continuously
under the threat of banishment to the Eastern Front and especially so should
they let a prisoner escape for whom they were responsible. They therefore
did their very best to dissuade their charges from such activities, and this
usually took the form of roll call parades which would last for hours on end,
sometimes in pouring rain, whilst the guards meticulously searched every
square inch of the barracks for escape equipment, radios, tunnels, civilian
clothing, maps, compasses or any of the other essential bits and pieces.
When the prisoners were eventually allowed back into the hut, the shambles
was of course indescribable, and usually allowed the inmates to find out who
amongst them were the 'black marketeers' and food hoarders for such little
nest eggs would have been unceremoniously disclosed.

Another more serious mass punishment was curtailment of issue of Red

Cross parcels, but this was never regarded as a very sporting retaliation, and even some of the more unpleasant German commandants hesitated before using such a weapon. Any such retaliation could, of course, make things even more difficult for the Germans, since they were far from being overmanned as a result of so many of their troops being required now on the Eastern Front and therefore any serious disturbance amongst the captives may have ended in unpleasant consequences all round, so an uneasy peace was maintained in which the prisoners did not go out of their way to make the guards' lives too tricky and they in turn let the prisoners get on with their amusements, including of course, digging the inevitable tunnels. The Red Cross parcels did, of course, have the advantage to the Germans of providing sorely needed nourishment for the prisoners they were responsible for, and eventually saved them from the dire consequences of starving their prisoners to death or causing illnesses and disease to spread.

As an example of the external influences affecting us, it was at about this time that British prisoners of war suffered reprisals for some incident which occurred in the war in the West. Without any previous warning or comment, one morning at an obviously high powered roll-call attended by numerous extra guards waving machine guns around and generally giving a fair impression that something untoward was about to occur, the Germans proceeded to tie the hands of each and every one of us with string, which looked surprisingly like string from Red Cross parcels. Everybody was duly tied up and no explanation was given.

Two rather different reasons eventually transpired and circulated through the unofficial camp news sources which originated of course from the toilets, and maybe that is the place to which the information should have been subsequently consigned, but the official reason never got down to such a lowly inmate as myself and whilst there must be some official explanation, the two different reasons received at the time were (1) because the Canadians had so tied or chained German prisoners in a certain prison camp in Canada and (2) because the British or Canadians at St Nazaire or Dieppe (if there were any Canadians at the attack on St Nazaire) so bound German prisoners they had taken there. Whichever may have been the real reason, the result was not to the prisoners' advantage.

The wretched bindings were a confounded nuisance in doing most things which one normally wanted to do, like swatting flies off your nose and squeezing lice to death, and in particular, going to the toilet. Hands were tied regularly every day at the first roll-call and then not removed until the last roll-call of the day. This did, of course, completely prevent us from carrying on a whole host of daily activities, sport in particular and even walking round the compound for it is not easy to walk with your hands tied in front of you and was a most effective punishment, but was not something which resulted from our own transgressions and left us bewildered and very cheesed off with the whole performance. This charade seemed to last about three or four months at least and when eventually we were advised that the retaliation was to be ended, everyone was to say the least extremely relieved. Of course, as usually happens with these performances, after a very short time we learned how to slip out of the knots pretty easily and the whole thing after a few weeks lapsed into a sort of daily formality of being tied, loosening the knots and passing the day with the hands appearing tied when guards were around, and tightening up again for the evening roll-call. There must be some doubt as to whether the Germans gained much from it, but they were I subsequently gathered in turn duly castigated in the British and Allied press as well as in the neutral press, for inhumane treatment of their prisoners, but it seemed to give some small insight into the pea-sized brains of the German high command who initially ordered such useless reprisals. Whether the Canadians did chain or tie their prisoners up did not seem to be the point. If the Germans thought it was a wrong thing to do, then why follow up and do it themselves? Two wrongs do not make a right.

Eventually I was given an interpreting job at the delousing centre, not an enormously auspicious post but one which was given to me by the Germans upon the recommendation of the British camp authorities; in the form of the regimental sergeant-major who, as senior NCO assumed the role of camp leader. That recommendation was given with a very sound though slightly subversive intention in mind.

As mentioned, with the advent of the Red Cross parcels everyone started bartering with the guards, not just for food but also for radio parts and even radios. Those were the days of the crystal and valve sets and there were an abundance of expert technicians in the camp who could assemble, not only radios, but transmitters also, and could very easily turn a few bars of chocolate into an excellent radio. But it was not long before the Germans became well aware of the growing number of radios around the place, which were of course most strictly forbidden, and several exacting spot searches carried out by them revealed the extent of the problem. For example in one search no less than twenty-seven radios were found and confiscated and this was only a small proportion of the full number clandestinely secreted around the camp. This only served to increase the efforts by the Jerries to flush out every last set and component, their view being, presumably, that the prisoners may get to know too much about the progress of the war which by then had become somewhat unfavourable to the Nazi cause and may, if opportunities arose, start taking matters into their own hands and become a more active enemy, for both prisoners and guards were always careful to remember that, although we may be in captivity, we were still the enemy and had the potential of being very disruptive behind enemy lines. The British powers-that-be then had to think up the most unlikely place for the searchers to look for radios and they came up with the delouser.

In the delouser there was always an abundance of old clothing etc, lying about and many cupboards, nooks and crannies, and it was not difficult to secrete a radio in an old coat pocket so long as the prisoners operating the delouser were aware of its presence and did not send it in for steaming. The Germans' only role at the delouser was supervising and guarding, and the operation of the plant was carried out largely by the prisoners themselves. Furthermore, there were ancillary rooms where it was not so difficult to set up a radio and tune in and listen, and even when the guard was around his attention could be very easily distracted by a packet of coffee whilst warning signals were sent around. There was no security risk at the delouser as the plant was within the internal camp command, and the gang of workers of about seven or eight was not even regularly counted and checked when assembling for work except to ensure that enough were present to operate the plant. So all this combined with the fact that I was able to listen to both the German or Russian broadcasts and understand them, as well as the BBC if it could be got, supplied the reasons for my appointment as interpreter in the delouser.

This all went well except for the unfortunate fact that I was absolutely hopeless when it came to any form of instrumentation, radios, cameras or even cigarette lighters! So putting me together with, what seemed like highly complex instruments such as crystal radios, was really taking on something, so I had first of all to undergo instructions in the very elementary stages of operating a radio, that is twiddling knobs in the right direction, something which did not come easily.

Anyhow, I eventually got the hang of it and duly found myself closeted together amongst a large pile of very old and probably flea-ridden coats in a room off the very warm main delousing unit twiddling knobs in utter confusion trying to obtain any available news broadcasts or snippets of news information which could be obtained from any source during the day. This had to be done whilst at the same time officiating as interpreter for the Germans, which meant that each time a group of prisoners arrived at the delouser, I had to be warned and emerged from my shroud of old verminous coats to relay the usual instructions to the new arrivals, and then after they were settled, to re-establish myself and try and get some sense out of the infernal machine. This was obviously not entirely satisfactory, especially since I found that the best news programmes seemed to come in the evenings about 7.30 to 8 p.m. when we were all supposed to be nicely tucked up in our billets.

Arrangements were therefore made for me to clandestinely remain overnight in the delouser to get these broadcasts, which was a cold, lonely and generally thankless task. It was fascinating to get the different versions of the war position from the different sources as I could receive reports from the various fronts and versions of the progress of the war in German, which was of course not at all difficult, Russian which was again relatively easy and the more difficult BBC programme which was directed to Germany and which could only be got fairly faintly being so far from the source and suffering impediments en route, but get it I did, at least occasionally. There were also garbled news snippets from Vichy France and from Italy which were not of much value being nothing more than second-hand German reports. Putting them together resulted in as good a knowledge of the progress of the war as anyone could get in Europe. We kept maps of the Eastern Front up to date with the daily news from the Russian radio of the fall of cities and towns in their magnificent advance following Stalingrad, and this added a substantial degree of excitement and indeed hope among the prisoners that the war might one day actually finish.

Hence the tremendous value of this news service, the contents of which was shot around the camp by word of mouth like wildfire and enabled prisoners to start putting at least metaphorically two fingers up to the Germans and generally start coming back to life as individuals. Such was the tremendous impact of getting our own news, of actually hearing from the BBC that massive air-raids were being directed against German cities and that the lads had done wonders in the desert against Rommel and were now en route for Italy, that this news 'broadcasting' was realized as being of immense value psychologically in keeping up our end against the Germans. Copying centres were established, all very much undercover, so that news sheets could be passed around, which was of course, fatal because the Germans intercepted them and re-doubled their efforts to flush out the radios but they never searched the delouser. We even got so sure of ourselves that it was agreed we should try to transmit the news to the adjoining Russian camp over the way, and which I had earlier been in. Whilst there I knew that there were a few, very few radios which had been successfully concealed by incoming prisoners or civilian internees and it was thought that, if we transmitted on a local wavelength they may be able to pick up something. The technicians duly obliged and there was no limit to the remarkable skills of the radio 'hams' in the camp at getting and assembling the little bits of equipment so that I eventually became an 'announcer' in Russian. I did make a few broadcasts but as to whether they were ever picked up by the Russian prisoners over the way was never discovered but one thing was very certain and that was that the German camp commandant of the British camp could have picked them up himself if he happened to be listening to the radio at the appropriate time and on the appropriate wavelength and understood the language and might have been very surprised to hear a broadcast in Russian from his own prisoners! It was in fact agreed that this additional service was imposing an unnecessary risk on the new reception effort and was discontinued before any irreparable damage was done.

Anyway, it was not really essential, for the delouser on many occasions accommodated groups of Russian prisoners and civilian internees who would be sent from various working parties to Lamsdorf to undergo disinfection in the camp delouser, still being operated of course by the British prisoners, and I got into the habit of writing out a daily transcript of the news in Russian which could be passed on to the visitors if the occasion arose. It was, incidentally, always a very unpleasant operation for the British workers in the delouser to have to pass the Russians through the delouser for they were so weak and emaciated it was terrible to have to witness the veritable bags of bones assembled naked in the delousing cage. We even had to treat groups of Russian women prisoners, and the sight of a hundred or so naked emaciated Russian women gathered together with their accumulated dirt was not a pretty one and likely to turn the observers off for life!

It would not be possible to over-estimate the enormous value of these clandestine broadcast receptions and the resultant distribution of news, for I at least had already seen the result where hope is abandoned, as in the Russian camp over the way, and that situation had to be avoided at all costs.

An impartial observer would, I am sure, have been very fascinated to obtain an in-depth examination of the various activities and emotional reactions which existed amongst that assembly of maybe 15,000 men of all types, from adventurous, clever or cunning, intelligent and caring types to broken, gormless, bloody minded and disillusioned creatures, all of whom retained just one spark of hope in the future: liberation and return to their nearest and dearest. Everyone had their own peculiar way of trying to overcome the current difficulties to reach the final solution, whatever that may bring, and in the interim period innovation and attempts at introducing some degree of normality into their lives to make the time pass more quickly and preserve mental and physical stability, was the order of the day. As time went by and the vague possibility of eventual release became more real, the demand for security and survival became even greater, and men looked to their minds as well as their bodies, realizing that both components may once again be needed by them to compete in the cut and thrust of a more normal life in civvy street. So people took exercise more seriously to try to improve the body state, and more serious efforts were made to use the grey matter by taking advantage of various technical and other correspondence courses supplied by the Red Cross. The correspondence was, of course, one way only, but the supply of technical books etc was by now quite extensive.

11

The Hospital

I t was not long, however, before I actually was given a more official interpreter's job by the Germans themselves. An international hospital had been set up by the Germans at a place called Gross Strehlitz, which is in Upper Silesia but towards the old German frontier, and three Allied medical officers were to be despatched to the hospital to treat the patients who were variously British, Russian, Italian, French, Poles and all sorts of other nationalities. They were, however, in the main Russian prisoners direct from the Eastern Front, severely injured or critically ill. When an interpreter was sought who could speak both German and Russian I was duly produced; in fact there were not a lot of applicants, if any, and I was duly posted to this, my last and maybe most rewarding posting.

It was particularly fortunate that I was in fact sent to work in a hospital as by now the repercussions of my past escapades were beginning to make themselves felt. It was still summer and the bronchial condition I had been left with was not too worrying. But this was soon to change with the onset of colder weather and the inevitable snow, which were a repeat of the conditions under which my chest had first suffered. I was, in fact, now a permanent hospital out-patient myself and had been physically downgraded to C3 (from A1 on entry into the army) so work in a hospital was particularly appropriate.

The main hospital at Gross Strehlitz was actually a large modern hospital built pre-war and well set up and equipped, although the prisoners did not officially have anything to do with the hospital itself other than to have the use of the operating theatres for emergencies – and they had to be emergencies. The prisoners were kept in a small compound not far away from the hospital and in the hospital grounds in a group of huts surrounded by a ten-foot high barbed wire fence, and in the wooden hut allocated to the British were billeted the three medical officers in one part of the building specially set aside for them as officers and in the other part about six other ranks: four medical orderlies, a cook and myself. The whole unit was there theoretically to treat any British prisoners who were brought in, which was very seldom and mainly consisted of the occasional shot down airman, British or American, but in the other half of the compound were several huts completely filled with about two hundred or so serious Russian medical and surgical cases. It was primarily a transit camp for the Russian sick and wounded, and the very bad cases were operated on there and then by the British, or rather Allied, medical officers either in the British POWs' own treatment room or, if warranted and available in the main hospital theatres. Since almost all the patients were Russian, with the few exceptions being Italians, Spaniards, French or Poles coming from local working camps or in the case of the Spaniards, the Blue Division, it could be fully understood that I was given every opportunity to further my study of all these languages.

Generally speaking, I was involved just with the medical officers requiring translation to and from the Russian patients, and to and from the German guards and medical personnel, but there were occasions when, in the hospital theatre during major operations, as they mostly were, I was responsible for interpreting between a British surgeon who was operating and, say, a Russian patient, Polish nuns acting as nurses, German supervisors and maybe the odd French or Italian hospital orderly. So when the surgeon ordered 'scalpel please', I had to sort out what language to use, apart from the difficulty of getting to know the foreign translations of numerous pieces of technical medical equipment and a multitude of diseases and illnesses and organs of the body, half of which I did not even know the English equivalent. Fortunately I had also learnt Latin at school and many of the words so required had Latin derivatives or the Latin term was understood by all in the medical profession, so I managed somehow to muddle through, and I am fairly confident that no one died through the interpreter not knowing the name of something at the crucial moment. The operations I found to be extremely fascinating and interesting and I became very involved with the whole thing, to the point where I was beginning to become a qualified hospital orderly as well, and, in view of the usual dire shortage of staff, I was usually called upon to act as one! I got over my first operation 'faint' early on. Nearly everyone sometime or another who attends such operations, suffers nausea and a fainting fit when faced with the more spine-chilling surgical butchery and I had my experience when watching the surgeon lance a ghastly-looking abscess on a poor Russian's face; the pus shot up so high it hit the ceiling and my stomach just turned over and exit one interpreter. A few moments in the fresh air outside the theatre and the return of the interpreter enabled the patching up of the wound to proceed satisfactorily.

The cases were all serious, but it was interesting to see the way the German supervising surgeon would almost always make the patient stand up afterwards, and if at all humanly possible, walk back to the billet. This was not done as an inhuman act, but as part of a growing doctrine amongst the German medical profession to keep the circulation going etc, by free and normal use of the limbs, and it certainly seemed to be very effective, although it looked at the time to be rather callous and rough treatment, and the British medical officers were a bit apprehensive of the results. Actually the medical officers were not all British; one was a New Zealander and one a Canadian. The latter had arrived from an attack on the French port of St Nazaire, and the former was an 'old hand' from the disaster on Crete much earlier.

There were some diplomatic incidents on these occasions, such as the time a Russian surgeon was assisting the New Zealander major who was the senior surgeon. The surgeons scrubbed up in the theatre, and then from a reasonable distance from the wash basin, the Russian 'gobbed' ('spat' for the more delicate) right across the room with a beautifully aimed shot which landed directly into the basin. The Kiwi major was horrified and instructed me to tell the Russian that in no way did he approve of this filthy performance carried out in the scrupulously clean theatre. The answer that came back, which I duly related to the Kiwi, rather took everyone aback. 'Tell your major that I equally disapprove of him blowing his nose on his handkerchief, putting the handkerchief in his pocket and then putting his hands in his pocket!' There seemed to be two sides to these customs and in this simple matter of basic hygiene I was unable to decide who was right.

This same Kiwi major nearly lost me my job, and it illustrates the awkward position an interpreter was always in. There was a severe disagreement between the major and a visiting high-ranking German colonel over the accommodation the Russian sick were being given; the Kiwi made the point that it was no use carefully patching up Russian wounds, beautifully cleansed, and then sending them back to filthy dirty overcrowded sleeping conditions. When the discussion became heated, the Kiwi said something like, 'You German pigs may be used to this' which I duly interpreted, and having delivered the precise and correct translation, it was of course the interpreter who received a crack across the face with the end of a revolver for his pains. After hurling around all possible invectives contained in the German language, the colonel suddenly realized he had got in me the wrong guy, and turned his attention to the major, but of course, being officers they did not engage in fisticuffs or swiping each other in the face. In fact there were no repercussions other than a bleeding and sore face once again for the interpreter – and who worries about that?

One particularly sad case which came our way was a young Russian soldier of only sixteen years of age, who had gangrene in a leg, which was rapidly galloping up to the knee. It was remarkable that a boy of his age should have been in uniform, but it appeared he was not unique and in the defence of Stalingrad and neighbouring cities the Russians rustled up all the males they could find and many females. Our officers requested a theatre for an amputation operation but the hospital was full with German wounded returning from the front, so the request, despite many entreaties, was rejected. As a result, and since the lad's condition was getting worse by the hour, the officer surgeon decided to operate in our own prisoner's billet on a wooden table, and there and then, with improvised tools, hacksaw, open razor and anything he could get, amputated the leg above the knee.

I was given the task of holding the leg still during the amputation, but the terrible thing was that there was no means of giving the Russian any anaesthetic. He was doped up as far as could be achieved with whatever morphine pain killers, etc were available, which was not much, but no actual anaesthetic. Everyone had the utmost admiration for the surgeon's skill under such impossible conditions and also for the boy's heroic acceptance of his pitiable fate, being all the time horribly aware that he was having one of the two legs he had been going around on for sixteen years crudely sawn off in a hostile country a long way removed from his home, parents and family and with a pretty bleak future awaiting a one-legged prisoner with no artificial limb or even aids. I only hope he obtained some temporary relief from the very compassionate treatment he received at the hands of those Britishers of whom he had probably by then only remotely read about in books, probably severely censored by adverse propaganda.

I myself was most fascinated by the meticulous, slow and painstaking performance of cutting skin and tissue, cutting and tying up arteries, sawing bones and tying the whole lot up together again. I did, however, feel a bit of a fool when the leg was finally sawn through and loose from the body and I was left holding a leg and saying to the surgeon, 'Please sir, what do I do with this?' The answer should not be printed, but it serves to illustrate the extreme crudity of the whole wretched business. The Russian boy, for that was all he was although officially a soldier, survived the operation, but only just. Every possible bottle or tin of special foods and dietary aids were collected from the British stores to supply him with something to fortify his shattered system and assist the recovery process and to build up the body strength again, but I and all the British team wondered how on earth he would get on when ultimately he had to be returned to the Russian quarters. The Germans allowed him to stay in the British billet only over the night following the operation and after that he had to be sent back to the Russian quarters. He was visited there by the doctors accompanied by me and more tins of calves' foot jelly, etc, and was still surviving when the British eventually departed. He must have had a pretty thankless and difficult life ahead of him, with only one leg to support himself on as there were no artificial legs available. He would be virtually helpless amongst a lot of prisoners who were themselves experiencing the greatest difficulty in surviving. It would be a miracle if he was alive today, but in view of the circumstances surrounding his probable future, death may well have been a merciful release, even at that young age.

One of my jobs at this camp was to interrogate the weary Russian prisoners as they arrived direct from the battlefront. The Germans themselves had very few people who spoke Russian, and certainly none at this particular hospital and camp, so they could not in fact talk to their own prisoners but could only do so through a British POW - me. The 'interrogation' consisted of the usual name, number, rank and occupation, and the Germans did not seek any further information. There would not really be any useful information such 'cannon fodder' could provide and there were so many of them that time forbade any more questioning by the Germans, but these essentials were left for me to register; from the 'occupation' part I used to elicit a lot of information which I duly noted at the time but did not of course pass on to the Germans. Such information involved details of munition and armament factories in Western Russia and in and beyond the Urals, and was given very freely. I would, for example, be advised, with a little prompting, by a Russian prisoner that he was engaged in working at a tank factory located twenty kilometres south-west of Smolensk making a certain type of tank, and that the factory had so many employees and produced so many tanks per day.

There was no reticence on the part of most of the Russians to disclose this information and in fact they seemed to be quite proud to boast about their factories. All this information I noted but did not pass on, and I found it rather fun amassing a private 'secret service' information folder in the disposition of the Russian war industry. Having carefully noted such information for what ultimate purpose I was not at all sure, carefully hiding the relevant sheets of information all written in Russian of course, and passed through countless searches, I ultimately brought it all back to the UK and have it to this day. At no time did I ever make any practical use of it and no one seemed to be interested in it when I ultimately returned to Blighty. No doubt today it is hopelessly out of date and valueless, but I had my little bit of fun acting as a 'spy'.

Some of the answers I got from my questioning of the prisoners used to be quite amusing and an insight into the peasant mentality, such as: 'What do you do?' 'I fix the left-hand front door to Mockvas' (Mockva was then the 'people's car' in Russia). 'Why the left-hand front door?' Answer: 'Because Ivan fits the right-hand front door.' But in fact after further discussion, it would become quite clear that in no way would he dare to fit the right-hand door because it had been made quite clear to him by his superiors that he was just not qualified to do so and his superiors, which seemed to include just about everybody, would never permit him to exceed his usual duties. The degree of regimentation involved in industry was obviously enormous and it was clear to me from my questioning that I was dealing with a mass of automatons or zombies, although no doubt underneath was a tender, emotional and fully intelligent soul trying to get out.

I chalked up a further 'first' during these operations, for at the time in order to alleviate the boredom of the long nights, I had taken up a study of Turkish – Lord knows why, other than the fact that I had somehow come by a German-Turkish grammar and a Russian-Turkish dictionary purloined no doubt from somewhere, and I now found my Turkish could be used, very haltingly, in translation from Russian soldiers from Azerbaijan, Georgia, etc, to their own Russian officers and comrades, who otherwise would not have been able to speak to them. Presumably they formed part of quite separate local regiments or army units, and their local dialect, which was much more Turkish than Russian, would have been the language in normal use, but when mixed up in the general mêlée of Russian prisoners they had to resort to the use of a British POW to translate for them to their own colleagues. But the example also serves to illustrate the very wide divergence of nationalities coming under the general heading of Russian, for I was frequently encountering in these cross-examinations soldiers from Mongolia, Siberia, etc, many of whom had little, if any, national interest beyond their own local 'Republic'. It seemed to me that the Russians sitting in Moscow would always have a difficult job convincing those from such outposts that they are truly Russian and brethren of, say, the Ukrainians.

293.

Rybinsk. Aeroplane fact.
Kalinin.
Jaroslav. Synthetic rubber: carriages.
Ljuberzi. Mech. agric: locos.
Wosnerensk. Chem. indust.
Ryasan. mech. agric.
Gorki Carriages. Steamships. Aeroplane. Elect. work.
Kasan. Steamships. tractors
Kolomna Locos. Armaments. tractors
Kuibyschew. Tank fact.
Tambov. Sinthetic rubber.
Woronesch. Su. Rubber: Aeroplanes.
Chernov. Tractors. Mech agric. bicycles.
Kiow. Mech agric
Dnjepropetrowsk. Copper + bran. Aeroplanes.
Woroschilowograd. Locos. Armaments.
Stalingrad. Tracks. Arm.
Eriwan. Su. Rub.
Sumgait. Su Rub.
Titrenov. Su Rub.
Solicamsk. Chem indust.
Tschiina. Tractors. Aeroplanes. Mech agric.

A page from my efforts at intelligence gathering at the Russian hospital at Gross Strehlitz where I interrogated the Russian prisoners on behalf of their captors who could not speak Russian! In so doing I discovered where they worked in Russia and what they did. I did not, of course, divulge the rather primitive information to the Germans.

There must be as much difference between them as between a cockney and an Indian from the North-West Frontier, and it is now established as to what happened in that case. British Imperialism could not survive, one wonders whether Russian Imperialism will.

I had a lot of opportunity, of course, to converse freely with the Russians and found their views on Communism and their life in Soviet Russia generally to be most enlightening. In the main, the average Russian at this level was not a political animal, and did not have any great views on his nation's external or internal politics, but it was pretty obvious to me then that, having regard to the very vast areas coming under the control of the central government, there was an enormous divergence of views according to location, and for example the Uzbeks (from Uzbekistan) were really only concerned with their local political scene and situation, and did not give two hoots for political ideologies or even know anything about the central government. There were always, however, the heavily indoctrinated youths from every region who shouted the political slogans and belonged to various Workers' Parties and Youth Organizations, and who had clearly benefited their own situation in life generally by attending the numerous political indoctrination courses held for the young Communists and Party Members, and who really accepted their beliefs as a means to an end – ultimately obtaining through their elevated position in the Party personal power and a permit to buy a radio or even a television set or maybe in the end a car or a free holiday on the Black Sea, or simply for the pleasure of having that power over their fellow men. This gave rise to continual arguments in the camp between the dedicated ones who tried to maintain their position of power and the ordinary and basically uncommitted citizen soldiers who took the opportunity afforded by the 'protection' of captivity to tell their political masters where to get off, and just what they really thought of Comrade Stalin and his Communism. I was frequently in the middle of such arguments, much to my discomfort.

When in the Russian billet, I would clandestinely be handed a slip of paper by one of the older Russian prisoners, maybe aged thirty-five to forty and on it would be written a few words to the effect: 'Don't believe anything Sergeant Ivan Ivanovitch may say – he is a political murderer and Party Leader and has got lots of our friends shot for what he calls subversive actions. Do not believe him. We are the real Russians, born and bred on the plains of the Ukraine and not just bully boys from the factories who would get their own grandmother shot if the party told them it was in the State's interest!'

Then the obviously loud-mouthed Ivan Ivanovitch, a youth of about twenty to twenty-two, would come up to me in the middle of the hut and well within the hearing of all the inmates and decry the 'oldies' in a loud voice: 'You must not listen to these old fools, Englishman. They are all enemies of the State and did not fight properly. They ran away, and that is why we are here now. They are all bourgeois cowards and are not the true Russian people.'

His words would, of course, not only be heard by the 'oldies' who may have there and then objected in no uncertain manner and were no longer afraid to air their views on Communism, but also by the close gang of the Party Man's immediate comrades, there to defend their creed against all non-believers, and also heard by the great mass of listeners from the Urals and beyond who really could not have cared less for either viewpoint and were heartily fed up with the whole political and military scene and wanted to get back as soon as possible to their farms and farm life, the occasional overdose of beer and vodka and the weekly bed-down with the most succulent Ivanova they could find. And there was I in the middle of it all, the only neutral recipient of the seething animosity between the groups because I was the only one who could understand their comments. I was rapidly being taught diplomacy in a hard school. I often wondered how they got it all sorted out when they were eventually all returned to Mother Russia and Father Stalin – presumably some pretty forceful further indoctrination took place!

It was indeed fortunate for me that I was now working in a hospital, for I was the one in need of treatment. The earlier episode on the mountain had left me suffering from a very severe bronchial condition which was generally referred to as bronchial asthma. In fact, the spasms were so bad that, in the middle of the night I would sit in vest and pants on the doorstep of the hut outside in the freezing night air in the snow and with a temperature many degrees below zero, and struggle for breath to the extent that, despite the extreme cold I would be ultimately saturated with perspiration which froze on me. I could well have been compared with the Yogis and dedicated religious men in Tibet and the Himalayas generally who may be required as part of their teaching to sit for hours with their feet in an icy mountain stream and dry off soaking wet towels placed aorund their naked bodies by means of the heat generated by will-power from their bodies. I seemed to be doing much the same thing, for the performance I went through to breathe at all involved considerable mental as well as physical strain – mental in the sense of basic determination to attain the next intake of air and expel the last. It is quite astonishing I did not get another dose of pneumonia, but in the end the medical officers came to the rescue, rather reluctantly, by giving me continual injections, first of ephedrine and subsequently adrenalin. The adrenalin, which of course is a pretty strong drug, had immediate effect but not long-lasting, and I soon began to become a drug addict which of course accounted for the doctor's reluctance at giving me the drug too often. I became in the end, however, virtually reliant upon the adrenalin and finished up riddled with intra-venal injection marks to the point that there was hardly anywhere left on my body to administer the further shots. The immediate effect of the injection was to leave me shivering and weak but at least able to get my breath, but I knew the doctor was very unhappy about the whole performance for very good reasons which I did not at the time fully appreciate. There was, however, no alternative treatment available to ease my tubes sufficiently to allow induction of air.

It was however, an insight into drug-taking in a big way. The relief obtained from the injection of adrenalin was instantaneous, and knowing this, I would have been absolutely screaming, if I could have screamed, for another injection every time the effects of the last one wore off. I would willingly have paid any money or rendered any service to get another shot. I was reduced to begging for the stuff, no doubt just as heroin addicts may do, and although the adrenalin had its immediate beneficial effect, I sought consistently more and more, until the doctors were at their wits end to devise some means of getting me unhooked. Fortunately, with the passing of the worst of the winter weather, or acclimatization to it whichever was the case, the asthma condition improved a little so that regular intakes of ephedrine and concentrated efforts to prevent the attacks increasing in intensity once they appeared had the desired effect of at least keeping the problem under sufficient control to enable the interpreter to continue interpreting. Ultimately, I suppose the inability to continue to be able to procure the drug at all, when supplies were just not there, obliged me to become 'unhooked'.

One of the officers who was a chest specialist said it was the worst asthma he had ever had to treat. Still, it seemed to come and go, and I still had to get on with my interpreting duties since no one else was able to deputize, and maybe that very fact assisted in keeping the problem a little at bay.

Of the three medical officers in the prisoner's billets, one was a member of Crockfords Bridge Club in London, the New Zealander was the reigning bridge champion of some sort in his country and the other officer who was Canadian, was also an extremely keen and efficient bridge player and a local champion back in his native land. And that left me for them to play with since none of the orderlies had any interest in or knowledge of the game. Nor did I since I did not play bridge and had not the least interest in learning, but I used to get roped in in the evening much to my disgust, to sit as a 'dummy' whilst the officers played the wretched game for what seemed endless hours. I was invariably partnered by the Kiwi, and all I had to do was to sort out my hand in suits and from that point on the Kiwi did the rest. A very efficient though unwilling dummy, which I felt rather summed up my whole army career. However, it ensured that I would never have any interest in the future in learning to play bridge, and not much for that matter, in any card game.

One freezing morning two medical officers and I were unexpectedly awakened at about six o'clock and told to dress. We were then marched out of the billet to a house in the neighbourhood, being taken there without explanation. At the house we were confronted by the most grisly sight for that early hour of the morning. In an upstairs bedroom, lying on two beds and seated variously on armchairs were a number of obviously very dead German soldiers. It transpired that six German soldiers had been billeted in the house the night before, and slept in this upstairs room. There was a gas fire in the room and they had left this on and shut all the windows tightly on the very cold night, and in the morning all six were found apparently dead from monoxide poisoning. Apparently the fire flame had become extinguished but the gas remained on. There was absolutely nothing the British medics could do for them, and all hope of resuscitation had passed, but the gruesome sight and smell remained very clearly in my memory for quite a while. The six who had died in various chairs and on the beds in the room appeared in grotesque positions in which they had eventually succumbed. Maybe however, they had passed on more contentedly than they ever would have done had they reached the Eastern Front they were clearly bound for.

We did not know of the progress of the war since unfortunately we were now no longer near any radios and were entirely dependent upon the Germans for news. Needless to say, the German news did not give us a lot of immediate hope, although one could read between the lines to some extent. Almost daily huge groups of planes, probably some hundreds, used to fly overhead, always at much about the same time of the day – about midday – and flying in a general direction from south to north at a considerable height, and the guards used to point at them saying, 'There goes the Luftwaffe, off to finish the destruction of London', which did little to raise our morale.

One bright day, after midday, as I was having a welcome spell with a cup of ersatz coffee after cross-examining the last of a series of Russian soldiers as to the exact nature of his pains, location, frequency, etc, and the medical officer had carried out his last examination for the morning, a particularly unpleasant little squint-eyed under-officer of the German guard came running into the surgery saying, '*Dolmetscher*, (interpreter), come and look at the planes this morning. The Luftwaffe have sent more than ever to bomb London. This will finish the war quicker and we can then all go home.'

Presumably he brought in the bit about going home as a moral face-saver for the previous cutting remarks about bombing London, which he knew would leave his prisoners feeling pretty bloody. It was just a little effort at compensation to the poor prisoners for having to draw their attention to the vast strength of the Luftwaffe and the fact that the prisoners would be unlikely to find anyone left alive in their homeland even if they were eventually sent home, which was pretty unlikely.

I had to comply with the request to go out into the courtyard to observe the hundreds of pretty German airplanes which could not be missed anyway as the droning sound of the engines was getting more and more thunderous as the planes approached the town. I just had to carry out such humiliating tasks, for it was always essential for the *Dolmetscher* to swallow his pride and do as the Germans required; the alternative in a place like a hospital could be disastrous since one guard, of the rank of under-officer, was quite capable of preventing vital medicines, paper bandages or other facilities from reaching the prisoners when required, so it was much more sensible for the *Dolmetscher* to accept the inevitable and do the Germans' bidding. Such acquiescence to the guards' directives did not of course extend to all prisoners, only to those in a position of responsibility and upon whose shoulders the burden of keeping the peace on behalf of the helpless sick rested.

So I went out in the sun together with the under-officer to view the pride of the German armed forces. There certainly were a vast number of planes, many more than the usual quota, and I had to estimate that there may have been as many as a thousand huge droning dragonflies blackening the skies above us, relentlessly pursuing their journey of death and destruction to be unleashed upon a pretty defenceless civilian population somewhere. Where exactly no one knew, but according to the knowledgeable under-officer it was London.

'There you are, *Dolmetscher*. That shows the *Reichsmarschall*'s [Goering's] superiority in the air. They can fly uninterrupted across Europe to England and blow the place sky high without any difficulty.' I hastened to agree that it was a tremendous show of strength, but there seemed however to be just something slightly wrong. The planes were very high in the sky and one plane at that height looked very much like another. And yet, whilst agreeing with the German for the sake of diplomacy, I was not quite clear on why they should be flying over Silesia.

And then the answer came. One minute I and the under-officer were standing in the courtyard admiring the terrifying view above, the next second there was an ear-splitting detonation of explosives seemingly right under our feet and we were all knocked off our feet whilst the ground under us shuddered and the buildings around us trembled from the combined effect of a number of 1,000 lb bombs which landed somewhere near the hospital, sufficiently close to have both under-officer and I dive for cover and cause almost all the bottles on the shelves in the dispensary to crash to the ground.

I was the first to emerge from cover to take quite another view of the air armada now retreating into the distance to the north, whilst some way behind the main formation, and at a very much lower level, were twenty or so huge planes flying in formation and obviously racing to catch up the rest. But, still more telling, there were occasional puffs of smoke and sounds of gunfire from the ground, clearly anti-aircraft fire, and those explosive sounds once and for all exploded the myth of the Luftwaffe flying to bomb London and a lot of other myths connected with it, such as the air superiority of fat Goering's Luftwaffe and even the more vital myth that the Germans were winning the war. These illusions were exploded in the face of both German guard and his British prisoner in one revealing moment of truth.

The under-officer and I duly extricated ourselves from our hurriedly sought shelters and I saw an ashen faced even more squint-eyed under-officer appear in front of me, covered fairly liberally with a coating of dirt. The man just could not believe what had happened in front of his very eyes. Years of propaganda had led him, a man of about thirty years of age and probably an ex-Hitler Youth addict, to believe every word he was indoctrinated with concerning the superiority of the German forces and the eventual victory which lay ahead. That the planes which had been pointed out to him first by his officer and which we had been told were, of course, German and were heading for the English coast, could be anything but German and that his officer who was the mouthpiece of all wisdom and also of all propaganda, could have been mistaken, or even, shudder the thought, lying, was almost inconceivable – nay, it was worse, it was unbearable. He looked at his prisoner dumbfounded, but at that moment of shock and disbelief, his prisoner did his best to save the German's face and retain a measure of goodwill in order to keep the flow of medicines and paper bandages going.

'There must have an accident, one of the planes must have crashed and its bombs exploded upon impact,' I ventured, knowing only too well that the Germans would be unlikely to direct anti-aircraft fire against their own planes, but it was an effort at conciliation anyway, however feeble it may have sounded.

At such moments, when you are a prisoner, you do not go out of your way gleefully to rub your guard's face in it. You are still on the ground a captive, a long way from home, and your guard's immediate and eventual reactions will still determine your own present standard of comfort and more particularly the standard of welfare for your sick and helpless colleagues and will also probably help to determine whether any of you find your way eventually back to your homes – so wisdom was very much the better part of valour. The guard could however, do no more than grunt and retreat to the guard hut where no doubt he had ample opportunity to discuss the new turn of events with his German colleagues, as well as to help put the beer bottles back on to the shelves and help himself to a liberal quantity of Schnapps (a sort of vodka). I for my part returned to a shambles of a dispensary to assist in the laborious, but under the circumstances joyous task of clearing up the mess, and to discuss with great glee an event which gave us all that very necessary hope essential to see us through to the end.

We found out later that this group of 'Luftwaffe' planes had dropped their lot on the local railway station and blown it to smithereens. Of course, they were not German planes at all, but American bombers flying up from bases in Italy or Africa, to bomb Berlin. The astonishment shown afterwards in the guards' faces was to be seen to be believed, and the elation on the part of the prisoners was so obvious that the British officers and I feared reprisals from the Germans. It did however, have a very sobering effect upon the Germans, and they began to wonder whether all the other optimistic things they had read about in the news were true, and whether in fact, the Fatherland really was winning the war hands down.

This bombing attack was only a prelude to a number of successive attacks in the area, and it was the railway junction at Gross Strehlitz which was apparently of quite considerable strategic importance. It is probable in fact, that it was of greater strategic importance to the advancing Russians than to the British and American Allies since there always seemed to be considerable troop activity in the area with German forces, supplies, tanks, etc, to be heard, with convoys passing sometimes all night long travelling to and from the Russian front which had become at that time rather unstable for the Germans and was now not such a very long way to the East of the hospital. Many times the drone of heavy vehicles on the nearby main road could be heard as long heavy convoys passed up the line all through the night and sometimes day and although the prisoners had had no occasion to visit the railway station other than upon arrival, it was then clear that there was quite a large marshalling yard there. The Germans obviously brought in anti-aircraft batteries to the area just in case and to everyone's local discomfort the prisoners and their guards all experienced their first baptism in being on the receiving end of real Allied bombardment, which was repeated on at least a further six occasions. The planes were always American and not always were the bombs direct hits, for some landed uncomfortably close to the hospital, in fact so close that a little while after one particular raid in which an American plane was shot down, a Russian prisoner sold me a knife made out of steel from an engine part (or is it titanium?) with a handle made from the perspex from the cabin windscreen.

It is amazing how, with such limited tools as they could muster, the Russian craftsmen could make such articles, and I have retained the knife to this day as a souvenir. It is fashioned like a Russian hunting knife, some ten inches long with a turned up point, and would make a very handy weapon, and I was very proud of the fact that, despite all the searches we had from time to time I managed to bring the knife back to England without having it ever discovered. If, indeed, it had been discovered, the consequences may well have been most severe for me, as prisoners were of course most stringently not permitted to carry any sort of weapons and this very definitely was a most handy and lethal weapon, especially in close quarter combat which could be encountered in a camp, and certainly would have the capacity to kill. The Russians also used to make cigarette boxes and other such ornamental articles from pieces of perspex obtained from crashed planes and their artistry and efficiency in the manufacture of such goods, for which they were paid in food, was astonishing in view of the lack of tools available to them.

The relationship of the Allied medical officers and staff with the Russians was very good, and the Russians certainly knew of and appreciated the material aid which was being given to their country by the British and Americans on the war front. At the same time, they were patently aware that they, the Russians, were bearing the brunt of the fighting on land and receiving the major attention of the German forces, and they were always asking whether the Allies had opened up a second front. They were, in the main, good natured despite the terrible conditions of their captivity, which now was very much worse than ours, especially since the advent of Red Cross parcels, and they were still able to sing with their magnificent deep voices on the occasional get togethers which were permitted by the Germans, and on which occasions they reached down into their boots to render 'The Volga Boatmen' and other Russian peasant songs of equally stirring capacity.

The Germans soon realized, however, that the British were becoming too friendly with their allies, and clamped down on fraternization, but there was no doubt that the medical officers and in particular the 'other ranks', all six of them, were able to help the Russian prisoners a considerable amount, not only with medical attention, but also by alleviating their conditions by persistent approaches to the German commandant for improvements in their quarters and by more material assistance in the way of food and clothing which could be spared from our own supplies. It was, in fact, quite probably a unique situation under prisoner of war conditions for British prisoners to be so closely connected with Russian prisoners, and one that surely would not last.

All of us began to suffer from the air raids so much so that we soon became accustomed to taking a dose of pure hospital spirit when the sirens went off, which we referred to as a 'quick dram' and then lay for some extraordinary reason under the treatment table in the wooden hut which served as our billet and entered a state of semi-oblivion until the raid had finished, the all-clear gone, and we could struggle up with a slightly dopey head and put all the bottles back on the shelves and clean up all the dust, etc, which inevitably covered everything after a few bombs had landed locally.

The effect of the hospital spirit was not, however, so easy to get rid of, and the medical officers soon issued very stern warnings about drinking the stuff. We were told it would send us blind, amongst other sobering prospects, but it does serve to indicate just how unpleasant the raids were that, despite such warnings, we still continued with it in some form or other. In fact, we altered the tactics and started to produce home-brewed wine; this consisted of getting some Red Cross dried fruits, prunes, raisins, figs, etc, and placing them in a succession of bowls to give a semblance of distillation, but always ultimately the delightful brew was completed by pouring the pure spirit into the resulting effluent to give it sufficient boost to gratify our quick action requirements as an anaesthetizing medium. No wonder today's bitter beer has always seemed to me to be a little unexciting!

Misha Popov and Pyotr (Peter) Ivanovitch were the most disappointed prisoners to be found in Gross Strehlitz early one morning in late October 1944, when they looked out of the tiny window of the hut in the Russian enclosure in the POW billets, to see their friends, the British, the three medical officers and the six staff, lined up by the Germans with all marching kit, which consisted in fact of all their worldly goods, and be suddenly and very unexpectedly marched out of the camp, never to return. I too was a most disappointed young man, for I had come to enjoy my work as interpreter which involved helping those who were even worse off than I was, as a prisoner of war, and projected me each day into a number of exciting new challenges and situations thereby considerably improving the normally humdrum existence of a prisoner.

Misha and Peter had become especial friends, and I frequently walked round the small enclosure with one or the other for long periods talking, in Russian of course, of their past lives and their future prospects, if any. They were complete contrasts in background and outlook.

Misha was the older, a little chap about forty years old which seemed old for a front line soldier, but on the Eastern Front the Russian soldiers could range in age from fourteen to sixty-four. Everyone was dragged in, from the factories, the farms, etc, and at the time of the rapid advance of German forces into Russia you could find yourself armed with a rifle and fighting in the front line just as a result of the fact that the front line had reached your doorstep. This was much the case with Misha, who was a gentle, polite and educated man of good bourgeois middle class family background, not a typical Bolshevik by any means. He was a *Gospodin* (gentleman) and not a *Tovarich* (comrade) and had absolutely no time for Communist ideals nor for the methods by which those ideals were to be achieved.

He really had no interest whatsoever in the war and regarded the whole performance with utmost abhorrence. He first came to my notice when I was standing in the Russian billet relating instructions from the Germans to the Russians. He passed me a note, surreptitiously, which I smuggled into my pocket to examine more carefully without the presence of the Germans. The note still remains in my possession to this day, and ran as follows, (translated of course!):

Dear Friends,
Thank you for your help. For us too each day is a matter of survival. The officers in this camp have been here since 10th September 1943. In our camp the food is terrible. We all hope for a rapid end to the war. I am from Murmansk. With greetings – Sergeant Popov.

This short epistle was followed by an even shorter note passed the same day in the evening, which simply went: 'I will write an answer tomorrow and bring you a book.' That response came following a brief note clandestinely sent round to Misha from me via one of the patients during the day, and amongst other things, asking whether any of the Russian prisoners had Russian books they would sell or loan me. I had, of course, by now become an inveterate scrounger, and where there were Russians there may be Russian literature through which I could advance my understanding of both Russian and its peoples. Hence the strange request, since I was well aware that any of the Russian prisoners would sell his soul for a piece of bread, let alone an old copy of Pushkin.

A longer note came the next day, which read:

Dear Comrade Prisoner,
We Russian prisoners thank you for your sympathy towards us. Your nation is helping very greatly our country to carry on the fight against the Germans. The Germans do not regard the Russians as people. What they have done since 1941 we shall never forget. In Kiev they machine-gunned down sixty thousand people, in Odessa eight thousand, Lvov ten thousand. About thirty-six thousand prisoners have died. We await the day when we will be able to pay them back. We shall not forget the state of the account. 9/Nov.

This letter was simply signed 'prisoners'. Presumably it was too incriminating to put a personal signature to, but I was well aware that it came from Misha.

Where Misha had got his figures from, I had absolutely no idea, but it was pretty clear from the letter that there was little love lost between the Russians and the Germans. The atrocities clearly carried out by the Germans in the course of their rapid advance into Western Russia were accompanied by the most horrific massacres of civilian population, especially of course the Jews, and it was small wonder that the German soldiers had the greatest fear of being sent up to the Eastern Front where they could expect very little mercy from the Russians, bent as they clearly were, not only on wreaking full revenge on the Germans for their earlier inhuman behaviour, but also ensuring that never again would Germany rise against the Russians and repeat the massacres they had now so callously and tragically carried out.

Misha passed one more letter to me behind the backs of the German guards, which ran:

Dear Friends,
You receive letters from home but we do not. I would like to send a letter to my family in Murmansk through you. There are now no prisoners coming from the Russian front. One airman came from the town of Orego on 2 August (the Germans wrote that they gave up the town of Orego on 4 August – this was not true) but they sent him to Czechoslovakia. He was however with us a few days in the cells at our camp and told us that at the present moment on the Eastern Front the Russian Air Force is in complete command in the air and on the ground our tanks, certainly obtained with our most grateful thanks from your country, are in command. It is with the help of your country that we have these aeroplanes and tanks.

They do not give the Russian prisoners in the camps much to eat. Those who are on working parties get 100 grams of tobacco. As far as food goes, it does not matter whether you work or not. Bread on Saturdays and Sundays, one loaf to four men, and on the other days one loaf between seven men. Margarine only on Sunday. Two litres of soup each day – potatoes in the soup not cleaned, and Tuesday and Friday the soup is just swedes. Book will follow. Misha.

I had asked Misha for a Russian book with which to further my studies, but I received eventually a book containing a number of well-known Russian poems and folk-tales including the 'Song of Stalin', a song by Vertinski, 'The Caucasian Prisoner' a poem which is a dramatic recital of the hardships undergone by suffering Russian peasants, as well as 'The Railway' (Nekrassof) a dramatic poem covering hardships undergone by workers on the construction of the infamous Trans-Siberian railway under the Tsarist regime. Also 'Gavciliada, Stenka Razin' (a sort of Russian Robin Hood). All these poems and songs taught me a lot about the Russian mentality. They rather gave me the impression that just about everybody in Russia specialized in suffering in some form or another.

Amongst the most dramatic and illustrative was 'The Railway' which commenced with the following opening gambit:

Vanya (in coachman's uniform: 'Old man, who built the railway?'

Old man (in top coat sitting on red luggage): 'Why, Count Pyotr Andreevitch Klienmihail, little friend.'

It then went on to describe in such an eloquent poetic masterpiece the horrific hardships undergone by those who really did build the wretched railway, the forced labourers and slaves and not the esteemed count who took the honours. I was very much impressed by the cynicism and heavy tragedy contained in such works, and no doubt the publication of 'The Railway' was very much with the blessing of the Party authorities; its satire emphasized, for political interest, the contrast which they are stating existed in Tsarist days between the count, who got all the glory, and the poor bloody workers who got all the stick. I began to understand then why it was only

Charles Dickens whom the Russians had ever heard of amongst British writers; no doubt he was excellent propaganda on the same theme. Shakespeare of course, was a Russian, or so I was advised by my highly indoctrinated new colleagues from the Soviet territories!

The exchange of the notes was followed by more frequent discussions with Misha who accepted that, as far as he was concerned, life had come to an end. He did not really expect to see Murmansk again nor his family, a wife and small son, and he concentrated solely on staying alive to face the next day, but for what reason he could not really say. There was no hope and Misha was realist enough to accept that fact. Even if the Russians conquered the Germans on the Eastern Front, he would probably never get all the way back to Murmansk. The Russians did not treat their soldiers who became prisoners and were subsequently released, with anything but disfavour, and they were regarded frequently as being no better than deserters (which of course many were) or at the best, severely tainted with counter-propaganda and Fascist doctrines which would have to be forcibly removed from their minds before they could take their place in Soviet society again. They would have to be treated like dangerous outcasts having been contaminated by contact with Westerners. And so far as Misha was concerned, because of his age and background, this was more likely to take a very long time. The best he could hope for, upon release, was a concentration camp somewhere in Siberia, and maybe after many years, if he survived, he may be returned eventually to his homeland to die.

Peter Ivanovitch, however, was a quite different case and did not share Misha's realistic but morbid outlook. I really got along better with Peter, but maybe primarily because he was much younger, only about nineteen and more in my age bracket. Where the conversations with Misha had always begun with some deep philosophical undertone such as, 'Graham, why are we living?', with Peter the discussion was more positive and revolved around the current opportunities Peter may have for earning more bread and what the future held for him after the war. I was indeed fortunate to have two such entirely differing personalities with whom to discourse and to learn about the life style in Communist Russia.

Peter Ivanovitch came from Novosibirsk in Western Siberia, just the other side of the Urals and in the general region of the quaintly named cities of Omsk and Tomsk. Novosibirsk was a 'new' city, having been constructed as part of the great Bolshevik plan to develop Siberia with a number of major industrial cities. Not only was it a new city but it was a young city and the people in it were young and virile – they had to be to survive the climate! And Peter was no exception. He was a physical training student and hoping to become an instructor when fully qualified. He was not regular army, but a member of all the various Communist Youth Organizations, many of which provided their members with quasi-military training. Not so very different in a way from my own military training via the territorial army – an occasional evening after a day's gymnastic training, and involving a brief instruction on the workings of Russian infantry arms, etc. He lived with his family and had apparently become quite advanced in his relationship with another young gymnast of the opposite sex for whom he now yearned.

His views were most optimistic for the future, and he looked forward to getting back to the life he had left, a life which, as far as I could gather, he had found enjoyable and rewarding despite the harsh climatic conditions. He was not a furious Communist supporter, but had grown up into a system which he had to accept since he knew of no other. He had been very well politically indoctrinated to the extent that he did not actively seek any alternative to the way of life he had pursued to that point of time, and was content to let others get on with the politics whilst he concentrated on the physical development of his body, which appeared to be well suited for such an occupation. In the camp he concentrated his efforts entirely on obtaining food to sustain that body and keep in trim – he even undertook some exercising apart from the long walks round the enclosure with me, and much to the astonishment of his fellow prisoners – and in the effort to earn more to eat he undertook jobs in the British quarters, with German approval, consisting of cleaning duties and general 'dirty' tasks, for which he was handsomely rewarded with tit-bits from Red Cross parcels and whatever else could be spared.

In his discussion with me, Peter discovered for the first time that there was an alternative way of living to that to which he had become accustomed in Russia. In explaining to him the various freedoms which I enjoyed in my homeland, such simple freedoms which I took for granted – choice of profession, choice of domicile, freedom of expression by speech or otherwise, self-determination for the future, free choice in disposal of funds, even methods of relaxation, reading, choice of sports, ability to travel anywhere in the world (subject to availability of funds!) etc, Peter came to realize that in all these areas he was not free in the full sense of the word: his future was determined by the local Youth Cadres and factory units by whom he was treated as one of many, and he had no means of disputing their decisions and no right of objection and certainly no opportunity to express his own individualism. He was unable to follow his own desires for the future – not that a great number of alternatives were on offer – and I think he came to appreciate that, at much the same age, we both were experiencing entirely different life styles, regulated by the fundamental factor of freedom of personal will. I explained to him that I was fighting to maintain that freedom. He explained to me that he was fighting in defence of his homeland. Had we asked young Hans the guard what he was fighting for, I wonder what answer we would have received?

My association with both Misha and Peter had not only given me further opportunities to extend my conversational Russian, but had given me great insight into the living conditions in Soviet Russia and the innermost views of its people, unrestricted by any form of control such as the listening Party member of OGPU (KGB) any of whose officers would report any divergent views expressed to a so-called Security Department for action. Misha's views were, of course, traitorous by Communist standards, and no doubt Peter's apathetic and slightly questioning attitude towards Communism particularly in the matter of his freedom of speech and action compared with my own would not have been smiled upon by the upper echelon of the party.

So I was very sorry that my close connection with the Russians had now so suddenly come to an end. I considered with great misgiving the doubtful future with which I left my two particular Russian friends, and many times thereafter wondered how they, as well as the young lad who had his leg amputated, fared after the Russians had overran the area, which would be in about eight or nine months' time. I could only hope they would survive until then and that their Communist masters would eventually give them an opportunity to re-make their lives in their own home towns and with their own families, but I doubted that.

I understand that the Soviet State did not welcome their returning prisoners of war, nor in fact anyone who had been imprisoned or forced into labour in German-occupied zones of Europe, be it from Poland, the Balkans, Germany or even Norway and Finland. The problem of course was that such former prisoners of war had been irrevocably 'tainted' or maybe 'polluted' is a better word, by having had intercourse with people living in the 'free West' against whom the violent propaganda and mass education within Russia over the past twenty-five years or so had been directed. The education of the youth of Russia, and in this category came a very large number of the Russian POWs eventually freed either by the Russians themselves or, worse still, by the Americans or British, had been directed towards indoctrination of the view that the Russian police state was a superior system to the decadent bourgeois system operating in the West. However, several millions of returning POWs and internees flooding the streets of Moscow, Leningrad, etc, and dispelling the veracity of this fact could not be acceptable to a regime which kept itself in power by enforcing strict acceptance of the doctrines it taught, so the great mass, if not all, of the returning POWs, including my erstwhile friends would, I feel, have ended up with ten-year sentences to concentration camps in Siberia, largely for re-indoctrination into the Soviet political system.

It is most repulsive to me to think that a young man like Peter should have his whole future life wrecked, after surviving the horrors of German concentration camps, and what on earth would have become of that young Russian warrior who had his leg amputated and which I was left holding aloft? It seems incredible that the Russian state should inflict such further punishments on those who had already suffered so horrendously, and whose only crime probably consisted of being under the command of some inane Russian general appointed by an ultra-security conscious state for his political prowess rather than for his military tactical abilities.

An alternative always existed for the Russian prisoners in German hands: namely, to join the battalions of the so-called 'free' Russian army led by the former Russian general Vlasov. This was a body of Russian POWs who had been offered by the Germans the opportunity of fighting their own kith and kin in exchange for a uniform and some food rations.

I suppose they faced even worse retribution upon release at the end of hostilities, branded of course traitors which I suppose technically they were. But if the critic of their actions had been put into the same conditions as they existed under in the German concentration camps, I wonder whether he could not, in all honesty, admit some element of sympathy for their 'traitorous' actions. If you have absolutely nothing to eat or drink, and this state must surely be incomprehensible to the great mass of those who criticize such 'traitors', and worse still no future and no hope, knowing that if and when you are freed by your own side you will end up in another concentration camp this time in freezing Siberia, who can really blame those who accepted the 'Vlasov' alternative, to get a bath, clothing and some food. No doubt most of the defectors would not in any case have fired upon their own brothers, and would have ditched the disguise as soon as escape to their own ranks became feasible; but these poor chaps probably suffered or are now still suffering life sentences to Siberia, just for displaying the fundamental reactions of humanity.

It seems so utterly unjustifiable, by any standards, that the older and cynical Misha and younger Peter, so enthusiastic for the future, should have no such future by decree of an ultra-suspicious and scared regime dominated by one evil and fundamentally frightened Georgian peasant Stalin – that the police state which their parents forced into power to replace an unbending autocratic Tsarist rule should dispose of lives so callously. Those of us who are fortunate enough to live in a 'Free World' probably do not understand the meaning of the term.

I saw in the treatment of the Russians by the Germans at that time the same callous disregard and brutality that I myself had experienced when captured some four and a half years earlier. Now of course the situation was vastly improved for me and my British colleagues, but my memory was not all that bad. When the Germans thought they had won the war, the treatment meted out to any national, be they British or Russian, was quite abysmal and I could now see in their treatment of the Russians a reflection of their treatment to me some four years earlier. I shuddered to think how that treatment could have enveloped my own homeland and probably lands further afield if Hitler's victorious all-conquering armies had not been stopped. There was not the slightest doubt in my mind but that the Germans had a very highly cultivated ability to treat those fellow human beings who fell into their power with callous disregard for their status as fellow humans and knew how to very expertly divest such beings of any last trappings of humanity.

I had no idea why we were suddenly sent back to Lamsdorf from the hospital at Gross Strehlitz, but could only assume it was in some way connected with the progress of the war. Maybe the town had become strategically important and maybe the war was coming too close for comfort, and maybe the Russian huts adjoining the hospital were now more urgently required for German wounded from the rapidly approaching front. Anyway, the day came when we were told to pack our bags and were transported by road back to the Stalag at Lamsdorf. The sad exchange of waves with the Russian prisoners we left behind to the mercy of their German oppressors did not in any way fully represent our feelings of deep sympathy for such people who, in the main, seemed perfectly solid citizens with whom I should have thought we could have lived in peace.

Presumably there was then no station left to take us to. We were all very sorry to leave and to have to load up on the truck all our equipment, for I in particular had had a most interesting job and reasonable conditions to perform it in, and we all thought that we were assisting in achieving something – alleviating other people's pain for a change, rather than just moaning about our own troubles. The officer doctors and surgeons had probably served humanity in those brief few months more effectively than they would ever be able to again.

12

The Evacuation

Lamsdorf was now a very different place from the spartan establishment it once was. A great part of the vast and very evident improvement could be clearly attributed to the regular supply of Red Cross parcels. The place was well disciplined with private ranks showing due respect for NCOs and medical officers, and most of the inmates retaining a growing sense of self-respect. A whole host of activities had been set up to cater for the inevitable boredom resulting from incarceration.

There was a theatre which put on regular shows, dramatic plays and revues, and the soldiers taking the part of the girls in such revues really needed protection going 'home' to their barracks after the show. The German commandant and guards regularly attended the shows and there was due international respect shown by both sides in the choice of suitable material. 'Hanging Out the Washing on the Siegfried Line' was duly avoided to enable the theatre to continue to receive the co-operation of the German Command. There were proper facilities for worshipping in most denominations, a good library stocked largely by the Red Cross and specializing in technical books to enable prisoners to continue the study of chosen vocations, a music centre with lessons available in many instruments and groups specializing in other varied hobbies, and sport was also properly organized with inter-hut soccer matches, basketball, etc (no cross-country running, unfortunately!).

It may seem, in retrospect, surprising that the camp church usually had a good attendance. For customers who, by and large, had little to thank God for, one could be excused for thinking that at best apathy, and at worst agnosticism would be the order of the day. That most certainly, however, was not the case. A philosopher, name of William James, once wrote in his book *Varieties*, 'Religion ... shall mean for us the feelings, acts and experiences of individual men in their solitude, so far as they apprehend themselves to stand in relation to whatever they may consider the divine'. These particular men had experienced and performed or been party to acts which must have left them wondering about the existence of anything or anyone divine. Strange to relate, I believe the general opinion seemed to veer in a direction supporting a theory of something which each man considered as 'divine' in his own way.

For myself, I could never quite reconcile the many escapes from death I had experienced with any theory that such matters were the result of chance or luck. The French officer on the boat at St Valéry and the civilian the other side of me had both had their lives instantaneously terminated, but I, in the middle, had escaped injury. At Schildeberg the soldier on the steps in front of me had been killed and the one behind me seriously injured, at Hohensalza the German officer who arrived at the camp seemed to come just in the nick of time to spare us a possibly fatal end. On the mountain, I came across those foresters just in time, at least for two of us. I had to wonder at this whole train of events and its relationship to Providence, as did I think many of my colleagues, and certainly there was never any evidence of apathy for the well-filled church attendances which were of course entirely voluntary. Men had time to think, they had experiences to consider and to reconcile with fate, and despite the discomforts such experiences had rendered, they appeared nevertheless to get people thinking quite deeply about religious matters and in many cases, I am quite sure, introduced a positive awareness which had not existed in the more uneventful pre-war days, at least amongst those who were prepared to think and had something to think with.

There was, of course, a general acceptance by the Germans that at this time, summer 1944, the Fatherland had not won the war hands down. The landings in Italy and the keenly awaited opening up of a Second Front in the West, as well as the phenomenal turn-about on the Eastern Front had all contributed to a new look by the German camp authorities and Camp Commandants started considering the safety of their own skin in the future, and were therefore pretty correct in their handling of their captives. Similarly, the captives themselves could start smelling the sweet scent of possible freedom one day; and the expression 'When I get back to Blighty...' could sometimes be heard in the huts, spoken rather timorously in case the Gods may hear and be displeased at such lofty aspirations, and in any case to be immediately and fearfully rejected by the many pessimists who realized just how many slips existed between the cup and the very parched lips.

The urge to escape had also dropped off, and the furious digging of tunnels all over the place which had been a major pastime for the adventurous members of the various escape committees, began to fizzle out, which in turn gave the Germans some sense of security in their dealing with their prisoners. The tremendous effort earlier to dig tunnels had exhausted the camps complete stock of bed boards upon which the prisoners were supposed to sleep, leaving them in an embarrassing position until the Germans discovered the tunnels and the use to which the bed boards were being put, and replaced them all with wire netting, which was much more comfortable anyway. When the wire netting was systematically removed by the prisoners for the manufacture of all sorts of domestic appliances, the Germans resorted to offering the string from the Red Cross parcels as a mattress support. This also had its uses in the make-do world in which the more inventive prisoners were able to produce all kind of utensils and equipment from such a limited supply of raw materials.

The relaxation in security now had reached a pitch where I rather enviously learned that at least one chap who escaped through the main gates in order to pay a much needed visit to a lady of the local village had the greatest difficulty in getting back into the camp, because the guard he had bribed with chocolate or coffee to let him out was not, due to a change in rota, on duty at the alloted time to let him in, and he had to wait outside and eventually give himself up and ask to be let back in!

Needless to say, there was not a lot of sex in our lives. For those who remained continuously in the Stalags, there were only dreams and a powerful imagination to provide solace, and after many years even the memories became a bit unexciting. For those out on working parties, we heard of the occasional episode of the more frustrated stalwarts bribing the guards and making their way to an equally frustrated *Hausfrau* to exchange solace, but whether such events were true or simply wishful thinking, I have no idea. Women of pure German stock were not, of course, permitted to consort with any of the multitude of foreign workers available and presumably British came under that heading, and the penalties for transgression were very vicious. The Germans did not favour the thought that their high class pure Aryan stock of females should be polluted by penetration from the lower grades of humanity.

That did not, however, deter the Germans from utilizing any available and attractive young Polish girls or other foreign nationals of sufficiently enticing beauty as compulsory and very unwilling items of solace for their troops travelling up to the front by rail. It was the accepted custom that a few such young girls would be literally thrown into the cattle truck or troop train carriage at the point of embarkation to be devoured by as many of the eager German soldiers as could be reasonably accommodated before the exhausted girls would be ultimately, and again literally, 'ditched' and a new supply taken on board at a later stage in the journey.

At the delousing plant we had many opportunities to be intimately involved with the Russian peasant women who were in the process of being made a little less verminous, but I think most of us would have preferred something rather less substantial – a baby elephant or something of that ilk. If any had made advances to us I think we would have run for our lives!

The incident when the chap was locked out was certainly not, however, a repetitive situation, nor was there any sloppiness about the German control of the camp, nor the British supervision, and every credit had to be given to both British and German officials in charge for producing such a well ordered and hygienic establishment for what was a very large number of inmates, run to the mutual benefit of all at a time when more strict adherence to the principle incumbent upon prisoners of war of causing maximum damage to the enemy would have only resulted in greater damage to their own men, and could have caused the Germans no further embarrassment than they already were suffering.

In fact, at about this period, legitimate possibilities of getting back to England arose through the initiation of exchange of more severely wounded and sick prisoners with their German counterparts in Britain. This was negotiated by the Swiss through the aegis of the Red Cross and under provision of the Geneva Convention. Lists of the more worthy contenders for exchange were being prepared and in fact some exchanges did eventually take place, but very few considering the great number of those who were suffering sufficiently to merit such treatment.

A few of the 'wide boys' amongst the prisoners cottoned on to the idea of feigning illness in order to qualify for such exchange. It was possible, by judicious taking of drugs obtainable from the camp hospital, to raise or lower one's heart beat and provide other similar effects on parts of the body to produce a condition which may be identical to a certain heart condition or other form of disease, and to bluff one's way in this manner past the various boards consisting of German and British medical officers who sat for the purpose of compiling lists of prisoners urgently requiring repatriation. Such falsification and endeavour to hoodwink the authorities, was however, considered very much taboo, and although the possibility of employing such a ruse did occur to me and I had much more reason to be considered for repatriation than most of my fellows due to my chronic chest condition, it was generally accepted that this bonus of repatriation for the very sick should not be jeopardized in any way by attempts at fraud, and in any case the numbers of the really deserving was so great that by gaining repatriation by false means would only be displacing another whose complaint was genuine and obviously deserving of such sympathetic treatment. It was something one just did not do, rather in the same way as no prisoner worth his salt would attempt to escape from a camp hospital which was, of course, far less heavily guarded – the deleterious effect upon the remaining really sick and injured, unable to look after themselves, could not be considered worth the escape. To embark on either such course would be tantamount to flouting, not only hard won provisions for humanity contained in the Geneva Convention, but the basic rules of common decency and consideration for one's fellow men.

It was under these more reasonable circumstances in the *Stalag* that I took my language exams under strict invigilation by camp officers and a padre appointed for the purpose by the Royal Society of Arts, and others took their various technical and professional examinations to provide for a future. Everyone helped in various activities, and it was surprising how, in a camp of several thousands of prisoners, one could always find experts to assist in tuition, in directing and producing theatrical shows, learning to play musical instruments, etc.

As time went by, however, the Eastern Front got closer, and it was not long before the 'lavatory' rumours started moving around that the Russians were not so very far from the camp. This induced me to polish up my Russian a little more and I even had preliminary discussions with the camp sergeant-major and hospital officers concerning interpreting duties and general behaviour should we suddenly be confronted with a sea of red flags being waved by our friends, the comrade soldiers.

It did not actually happen quite like that at all. There was at first in the far, far distance, the rumbling of what we all thought initially was thunder, but which was soon identified as artillery bombardment at a considerable distance. The German commandant, however, was well aware of the position on the Eastern Front, and preparations were put in hand for possible evacuation of the camp. However, a rather strange and unexpected train of events did occur which left the prisoners very bemused and only a little better off. Quite suddenly, and very much without any prior warning, the German guards departed from the camp lock, stock and barrel. The prisoners were all utterly shattered to look up at the watch towers and see nobody in them, and to see the main gates left unattended and open. Since there was now a lot of firing and bombardment to be heard around, a state of hiatus filled the camp. No one knew quite what to do, so the obvious thing was to continue as usual and not all suddenly billow out all over the place in anticipation of liberation. We all had to bear very much in mind that we were subject to two sets of discipline, German and British army, and that in the absence of the former we still remained very much under the command of our senior officers and warrant officers.

There were consultations between the 'powers that were', which consisted of medical officers and padres and the senior warrant officers, and very sensibly the order went out to sit tight pending a clarification of the military situation and to avoid any dangers which may be lurking outside the camp. No one was permitted to take advantage of the open gates and life just went on the same, without any guards. Anyway, we just had nowhere to go and in an organized group there was safety and some assurance of ultimate liberation, whereas odd bods wandering about all over the fields outside the camp would, without any hesitation, be mown down by either Russians or Germans who may be in the vicinity.

I went down to the German guard quarters just to look at the open gate. The German guards had been replaced by a British sergeant-major supported by a corporal, both of whom were there to stop the former prisoners from leaving the camp. 'The ruddy incongruity of it all' I muttered to another prisoner. 'Here we are, having waited for bloody nearly five years to get free, the gates of the prison are wide open, and all we can do is stand here and look at a fat, red-faced vicious-looking sergeant-major and not be able to get any further.'

The other sightseer alongside me grunted agreement and indicated his disapproval in the manner customarily adopted by all those inmates who had something to disapprove of, 'F— bastards. F— if I'm going to bloody well stand here and look at the f— open gate.'

Courageously he took a few strides towards the gate, and when the sergeant-major turned his not particularly attractive head in the direction of the advancing one, the effect was much more instantaneous and decisive than would have been the case had there been a full section of German guards on duty with machine guns. The complaining sightseer stopped dead in his tracks, viewed the glowering sergeant-major uncertainly from a safe distance and eventually turned round and shuffled grudgingly past me.

'F — bastard. Worse than the bloody Jerries' came the anticipated growl as the disenchanted and not so courageous one returned to his billet to let loose an articulate range of further choice expletives to describe the behaviour of his fellow prisoner, the exalted warrant officer, to a bored but inwardly understanding audience in the barrack block.

Disappointing it no doubt was, and I felt as frustrated as any after risking so much to escape three times and then see the gates open and not be able to walk through them. Sensible, without any doubt whatsoever, it was.

Anyway, it was not to be for long, for the Germans returned, looking maybe a little sheepish, and the rumbling noises died down a little. The brave little contingent of Germans re-occupied the guards' quarters, re-entered the sentry boxes and re-established themselves in control of the camp. It transpired that a forward prong of the Russian spearhead tank attack had advanced a bit ahead of the general front line, and had got to within a few miles of the camp, but the introduction of a German Panzer unit into the weak spot had soon rectified the situation and the Russians had pulled back. The German commandant and his guards had apparently received an order to leave the camp unguarded and return to a safer spot when the Russian advance first occurred presumably on the basis that the German High Command's first responsibility was to its own troops and not to foreign prisoners, but subsequent orders were to return, which they duly did, so the prisoners' brief glimpse of freedom was dramatically terminated and they were again behind wire and German domination. It all seemed rather ridiculous to us, but the fact was that once we had been captured and taken prisoner by the Germans, the latter had an on-going responsibility to care for us, not only to stop us from escaping, but to actually protect us from any danger. They were now guards in a different sense altogether.

There remained a very strange and unreal sort of atmosphere in the camp, one in which the Germans and their prisoners seemed to be as members of the same club awaiting the arrival of the opposing team. The opposition, that is the Russians, were, of course, theoretically on the prisoners' side and the Germans could expect nothing more from the Russians than probable execution or at the best enslavement in Siberia for a very lengthy period; what the prisoners had to expect from the Russians no one was very sure of, and it was to some extent this sense of doubt which led us to look at our captors, after all these years of hardship and a lot of maltreatment, as possibly the better of two considerable evils. The future did seem however to present two very clear facts: firstly that the process of liberation was not going to be simple and, secondly, that the Germans would clearly have to evacuate us from that camp or officially hand us over to the advancing Russians, thereby involving their own capture by the Russians, something they would wish to avoid at all costs. The further option remained of running away whilst the camp was free and being picked up by the Russians, but what then? Maybe the more sensible alternative would be to remain and be officially removed by the Germans, with luck to the West, to be freed in the end by our own forces or the Americans. On balance, and probably very wisely, the Powers decided on the latter course. I had no personal experience of course as to how those ultimately released by the advancing Russians fared, but I later learned that they encountered a lot of problems before eventually getting back to the UK, being transported in many cases across Russia to Murmansk and put on ships which were returning from delivering arms to Russia; the whole journey was long and involved much frustration and discomfort. My own future to liberation was not exactly to be a bed of roses, but maybe a little more geographically direct.

The reaction we may have encountered from the local civilian population was not at all clear. There was very definitely an aura of intense apprehension over this whole region of Upper Silesia and Western Poland, a region which had over many decades become acclimatized to chaotic military upheavals and political disturbances, and the anticipated arrival of the 'Ruskies' was cause for 'apprehension' rather than eager anticipation. Despite the atrocious treatment meted out to the Poles and to the slave labour of the region, I think it was also fully understood that the Russians were the historical enemy of Poland, so the local inhabitants were probably intent on keeping their heads down at this particular time and not anxious to be seen assisting one camp or the other. In any case, it was doubtful if they were in any position to help or hinder.

The Germans did immediately put in hand an evacuation. All able-bodied prisoners, and I was now no longer one of those, were assembled in several groups to be marched away from the camp to the West. This amounted to many thousands of men and those who were sent forth on this terrible march, and I counted myself very fortunate not to be amongst them, encountered the most agonizing hardships before reaching camps in the West. They were forced to undergo a march covering 600 miles through central Europe in extremely hard winter conditions before eventually arriving at prison camps in central and western Germany, and many thousands fell by the wayside from fatigue, illness, and the generally horrific conditions under which such forced marches were conducted. They were left to sleep in fields in the freezing cold weather with no proper accommodation or feeding nor medical services; they also suffered from aerial bombardment from their own forces and it would be difficult to imagine a less satisfactory way of approaching that ultimate goal of freedom which had been so nervously awaited for so long than via continuous bombing from planes sporting their own colours. To have survived so many trials and tribulations and no doubt so many close escapes from death over maybe many years, both in perilous conditions of front line warfare to the exacting conditions of prison camps, always maintaining at least a small hope of ultimate repatriation, and then to suffer from ultimate exhaustion on a march when approaching the probable end of such horrors or being blown to pieces by their own countrymen really was like rubbing salt into the wound.

Those who were left at Lamsdorf, including of course myself, and who were all disabled and sick, which amounted to a few hundreds, were left with a huge largely deserted camp, many scores of huts rapidly abandoned by the occupants who left most of their surplus gear, anything they could not wear or carry on a long march, lying about on top of vacated bunks or thrown into heaps around the barrack rooms. The remaining prisoners were not, however, allowed by the Germans to rummage through the discarded goodies, if the occasional moth-eaten well-worn pair of socks could rightly be considered a 'goodie', for the Germans patrolled the empty huts to ensure there was no looting. The reason for this behaviour was apparently so that, when the sick and disabled had been removed and the camp totally evacuated, the Russian prisoners from the camp over the way, and which I had earlier spent a few exceedingly unpleasant weeks in after my second unsuccessful escape attempt, could then be evacuated by the German guards and their Russian prisoners and the inmates established in the old British camp. This would then enable the Germans to burn down the old Russian camp, which contained all the signs of horror and torment associated with a concentration camp, and erase the scene of their inhumanity to the Russian prisoners from the advancing Russian troops, who would not have been overjoyed to see the way their fellow soldiers had been kept as prisoners by the Germans. It also enabled the Russian prisoners to take advantage of the discarded British prisoners' clothing and goods abandoned in the British camp, thereby enhancing the view, to the advancing Russian soldiers, that their own men had not been so badly treated. Superficially it may have sounded a bright idea, but nothing would ever erase from public scrutiny the atrocious behaviour of the Germans towards the people they had conquered, and certainly no such ruse would ever lessen the hatred which completely filled the breasts of the conquering Russians now rapidly infiltrating into territory formerly held by them and shortly to enter Germany itself. No mercy was ever likely to be shown and had not been earned.

Those Russian soldiers had advanced from almost the gates of Moscow reclaiming territory previously conquered by the Germans in their rapid and devastating attack in 1942. They had uncovered the real enormity of the inhumane and cruel treatment meted out to civilians and war prisoners alike by the Germans, a degree of cruelty which far exceeded anything they could have imagined possible, and the Russian evaluation of human life is not high compared with more Western standards. They had uncovered the mass graves containing, not hundreds, but thousands of civilians and enemy soldiers, mown down in cold blood for no better reason than that they happened to have been of the Jewish faith, or mere Polish civilians who may have displeased the occupying conquerors, or Russian prisoners of war who were an embarrassment to the Germans to feed and guard. I recalled the German camp commandant's piece of logic: 'I have a camp with a maximum capacity of 25,000 and rations for 25,000. Every month I get a further intake of 10,000, so I have to get rid of 10,000', resulting in the carts leaving the camp every morning laden with corpses for the mass grave pits. Now those same pits were being uncovered; Polish and Russian women who, having been collected en masse in the villages overrun by the Germans and had been raped and slaughtered and of no further use to their conquerors, the inhabitants of whole villages etc, etc.

The discover of such a holocaust was shattering to those Russian and Allied troops who were involved in the liberation process and who met with the irrefutable evidence in the course of their advances, the more so because so little information had ever escaped from the close frontiers of Hitler's occupied fortress of Europe to reveal to an ultimately incredulous free world just what had been going on. As those occupying troops advanced and uncovered these atrocities, their personal feelings of utter disgust could only result in revenge to be vented on any Germans who happened to be around at the time; their suspicions regarding culpability for an involvement in such crimes could extend to anyone or any group who happened to be then available to them. So the whole process of being set free, even as a British prisoner of war, promised to be very hazardous.

Eventually, after a further day had passed, the remaining British were allocated into two parties to be removed on two train transports; I was on the second of these transports, which was again very much to my good fortune, as the first was the victim of an American bombing attack and very many of the prisoners being transported were killed. Having come so far in the war, and been a prisoner for some four or more years already, the fate of being killed by your own side at this late stage, with freedom and return to loved ones in Blightly in sight, it was clearly very traumatic and all the prisoners now left felt they were living on a knife edge.

So when our turn came, the few hundred remaining crocks including the very severely wounded and sick were loaded on to carts and formed up in a pathetic group one very cold and frosty morning, to be led by the Germans for the last time through the pearly gates of the camp which had been 'home' for so many years, and led to the station, in as motley a group of weary travellers as you could expect to see. There were wounded on carts being pushed by men hardly able to walk themselves, colleagues hanging on to each other and shuffling along as best they could. There was, of course, virtually no guard, just a few Germans left to supervise the pathetic evacuation.

It is difficult to imagine the aggregated total of discomfort and despair and utter dejection which existed amongst those who stumbled out of a camp from which they may well have formerly hoped that they would emerge to the accompaniment of brass bands and much celebration. Neither of these two ingredients were present, just a pinnacle of abject misery reached on a freezing cold wind swept Polish plain, a new height of tension and foreboding for the future and a deep loathing towards the place of detention just abandoned.

We wondered where we were heading for and whether we would ever get there, but it began to seem to be the sensible thing to do to move in the general direction of the West, rather than stay in the East. At the station it was the usual routine, forty *hommes* to each cattle truck plus an additional ten or so for shortage of trucks, and then locked in to await the uncertain future.

That journey back from the East towards Blighty via a beleaguered Czechoslovakia and Germany had all the discomforts and horrors we earlier had experienced in the train journey from Bucholt to Poland nearly five years earlier, but with two vast extra problems: one was that we were now a group of officially sick and wounded with all the difficulties in mobility that presents, and the other the intense and ever present hazard resulting from the continuous Allied bombing, since the train slowly coursed its way through many of the industrial centres of southern Germany and Czechoslavakia, and although it had red crosses clearly painted on the roofs of the trucks, the Germans seemed to take delight in parking the train for interminable periods in the busiest stations, presumably for obvious reasons, and it would seem most unlikely, in any case, that a bomb aimer or whatever they may be rightly called sitting in a bomber 10,000 feet up would be able to pick out the red crosses on the trucks from such a distance and through the clouds of smoke which inevitably accompanied such raids.

Through the slit windows in the cattle trucks I was able to get some ideas of the enormity of the effects of the bombing raids on Germany, and the land at the side of the tracks was frequently seen to be littered with smashed and burnt out carriages and trucks and even engines, whilst most of the stations were partially or wholly derelict. The stations in the city centres we went through were smashed to smithereens, with buckled steelwork, bombed and crashed rolling stock and shattered buildings everywhere. The Allies had certainly wreaked havoc with the German industrial centres and in passing through Dresden I looked out at the skyline in the centre of the city and could see one, and just one whole building still standing outlined on the horizon. All the rest had been reduced to rubble and that had then been systematically turned over by further bombing. Of course, British cities such as Coventry took a terrific pounding and I could not, of course, compare the extent of damage inflicted on the major cities in each country, but the scenes I now saw in the course of that journey of three or four days' duration through Prague and the various major industrial centres of Southern Germany during a journey which seemed to take in a large part of that terrain, no doubt as a result of the day to day effects of the relentless bombing which was still continuing unabated and required us to take a very circuitous route, gave me a first hand idea of the results of such formidable aerial bombardments over the years, and I could well realize that Germany had suffered a holocaust of such proportion that it seemed inconceivable that it could be renewed and rebuilt within a period of even fifty years. It seems astonishing to think that it was in fact rebuilt in the main within ten years of the end of the war.

That journey was every bit as horrific and distressing as the earlier journey out. The plight of the very sick and wounded locked up in the cattle trucks was pathetic, especially since no one could do anything really to help. The Germans had allowed, in fact, one medical orderly per truck but he had to act virtually as a fully qualified doctor and surgeon to deal with the problems which continually arose. These problems were accentuated by a lack of reasonable sanitation, the usual bucket which was emptied through the slits, and a complete insufficiency of water and provisions. The accumulating stench of untreated wounds, stale bandages and vomit in the unventilated trucks and in many cases the dead corpses of those for whom it was too much, did little to improve the situation. Fortunately we had managed to save or get together some Red Cross food before leaving the camp, for if we had not done so, and in view of the fact that the Germans completely relied on our having Red Cross food and did not supply any themselves, we would have been in a much more weakened state upon ultimate arrival at our eventual destination, the city of Nuremberg. We seemed to hang around in various stations and outside stations so long that when we saw Nuremberg come up, and even saw the old stadium of such great fame resulting from Hitler's early salad days, little did we realize that this was it, that in fact we would ultimately leave the remains of this city as free men.

However, the greatest difference between that journey and the previous nightmare from Western Germany to Poland was that we now had a clear resurgence of hope in our minds. In 1940 we were being transported away from our families, from the lives we knew and understood and by and large enjoyed although we may not have appreciated that fact, to a future in the East as captives and with no ray of sunshine anywhere on the horizon. Now, returning back in the direction of our homeland and to those we loved, the psychological effect was enormous; despite all the discomforts and difficulties, there seemed to be some hope that we might actually once again see Blighty. What sort of Blighty we had no idea, but it must be an improvement on the land in which we had spent the past five years!

This change in our view of the future brought about a quite new spirit amongst us, a spirit of comradeship in the full meaning of the word. Everyone did his best to ensure that those around him would not fall down at this late stage in the game and not enjoy the return to sanity and pleasure that beckoned to us. We began to feel that we were not just living for our own survival, but to help the survival of the whole group.

There was a nightmare march from the railway station at Nuremberg to the camp and transport only for those who were stretcher cases and could not stand up, or walk. The rest had to struggle along as best they could, staggering rather than walking, and the journey was quite a distance and in the dark.

My chest had by now given up the uneven fight and probably accentuated by the extreme nervous tensions conjured up by a combination of air raids, privation and uncertainty, I found the utmost difficulty in breathing at all, let alone marching. How I made it I shall never know, but it was an occasion for me to experience one of the most gracious and kind acts that I had to that time ever experienced from another human being; although it may now sound ridiculous, the kindness came from a Geordie who carried my meagre belongings for the last few hundred yards and gave me a push and supporting arm up the metaphorical and factual hill. It is, perhaps, easy ultimately to forget kindnesses rendered to one in times of difficulty, but this possibly small, insignificant act always stuck in my mind as an act worthy of continual remembrance and thanks. To whom I know not, but wherever and whoever he may be I was and still feel very indebted, and I can only now hope that my gratitude expressed in sincere thought may have at some time since lightened that Geordie's own load through life. It was not just a matter of a supporting arm and carrying a haversack; that sounds simple enough and in the cold light of day of relative insignificance, but under those extreme conditions when no doubt the Geordie, who must have himself been an invalid to some considerable extent, for the Germans only accepted as sick those who were half dead, and no doubt was equally as exhausted as the rest of us and probably felt he was barely able to take himself along, to assist another at such a time was an extreme sacrifice which cannot be properly evaluated except when the circumstances are fully appreciated and experienced. It was, in fact, such actions and the impressions they left that can only rarely be repeated in the ordinary mundane day-to-day lives people usually lead, and in a world to-day in which so many people feel it is their duty in life to make the other man's lot a little bit more difficult rather than easier, it certainly seems that adversity brought the best out of us.

In a strange way, I was thankful, looking back at the events in retrospect, that I was given the opportunity to experience such deeper feelings expressed by fellow humans, and which one really does not encounter in the pursuance of ordinary more civilized and ordered social lives. It was not even that the belongings involved were of any instrinsic value or had any value at all, but to prisoners at that time any personal goods of any sort, shirt, pants, a sock or even a pair, seemed to be a focal point to hang on to at all costs and such articles had a theoretical value far beyond any practical or actual value. One just had to arrive at a camp with some material possessions, which formed some sort of link, the only one maybe, with the past, and provided one with some sort of vague sense of identity coupled with a base in ownership of property something one could call one's 'kit'. Probably the millionaire estate owner would never understand, within the orbit of his property portfolio, the relationship we then had with our filthy and well holed socks.

The camp we arrived at was a very large camp and obviously a purpose-built military establishment of some kind. There were already a number of prisoners there and at a guess it may have had a total capacity of between 7,000 and 10,000 men. The inmates seemed to be of different nationalities but predominantly British and American, and there was an attempt at organization although not quite like Lamsdorf. Obviously everyone was very aware of the impending ending of hostilities and the possibility of release from this camp by advancing Allied troops who were not all that far away, and there was a general air of expectancy and hope. Presumably someone in the higher German commands had had the unusual wisdom to realize that, by bringing prisoners nearer to the new Western Front there was a good chance of the camp being overrun by the advancing Allies and the prisoners so getting released; they would then no longer be a burden on the meagre German resources and represent an embarrassment to the advancing troops as well as being an additional hindrance to the Allied artillery and aerial onslaughts.

However, the predominant feature of the stay at the camp was certainly the incessant air-raids. These were now occurring both day and night, daytime raids by the Americans and night raids by the RAF. The Germans used to say that during the day the safest place was in the centre of the city, and at night time it paid to get out of the city, but this maybe was a little un-just to the American bombers. Whatever was the case, the appearance of hundreds of droning bombers, wave after wave, adding up to maybe five hundred or sometimes a thousand planes or more, was an absolutely terrify-ing sight and when they dropped a marker bomb somewhere near the camp and one knew that all the following planes would drop their load in that area guided by the marker, the inmates knew they were in for a tough time. The camp was hit and many died and were injured and we lived day by day in abject fear of our own bombers. At least as a civilian you could get the hell out of it, but we were enclosed within many layers of barbed wire so there was no escape from the ultimate carnage, and I do not think that the Germans were particularly upset at British or American prisoners being killed by their own side's bombers.

The bombing went on for several days and with increasing intensity and then one day the order came for the prisoners to dig pits for themselves in the fields outside their huts but within the camp enclosure. 'We gotta dig goddamned foxholes', belligerently muttered a newfound American colleague, a a New Yorker who had advanced a bit too far ahead of his tank support on a patrol shortly after the Normandy landing. There was a vast contrast between Ed Hughes and myself, although we were both much about the same age. Ed had lived the past five years or so as a free man and had enjoyed his freedom in his own prosperous city home in the US and during the past twelve months or so in the pubs of Southern England accompanied by the best of British maidens. His fortunes had been very different from mine and each of us was fascinated to relate and exchange experiences which were on such a different level. Fortunately for my part, I could not somehow show jealously for the American's better fortune, and the American, in his turn, showed genuine sympathy for mine, not just polite interjections of 'Oh boy, that musta been god-damned awful', but a real interest in considering his own reactions to the situations I had been in. I, in my turn, of course learnt a lot about the lost years in terms of home and international news, so each of us had something to offer the other, although I did find at times, I would have found it much easier in conversation to understand a Russian than the New Yorker, who used many terms and expressions completely foreign to me.

'Maybe they are expecting an attack or something on the camp', I suggested when vast supplies of spades and shovels were dumped on the parade ground. Still, we equipped ourselves with a tool each and started digging. I had in fact little idea as to how to set about digging a foxhole and kept an eye on the American's more efficient effort. Apparently, I soon discovered, American front line troops live in foxholes, and Ed was an expert, but in the end I struggled through to produce a sort of short ditch, heavily but humorously criticized by Ed. 'Who are you going to bury in that god-damned thing?' Everything seemed to be 'god-damned' just as the American must have thought that everything emanating from the British soldiers was 'f...ing'. Still, there is no shortage of quaint customs amongst soldiers.

The following day we were all told by the Germans to get in the foxholes and stay there until allowed out. We had no idea what was to come, but after some while we were issued with cottonwool or something the equivalent supplied by a nation which seemed to miraculously survive on artificial substitutes, and told to block up our ears and leave it there.

'There is gonna be a big bang', forecast Ed, omitting the god-damned in the urgency of the occasion, and hardly had we settled down in our holes, cottonwool in place, when all of a sudden without any prior warning, there was the most almighty explosion anyone had ever heard or is ever likely to hear, an explosion which nearly shattered our eardrums despite the cottonwool and made the earth all around shudder and even the trenches fall in and the buildings rock; then, to our our utter amazement the whole camp suddenly became inundated with whole branches of trees, even whole trees clouds of leaves earth, bushes and Lord knows what else, all flying through the air above us and across the camp. There seemed to be even complete trees flying about and everything was covered in dust, earth and leaves and general debris.

It transpired that the Germans had blown up an enormous underground munitions works situated under a forest a short distance from the camp and the forest had gone up in the air with the force of the explosion and the winds had carried all the debris over the camp. Never a dull moment! The air was ringing, not only from the reverberation of the explosion, but also from the reverberations of 'god-damns' and less elegant British ejaculations.

No one seemed to be hurt, and we all clambered out of the foxholes and returned to the huts furiously trying to clean off the accumulated dust which had got into everything and which continued to settle over the camp for the next hour or so. Both Ed and I were happy to accept that the episode was just another in the closing stages of the Third Reich, and to Ed, only a prisoner for a couple of months, release was almost an automatic event to be enjoyed within the next few days. To me, release could most certainly not be counted upon, and if it ever happened and if I lived to survive until then, it may occur before Christmas (nine months away) if at all. Such was the enormous difference the past experiences had left each of us with.

The ultimate event I had waited for with varying degrees of hope over the past five years came in the end as a bit of a shock, as well as of course a tremendous relief, but not before we had all been exposed to further diabolical psychological as well as physical danger. The advancing Americans started shelling German positions located somewhere behind the camp and the Germans retaliated by shelling the advancing Americans with the extremely unpleasant result that the camp had salvos of shells whining across it for a whole day and night continuously, the inmates never knowing when the next one was going to land in their lap. One or two did land adjacent to the camp killing several prisoners and maiming others; when this happens in the front line you more or less expect it and accept it as your bad luck – 'It had your name on it ...' – but when you have waited through thick and thin, mostly very thin, for five years for an event of insuperable joy to happen and for release into the world and freedom to move where you will without a shadow with a gun to prod you around, and then you get killed by one of your own side's shells, bombs or even machine-gun fire, then the unwarranted interference with your uppermost dreams comes as a horribly dramatic climax to all one's suffering, and even the very thought ot terminating one's life when freedom and the hope of seeing the Home Country, relatives and friends is so close is unbearable in the extreme. And there was an assembly of some thousands of men all suffering the same traumatic thoughts: 'Please God, not now, at the last knockings.' But die some did and one can only feel for them, understand their agony and the agony of those they failed to be reunited with, and trust that a merciful Lord may so perform in an effort to spare them some future agonies. There must be some rhyme and reason to it all, or could it really be just the 'luck of the draw'?

And then it all happened. In the true traditional manner upholding the very essence of dramatic American Hollywood films, a section of American tanks suddenly came charging through the shell fire, which by then had decreased, and barged very unceremoniously straight through the camp main gates without even so much as stopping to open them and up the principal road of the camp accompanied by the wild and enthusiastic cheering and exciting antics of the overjoyed spectators (except the guards). The tanks were followed by a minor disaster. Along came supply trucks and various mechanized units (nobody seems to walk in the American army) and the occupants handed out to the half-starved inmates of the camp – what sort of sustenance? Why, bottles of rum and cigars! Anybody would think we were a bunch of well-fed businessmen who had just landed a fat contract and been invited to lunch instead of a load of very sick and emaciated beings for whom any strong liquor or tobacco was almost deadly. One can fully understand the thinking behind our benefactors' action – marvellous stuff to celebrate a victory and very well meant – and of course the recipients of both rum and freedom will always be eternally grateful for this action which led to their final release, but how much more satisfying it would have been to have received a nice ham sandwich and cup of hot coffee than a bottle of rum!

The spirits had their obvious effect and many of the released prisoners in a short time had no idea whether they were released or still prisoners, especially those who had been 'in the bag' for many years and had lost the bodily resistance to alcohol, but the great number tempered their thirst and desire for celebration with a matching desire to get some proper feeding arrangements organized and keep a clear head with which to celebrate in a more modest way with a beer. Our American friends were not slow, however, in making these arrangements and they certainly seemed to be well supplied with food and drink to pour into the newly opened up prison camps. One could almost expect a regiment of glamorous blonde American drum-majors to follow the victuals, but no such luck and anyway in view of the sorry state many of the prisoners were in, the young ladies may have been sorely disappointed!

What to do with one's freedom? No guard at the gate, in fact no gate, so experimentally I walked outside the camp barbed wire, all the time looking back to see where my shadow, the guard, was. The novelty of being alone at all was extraordinary, for during the past five years, except when in solitary confinement in a punishment cell, I had never been out of sight of other prisoners and guards, and now it was possible to actually move 200 yards away from other people and think what an absolutely wonderful world it was after all, a fact which had progressively escaped me during the long dark years.

There were now buttercups to be inspected, right of personal will to be exercised, dignity to be restored and all in all, life to be lived. Oddly enough this feeling of freedom seemed so very strange to me in the first days that it was almost frightening and remained as a novelty producing an odd feeling for a very long time, and even when I was back in hospital upon return to England, in Wimbledon, and used to walk across the Common I used to be still frequently looking round to see whether the guard was keeping up with me, and felt quite pleasantly lonely to see no one, just no one, around. It was clear that whilst the years of captivity had taken their physical toll, there was a much deeper and complicated psychological toll to be exacted, the precise results of which could not then be assessed, but one fact was clear: no one who had survived five years of prisoner of war life would ever be completely the same afterwards. The time had now arrived to discover the true cost of the past years of suffering. The starry-eyed one had certainly become anything but starry-eyed and knew by now all the answers (he soon found out of course that this was not so by a long chalk). But there were still shocks to come.

13

The Freedom

The shelling ceased and the general turmoil ended and we all started to concentrate our minds on the one and only great thought: 'How quickly and by what means do I get home?' The fact of freedom still hit us as a most strange phenomenon, and we automatically sought to be regimented whilst all the time feeling that military discipline would automatically be accompanied by the toe of a German jack-boot or butt of a German rifle. Old habits die hard, and now each time someone in authority shouted loudly, the adrenalin started to flow again and fear instantly assumed prominence in our nervous system.

There were, of course, amongst us many who had only been POWs for maybe one or two years and some only weeks or months, like my mate Ed Hughes, and my views would not necessarily coincide with theirs, but the veterans of the piece who had been under enforced control and ordered about by just everyone over a period of four or five years found difficulty in even accepting a situation where there was freedom of choice in both movement and action and even thought, and we seemed to seek out regimentation and the security of group action rather than being on our own. It was as if we had lost the confidence to act on our own, and in fact to a great extent we had, and maybe to even think for ourselves was something we had become quite unaccustomed to after years of being told what to do, where, when and how to do it, and we were now very lost in new found freedom and looking round for someone to tell us what to do next.

I ventured outside the gates for a walk around, all by myself, but a short way from the camp, in walking down what may once have been a pretty German country lane. I came across a shot-up and bombed German artillery unit and was immediately painfully remained of the carnage of five years ago in France. There were dead Germans lying around in grotesque postures, smashed equipment, trucks, guns, etc, upside down in ditches and general havoc, and together with the foul stench of rapidly rotting flesh it all quickly turned my stomach. I had seen it all before and never wanted to set eyes on it again, such horrendous and useless waste of lives and human effort. It was just not acceptable any more, not exciting, and gave the lie to the pre-war stories one heard of the heroes and their noble deeds and fruits of victory. It was all too horribly obvious that there were no heroes, no deeds that were noble but all executed under the exigencies of extreme fear and dire threats, or unconscious and automatic reflexive actions, and the whole so utterly futile and a complete waste of human effort and sad indictment of human intelligence.

I left the sordid scene as quickly as I could after studying, from a respectable distance, the agonized faces of young, very young German blond-haired youths who no longer would strut around the cities of conquered Europe and who probably before their recent demise had suddenly come themselves to appreciate that there were even greater gods than them around, in the guise of a distant and massive American war industry producing even bigger, better and more weapons of destruction with which to put them in their place. I contemplated that their families at home somewhere in the heart of Germany, who had such proud hopes of sonny Hans, would at least be spared the ghastly sight of their beloved young man's last minutes of anguish discovering the facts of life and particularly death, gradually stiffening in the last rigors of an agonizing and lonely death into the most frightening and ugly forms of mutilated human life, so that those families would just be left with a memory, a very very sad memory, for the rest of their conscious existence which would never go away and never allow them real relaxed pleasure again in their lives. All because one shell happened to be directed by some equally unknown and little-caring Hans from Philadelphia who ultimately would receive his earthly reward in the form of a Purple Heart to proudly display on his mantelpiece far, far away, something to remind him of the death and destruction he had managed to dispense during his younger days.

I retraced my steps to the security of the camp after my brief excursion to witness the pitiful results of human beings playing at being humans in a free world which apparently really had little freedom to offer after all. We had all, in any case, been warned that there were still German snipers lurking in the trees in the adjoining forest, so as a result not many of the prisoners ventured very far into the free world. We were, of course, still in a front line, despite the rapidity of the American advance, and one could never be sure of the possibility of counter-attacks, so we were strongly advised to remain in the camp until order could be established and arrangements made for our evacuation.

I had heard that the German camp commandant had been taken out and summarily shot by the Americans which, if true, struck me as being rather sad and unmerited. The guards and their commandants generally had been as reasonable as they could be in the latter days of my captivity and a lot of privation I had had to undergo were certainly not of their making, but were the result of the dire economic straits to which Germany had been reduced at the end of the war, and I had, in the course of my interpreting duties had many dealings with the camp commandant at Nuremberg, whom I had found to be quite a pleasant and reasonable old chap, probably more at home behind his desk in a local bank, so I was upset to think he had been shot out of hand. On the other hand, I can now in retrospect well understand the feelings of my American liberators who may well have earlier liberated concentration camps which were in the area and been witness to the terrible events of the past five years in such hideous establishments as Buchenwald, for instance, now emerging to the critical examination of public view, and any American army commander at front line level who may have ordered the immediate execution of a prison camp commandant may be perhaps forgiven in his lack of desire to await the formalities of justice.

The guards, however, were locked up in one of the huts and given, amazing to relate, a load of Red Cross parcels to survive on! Maybe they had never had it so good for a long time, but I did not witness any revengeful acts by the prisoners against their former guards and revenge was something which certainly the older prisoners amongst us (that means older in service, not years, for I was old in service but only twenty-two then) had no heart for revenge, for the futility of it all had long since terminated any particular feelings of distaste for the Germans, despite the treatment in the earlier years of captivity which had been so far from humane. Now when the tables were turned the imprisoned German soldiers and former guards were no more nor less than fellow sufferers and not souls to be further tormented. No doubt they would feel the pains of imprisonment as their former captives had, not to see their nearest and dearest for at least a fairly long time, and to suffer the same mental tribulations and anxieties; but it was doubtful if they would suffer in conditions of such hardship as had been laid on for the benefit of British prisoners, especially in the very early days of captivity, and in any case, they could look forward to an early end to the war, whilst our period of captivity as viewed at first at St Valéry, was for an unknown period, maybe for all time.

The arrival of the Americans and breaking down of the imprisoning wire was by no means the end of all problems. An address made by an American officer shortly after our release put the former prisoners firmly back in their place as continuing members of the military forces, and rightly so too. He made it clear that military discipline was absolutely paramount at this time since we had all again become, in effect, front line troops. The fighting was still being very actively pursued all around us, and as he made quite clear, at any time the Germans could instigate a Panzer thrust against the American forward positions and we could all be at risk again. So he correctly insisted on complete military order and discipline throughout the camp, including no excursions beyond the confines of the camp. He would make arrangements as soon as practicable for the evacuation to rear lines and hospitalization, etc, but for the moment we were to stay put.

This situation was frustrating, but completely understandable to those who had the intelligence to think, whilst those who were not so blessed resorted to the use of the inevitable four-letter expletive as a soothing palliative for their shattered and frustrated desires to go and chase local women who were no longer there and probably not interested anyway, or find solace in alcohol in the nearest remains of a town, alcohol which would certainly wreak havoc on a stomach the linings of which must have severely deteriorated over years of near-starvation. However it was only a day or so before the more extreme hospital cases started to be moved out of the camp and I, for no good reason at all but probably because I happened to be handy at the time or because I spoke the local lingo and was a hospitalized case, was packed off in one of the first trucks with about twenty others and an American negro driver and medical attendant at about nine o'clock in the evening, some couple of days after the arrival of the liberating troops.

I said my goodbyes to Ed, now about my only remaining friend in the camp, for all my former colleagues had been dispersed all over Europe. 'Bye, Edward' and a firm handshake was about it. The parting from those with whom I had temporarily become close and between whom all personal histories, hopes and views over all manner of things, ranging from the existence of God to the merits or otherwise of consorting with prostitutes, had been exhaustively and very honestly exchanged – probably never again in my whole life would I get to know other men so intimately as to be able to discuss such matters so freely and truthfully.

'My god-damned name's not Edward,' retorted the American with a broad grin and keeping up a banter which he had fallen into to relax our minds from other more pressing problems. I had not accepted 'Ed' as being a name, and had presumed it to be contraction of Edward. It appeared, however, that Hughes' parents had actually christened him with the name Ed, which had surprised me considerably, and made me wonder whether the folk the other side of the Atlantic, of whom Ed must have been one of the first I had ever met, were quite right in the head. I had occasion in the future on many occasions to raise the same question, but that had nothing to do with Ed.

Addresses were exchanged, one in Brooklyn for one in Sussex, but it was to be pretty meaningless. We both really knew that we would never contact each other again; no one wanted to be reminded of the war years in captivity, especially if you had been there for five long years. 'Nice chap – hope he gets home OK,' I thought. 'Poor guy – hope he makes it,' probably thought Ed, and that was that.

I made for the waiting convoy of trucks, and took up my place amongst those with limbs missing or damaged, stomachs which would not last much longer and the rest of the human debris now being very tenderly, for the first time for a very long while in many instances, assisted on to the waiting trucks by the American army ambulance corps soldiers; the helpful attention came as quite a shock to those who had grown to forget there was tenderness in the world and who had grown up to assume that if you were missing any limbs or suffered other physical disabilities you just had to accept the fact and fight the battle for survival as if they were all sound and complete.

We had no idea where we were going, nor as far as I could see did the driver, and we spent a considerable amount of time going down roads and reversing and turning round and generally giving a very good impression of being lost, which no doubt we were. The destination I had gathered was a camp adjoining an airfield for the Nuremberg Regional Command but situated some fifty or sixty kilometres away, and whilst the driver did appear to have a reasonable idea of the general direction, as he clearly explained, 'The goddam Krauts keep up rearguard actions which foul up the routes'. I think that he was continually being warned by American patrols and radio to take diversions which got him pretty lost. This was all in pitch blackness and with the continual rumble of front line activity to be heard all around, and it was becoming rather nerve-racking for those cooped up in the rear of the truck, especially being so near and yet so far from the principal objective of our life; return to Blighty. This was very clearly brought home to us as, when speeding down some road adjoining a forest, we heard the rat-tat-tat of machine guns pretty close above the general more continuous sounds of explosions, and suddenly found the canvas sides of our truck, at high level fortunately, had become perforated by machine gun fire. This was not helpful to our shattered nervous systems and many very intense and heart-felt prayers were offered to any particular deity who may be on hand for assistance, to which thankfully a helpful response was forthcoming. The driver managed to orientate himself correctly, probably urged along by the machine gun attack and we eventually arrived at a blacked-out American army camp in the middle of nowhere. We were duly put into a hut with beds and, astonishingly enough, sheets which I had not seen for five years, and I was not sure whether I should sleep in them, blow my nose on them or use them for bandages, or better still, roll them up and purloin them for they may come in handy for an escape! Such luxuries as beds and sheets were almost unbelievable, especially so near a front line, and I was full of admiration for the astonishing American ability seemingly unique to their army to provide home comforts under even the most extreme conditions.

Having spent a restless remainder of the night between the sheets which did little to assist in sleeping, sleep itself being a luxury which from long practice we had learned to dispense with during times of nervous activity, we were assembled outside very early in the morning and sent off to a hut for breakfast. This meal was quite astonishing for it was eaten off a plate. Not for five whole years had I eaten off a plate since my only eating utensils had been empty Red Cross tins which served to contain both food for eating and drink for drinking (separately of course!), so the appearance of plates and such ancillary and unnecessary items as knives and forks and cups was all very bewildering, though of course the newer prisoners of only a couple of years' service or so were still able to remember what they were for. It may all sound a bit ridiculous, but none of these little customs had been indulged in by me for many years and only perhaps some of the plutocrats in the camps such as sergeant-majors and cooks had in fact enjoyed the delights of such luxuries, but the eating of the first meal under civilized conditions and subsequent showering and use of some strange substance called soap completed my initiation into the wonders of modern society. Soap we had received, of course, in Red Cross parcels, but when it had not been mixed up by envious German commandants with toothpaste and treacle, it had been reserved by many of the prisoners for bartering with the natives, rather to be wasted in such luxurious and wholly unnecessary performances as cleansing the body.

The Americans wasted very little time in getting rid of us, and that same day we were assembled for embarkation on a transport plane to England. I had never been on an aeroplane before, and this was all a terrific new adventure which was helping to clear some of the very dull film from the former starry-eyes and bring a new sense of adventure into living again.

Often in life when the way ahead seems clear, the most unexpected things occur to remind one that fate still lies around the corner prepared to disrupt one's dreams with the utmost callousness and disregard for any rules of 'fair play'. As we walked across to the waiting Dakota C47 transport plane, in the evening darkness, we were all silently offering up prayers that nothing would now go wrong at the eleventh hour. Someone up there wasn't listening or maybe just thought it may be good for our moral fibre to be further tried and tested.

We sat in the plane on any packs, goods and chattels or coats or whatever, if anything, we still possessed, on the floor in the fuselage of the Dakota, about thirty of us in two rows facing each other and were told to hang on to anything we could find, which was an occasional strap hanging from the roof of the plane. A far cry indeed from a 747 with plush seats and a gin and tonic and smiling hostesses all of which would have been so very, very acceptable at that particular moment, but that plane at that time was to all of us the most beautiful object in the whole world; it represented a vital link between the normalities of civilized life and the exceedingly low state we had been reduced to over the past years. We had a rough ride over what presumably was an improvised airstrip and were soon airborne. It was bumpy but marvellous, and as a first taste of air travel, seated on the floor of the Dakota feeling every wind current and bump and pretty cold, things seemed just great and I was experiencing my first and most wonderful air flight with great pleasure. After all the waiting and all the hoping and consequent despair, things were at last coming right. We could get back to life more or less to the point where we had left it off, or so we very erroneously thought.

I had a strange feeling as the plane rose upwards over the lands where I had spent the last years of my life, in fact not far off one quarter of my whole life. It all seemed a little unreal. All that time spent wondering whether I would survive to ever return to my native land, and now the plane was actually moving at a relatively rapid speed, although it may have been barely 200 mph back towards the land I had unwillingly been dragged from by foot, at maybe 2 or 3 mph or in the slow-moving packed barges and cattle trucks full of suffering and protesting men. Now I was actually travelling so fast it was probably only a matter of hours before I would actually set foot in beloved England, all being well. I could never leave the place again, that was one thing very certain. I would also concentrate on eating, for I must build up the exhausted supplies I had come out with and lost over the years. People would probably look very different – my parents must be older and less fit, maybe ill; maybe the whole country would look very different because of the bombing and obvious war effort, and I tried to cushion my hopes to accept many shocks which inevitably I would have to meet. Nothing could mar the pure elation of being a free man, but even free men do not have everything going their way, and in any case, I supposed I would get so accustomed to being free again that I would be just like all the rest and no longer value that freedom. No, I decided, that would never happen. There was no doubt about it, freedom, the right to decide your own course of action even if it only involved getting up and going for a walk without asking permission and without having an escort, that was something I would always cherish for the rest of my life.

And so the thoughts wandered as the plane sped on its way 'home' with its silently pensive but inwardly rejoicing cargo. But it was when these future hopes were uppermost in our minds that the exciting anticipation for the future was rudely disrupted when the plane suddenly and very obviously climbed to some freezing heights, and we all began to shiver like fury and find some difficulty in breathing, which to me was a particular discomfort. The poor old crate, which of course was not particularly old then, seemed to be straining away to overcome some extreme pressures which had been suddenly imposed upon it, and it was very clear to all of us at the back that something was wrong.

Those nearest the 'driver' did not hesitate to enquire as to what the hell was happening, and after a little delay during which time the crew were fully involved in getting and keeping control of the aircraft, the navigator gave his explanations, which were duly passed down the fuselage.

Apparently what had occurred, as we understood the information proceeding from the 'cockpit' was that the corridor route via which the plane had flown into Nuremberg was now the subject of attention from the Germans and had become liable to anti-aircraft fire and fighter attack, and the pilot had been warned not to use that route and to divert by going over a mountain range. Well, to-day the modern jets take that in their stride, but at that time the Dakota was not at all happy about the decision and was not equipped for such an event. Not only was the Dakota struggling, but so were its passengers for we still only had pretty scanty clothing and it became absolutely freezing in the unheated fuselage, and despite the appearance of some primitive oxygen masks, breathing became immensely difficult. I had no idea as to exactly what height we had ascended to, but we all huddled together with teeth chattering and hoped for the best. This was definitely something we could happily have done without at this particular stage of the game, and all the old tensions and worries reappeared as we began to wonder about our future, but by then we were well acclimatized to assuming the worst, anything less being in the nature of a bonus.

We survived the brief ascent to the heights and the plane descended thankfully to a much lower level somewhere on the other side of whatever it was we had to go over, and was now flying over Allied occupied territory, so the dangers of attack were hopefully behind us. All must now be plain sailing; but was it heck! There was another problem.

When we eventually arrived over England and the pilot tried to get the retractable undercarriage to drop, he found he could not do so. We were given garbled reports from the three-man American crew up front about the undercarriage having got iced up during the high level flying, and just to make us a little more apprehensive, those nearest the crew's cabin heard radio messages being sent out to the airport at Swindon that we would have to crash land, and requesting fire tenders and ambulances to stand by. What a delightful way to end five years of imprisonment, to be crushed into the earth in a sardine tin from a few thousand feet up. All the hopes, all the joys once more were extinguished and replaced by considerable fear for the immediate future, for not only our thoughts of re-union were being dashed, but there was the distinct probability that we may, after all, finish up as dead corpses to be returned to our loved ones.

The pilot told us he was proposing to crash-land and instructed us all to get up to the tail end of the fuselage and hold on to anything we could for grim life. All the baggage, what there was of it, was shoved forward.

He then jettisoned all the remaining fuel and down we went. It would be impossible to describe our apprehensions and fearful thoughts in the few moments it took for the plane to approach and touch down on the runway, and we just froze again, this time mentally, crossing fingers and praying once again fervently for divine intervention. It seems extraordinary how frequently one has recourse to seek assistance from the Deity when all earthly hopes of advantageous intervention seem to have disappeared. Many of us who may have sent forth such earnest supplications could well have been amongst the first to decry the very existence of a Divine Being when gathered together in unholy celebration at a public house, but at times like the present, it seemed we would have gladly reversed such shallow views to accept a last favour from an ever-forgiving God, to enable us to preserve our miserable bodies for further visits to the pub and opportunities to deny the existence of a Divine Being.

The earth came up rapidly to meet our swiftly descending casket which was lacking any wheels upon which to land, and upon impact with mother earth, the grinding crashing sounds were deafening, and served to some extent to block out of our minds what else was happening, but what did, of course, happen was that we were all shot from the tail end of the plane to the front in a jumbled sea of legs, arms and bodies with astonishing rapidity. The front of the plane was a crumpled wreck and when the immediate dust had settled and we had been able to take stock of the shambles resulting, we all jumped or scrambled out through the remains of the doors through gaping holes of the wrecked fuselage as best we could into the welcoming arms of ambulance attendants, fire fighting men, etc, who were immediately on the scene. There were a few broken or damaged limbs and many bruises and cuts and I received a small share consisting of a few minor scratches and bumps, but really nothing too serious amongst the passengers. However, we later heard that the three American aircrew, who took the brunt of the crash in the front of the plane, were killed, and this would not at all be surprising although we never officially were given information on their fate. From the chaotic state of the crushed foreward compartment of the plane it would be difficult to imagine anyone could escape at least the most serious of injuries, and it was to this area that the rescuers directed their principal efforts at recovery, though we were in no great condition to observe the results. We were hastily removed from the scene. I think that the American crew must have done a terrific job in landing the aircraft as efficiently as they did, bearing in mind the complete absence of undercarriage. It would seem they must have slithered the craft along the landing strip rather than nose-dive into the ground, and I am sure we all owed them a tremendous debt. Certainly, the front of the plane was most severely damaged, and I only hope the rumour that the crew were killed was incorrect. By their undoubted skill, they had most certainly saved the lives of their passengers.

We were soon taken off to a hospital wing and a lot of patching up, and so ended my first of very many air flights. Hopefully it would be the most eventful, in so far as aeronautical results are concerned, but it certainly was a most dramatic way to return a once starry-eyed young man in more or less one piece to that land which had been no more than a dream over five years and which at many times he had never hoped to see again.

14

The Review

After only a day at Swindon we were put on a hospital train for a journey full of joy and anticipation, to Leicester. What a wonderful change from the cattle trucks – comfortable armchair seats, drinks, cigarettes all provided with great generosity and forethought by a nation willing to welcome home those scarred in its defence, to whatever comforts they could still provide.

The problems now were really over, and only the formidable task of re-entering civilized society and eventually making our various ways in civvy life lay before us; the task was specially formidable of course for those who had been in captivity a long time. I still kept looking for the guard with the rifle behind me every time I walked out alone and could not get used to the idea that I could go wherever I wanted without permission or escort. At Leicester we were given a civic reception worthy of conquering heroes, though I could not actually recollect having conquered anything. We were met at the station by the mayor and his corporation (which corporation we were very envious of in our somewhat emaciated state!) and they really did the returning soldiers proud with band and civic reception. We were each allocated a Home Guard member to assist us from the train to waiting ambulances, and whilst I had, of course, never set eyes on a member of the Home Guard, the gent detailed to assist me appeared so frail and old that I was not at all sure that maybe our roles should not be reversed and I should be carrying the old chap into the hospital! The reception was great, and supported by a supply of welcome beer and cigarettes rustled up from Lord knows where, and we were made to feel very welcome in our homeland, a fact which has since left me with a particular soft spot for the good burghers of Leicester.

We were duly placed in suitable hospital wards in the spacious Leicester General Hospital and given the usual hospital 'blues' the special clothing worn in and out of hospital by war invalids, but before being tucked up in bed with a nice supper, we were duly given a bath by young nurses who felt that the patients were too weak to bathe themselves, an ordeal which I in particular found hard to accept after five years of enforced celibacy.

The people of Leicester treated us magnificently and when I was eventually let loose in the city in my blues, I could do no wrong. At the time I was trying to learn to smoke a pipe and I went into a tobacconist shop to buy a pipe but the owner presented me with a magnificent Dunhill, refusing any payment. In the pubs I was offered more beer than I could drink, which was not a lot at first, and all in all I certainly began to feel that I may have contributed something to the war effort after all, which was now at last coming to a victorious conclusion.

I was very struck by the obvious sense of communal effort which seemed to exist amongst the civilian population in Britain. For so many years I had lived in a country or in countries under the domination of a tightly controlled dictatorship, where everyone seemed to be prepared to spy upon and to gain advantage from the momentary lapses of their brethren and where a war effort was very much a matter of compulsion with the principal aims of the war being largely forgotten and compulsion being the order of the day.

In Britain I sensed a quite different set of circumstances. Whilst the civilian population had clearly suffered severely during the past years, there seemed to be more natural unity of purpose amongst the people who showed very clearly they were all on the same side and were prepared to make personal sacrifices for the general good without obvious sense of reward; in Germany it was always difficult to know which side anyone was really on and people seemed only to do as much as their station required of them – there had clearly arisen two unequal and opposite elements in society in Germany – the Party and the People, and the division between the two was very clearly marked and the absence of such a division at home was very noticeable and great to see. There were 'Parties', but they confined themselves to bickering in Whitehall – the people seemed all to be on the same side and working for the same end.

I did not get completely away from hospitals for a further nine months, but at all times found the treatment afforded invalids and wounded returning from the front to be so tremendously generous and sympathetic. I wondered at the generosity, for it had to come out of somebody's pocket, and the people so freely buying us drinks did not look too plush themselves. The tradesmen, especially the older ones, may have been relieved that the war had resulted in victory and safety for themselves and their families, and the appreciation shown by such establishments as cinemas, for instance, which opened their doors free of charge to the 'boys in blue' must have cost somebody something. Maybe they had all made a fortune during the war and were prepared to make a payment of 'conscience money' to those who had not been so fortunate. Maybe, however, it is just a part of the truly generous spirit of the inhabitants of these islands, and happily I felt that the latter was the case, for I experienced many encounters and expressions of genuine sympathy and help, not necessarily material, that I began to realize that our years of suffering may not have been in vain and that we had in fact represented a very small part of a truly united effort by the people of these very little islands to upset a most unpleasant invader and defend the most valuable of all our assets – our freedom; no one knew better than I just how unpleasant that potential invader really was, and I did not hesitate to relate to others the experiences of our imprisonment, and especially the treatment by the Germans of their captives, so that they could all begin to appreciate what horrors they had been spared in these islands, and how, by their efforts, those in other lands had been saved from the tyranny of a pernicious form of slavery and how millions in Europe were now being liberated from the oppressive rule of the Germans with their complete lack of respect for the individual human dignity.

Anyway, it was all over now and in the comparative luxury and comfort of a hospital bed in clean sheets surrounded by attractive nurses, one could reflect upon the whole sordid business of the past five years. It had really been a life within a life. It was so entirely different in all its varied aspects from the lives people would normally expect to live, that, by its very difference and resultant excitement and also its quite considerable duration, despite the hardships and frequent long periods of monotony and depression, I regarded myself oddly enough as being privileged in living through and surviving this wealth of varied experience which clearly would never again be repeated for me in my lifetime (at least I hoped not!).

The immediate view, and the view I persist in to this day, was that, despite the considerable hardships, this was as great an experience of life in all its human facets that one could ever expect to meet with in the course of one human incarnation. The extremes of suffering, famine and thirst, heat and cold and the extremes of emotion, fear and hope, horror and joy and the participation in life and death struggles in the company of others was something which it would be difficult to imagine under any other circumstances and impossible to understand from books or other media. One can lead a life in which the most emotional event in the whole lifetime may be the loss of a loved one, and that fortunately does not occur too frequently, or the height of emotional activity maybe the refusal of a loan from one's bank manager, but such relatively trivial affairs will always be just parts of the general performance of living in a civilized society; the more extreme events which occur in the course of surviving in a pretty uncivilized society during a long major war are something which may occur rarely to people and the experience gained, though achieved in circumstances of extreme discomfort, tension and emotional upset, make for very lasting and impressionable experiences when undergone at a relatively young age and over a quite long period. The results will always be with me and my day to day views of everything that occurs around me must be influenced to some extent at least by the knowledge of the extremes in behaviour which my fellow man is capable of reaching, and the lack of endurance and sufficiency that may exist in the material things in life. For three score years and ten we are presumed upon to endure the vicissitudes of an uneven battle for existence and sometimes events of a very traumatic nature can occur to substantially affect our whole perception of living.

During that period I suppose relatively few people live knowing that a sentence of death could be executed upon them at any time during each twenty-four hours over as long a period as five whole years, for the uncertainty of survival, most especially during the early part of those five years and even right up to the conclusion, was always a factor one had to reckon with. Maybe that fact was exaggerated in my case during captivity by being an 'ordinary soldier' and probably rather more expendable therefore as a captive than may have been the case with one of officer rank or even in many cases with naval or airforce personnel, and further as a result of embarking on hair-brained escape attempts instead of joining the official communal efforts. Survival initially in France in action was purely a 'hit or miss' matter of fortune, but the uncertainty was still very much present. At any moment during those five years I could have met my end.

At the end of the war the immediate reaction resulting from five of those years must have equated to very many more years experienced at a more normal tempo, and left me with a rather deep cynicism, of consideration of the world through eyes which no longer were starry, but which viewed the whole theatrical performance with deep suspicion and every move and every action of my fellow humans with some disquiet. That things could occasionally go right could not be disputed; that they were much more likely to go wrong must most definitely be allowed for. There were few certainties any more in life other than the certainty of death, and that was something which was pretty easy to encounter at any time.

Anyway, that was it. A multitude of experience, good and bad, an in-depth look at my fellow humans and a hell of a lot of luck and ultimate survival which had been achieved when many others around me, British, French, German, Russian, Pole, etc, with whom I had on some occasion had very dramatic encounters, did not have the benefit of such luck. Where are they now? Did they survive? Are those cruel Germans still jumping on pregnant girls' stomachs, denying thirsting people water? Are those Russian prisoners I was involved with and even the brave German soldiers who guarded us now suffering enslavement under horrific conditions in Russian concentration camps in Siberia or beyond the Urals? Or are they free and trying to do their best somewhere to alleviate the difficulties humans encounter on their way through this earthly paradise and not making little Hells for their fellow humans? Or are they no longer enjoying that paradise, but maybe their consciousness, wherever it may exist, is still reflecting upon the enormity of the deeds perpetrated during those five long years?

I often wonder what indeed has become of my contemporaries in Germany and Russia during the war, the young Hanses and Ivans. I am, however, reassured by Hans' actions collectively since the war, for I do feel that the good Hanses have come out of hiding and play a much more helpful role in this world of ours. As for Ivan, well, I am not too sure that he has had much of a say in directing the affairs of the world. He was, for the most part, a good lad, a bit solid and heavy going at times, but true and reliable. Pity he was not able to make his own voice heard, instead of having his life mapped out for him by a series of soviets, whose Party policy is dictated by one all-powered ancient mogul at the pinnacle, without any reference to Ivan.

And I wonder what Hans and Ivan think to-day of me and the likes of me from those war years – the relatively few who tramped around for years in a Europe severely dominated by tyrant Adolf? I expect they forgot about us many years ago.

The Man in the Grey Mac

He is a pretty familiar sight around here, wearily trundling down the road wearing the same old dirty macintosh year in and year out, shuffling rather than walking, for he seems to have a gammy leg; preciously held by one gnarled hand is the inevitable plastic supermarket container in which he has collected his earthly requirements for another two days, the result of meticulous and careful forward planning to ensure enough sustenance to keep the body together for what reason he is not too clear, purchased with the aid of ostensibly grateful thanks of a nation who once professed pride in him and in his efforts.

There are thousands and thousands of men in grey macs throughout the conurbations of our glorious land all struggling to get into the next year. They do not appear to be of any further use to anyone now and have been finally deposited into the bag marked 'With sympathy but minimal care'. That sympathy emanates mainly from the older generation today and the subject of the sympathy and indeed the older generation themselves are fast diminishing, eventually to the point where the men in the old grey macs will be no more and Society will be rid of any embarrassment, however slight.

Watching very disinterestedly the old man shuffling along is the young one with the multi-coloured hair and an arrogance born of an overdose of security and care fostered upon him as a result of the rapid growth of a materialistic society and some severely over-accentuated views on freedom and child care. The old man in the dirty mac is, however, my brother, not literally but he is the chap in whose company I spent the five years of war; he cursed with me, drank with me, slept with me and may well have sacrificed his life for me to support a cause he probably never fully understood nor cared too much about. He never graduated any further than the position of a soldier holding a rank of private in the PBI (for the uninitiated the 'poor bloody infantry') and lower than that in terms of basic soldiery you cannot get. He was the last one on the list to receive the orders, who grumbled furiously and got on with the task in hand to the best of his limited ability and got the kicks when it went wrong and seldom any glory. He was my mate, and I was glad of it. He left the war years badly wounded with an injury which would cause him perpetual pain and render him unable to compete in the great 'Rat Race'.

Many books have been written about the war of 1939–1945, in the main by those of an acceptable status of education and intelligence, officers, men of the RAF and Navy and the departments in the armed forces where technical know-how and not just blood and guts are required but few by the 'ordinary squaddy'. The circumstances under which these different classes operated were poles apart.

This is not a story to evoke sympathy for the writer and most certainly not to enter the lists of political debate. I do not have a dirty grey mac. I am fortunate enough to have a reasonably clean anorak as worn by many of my fellows in the fairly prosperous town in which I live. By the benign smile of fortune on my post-war efforts I am not so concerned about the deployment of funds to ensure a supply of basic necessities. Nor is this book a critique of the life style of our modern youth. You simply cannot have a world war every generation in order to educate the populace in the fundamental meaning of the word 'adversity'. Such a thought is horrific. In any case, man seems quite capable of generating sufficient animosity towards his brother without having ultimate recourse to going to war. Presumably the one with the multi-coloured hair will meet his own special form of adversity sooner or later – be it drugs, glue or the frustations of unemployment; maybe just the lack of a *raison d'être*. I just wish he would refrain from sneering at the man in the grey mac automatically assuming him to be in a category of those who have failed to make it – 'I don't want to finish up like him' – without having any in-depth knowledge of the circumstances which led to the dirty grey mac. He has probably never heard of the Star and Garter Home in Richmond, but one brief look inside would dramatically vary his criticism of the old soldiers.

I don't blame him for not wanting to finish up like the grey mac one. I very much hope he doesn't. But I feel his education has been sadly neglected when he fails to understand in depth the events which affected the lives of so many ordinary soldiers during and since the holocaust of 1939–1945. Not all those who particpated are today just involved in regimental re-unions to mull over past heroic deeds. Many were just pushed around from 1939 in a sea of ignorant oblivion and had no heroic victories to chalk up. The chap in the grey mac and I were apparently both in that category. Many have continued to be pushed around ever since.

This factual story may well reiterate the dramatic experiences which many young men in 1939 of my age, seventeen and almost straight from school, lived through and which probably succeeded in transforming them from 'starry-eyed youngsters' to hard-bitten cynics and bringing them en route face to face with the ultimate reality of death, in various guises and in some cases a fate far worse than death, a prospect of unending misery. It is, however, written from the lowest rung of the ladder of success, or almost the lowerest rung, for as a corporal in an infantry battalion I was almost scraping the bottom of the barrel, and my life was dependent directly upon the actions of the chap in the grey mac, much less directly upon those in elevated positions who issued the more general orders.

That other corporal, Adolf Hitler, was at the top of the ladder. I am only too pleased I never got around to dispensing anything like the death, misery and destruction around Europe that he managed.

   Those five years represented a quite unique period in my passage through life – a period which, for some strange reason I would never have wished to be without. It is so unfortunate that there has to be a war to provide the opportunity for such an experience. The chap in the old grey mac and the young man with the psychedelic thatch will probably never meet on equal terms, which is a pity, for neither will have the patience to listen to the other's viewpoint nor probably have the experience to understand it.

   It has been suggested to me (obviously for very good reason!) that my experiences during these quite dramatic war years may have had a permanent effect upon me, mental and physical.

   I think the predominant mental effect which may have resulted, and no doubt this has afflicted very many others than I who were exposed to the more seamy side of the war for a long period, has been to evoke a high degree of cynicsm in all things perpetrated by my fellow men. The ultimate values in life, and death, have been severely eroded and having personally experienced the proximity of the 'Great Reaper' on so many occasions and seen so many reaped, I must admit to a somewhat disinterested acceptance of the finality of all material things. I suppose there must be many other effects subjectively not apparent to me, but I have never been locked up since the war, neither for criminal nor mental aberrations, so I presume society must have accepted me as reasonably normal; maybe the young gent with the earrings and necklace may not however agree.

   Physically I received a setback after the war having the handicap of a chronic asthma, and spent nine months in hospital after return to this country. Even this physical disability could be overcome, and in 1952 I had the honour to compete in the Olympic Games for Britain at Helsinki in what must surely be one of the hardest physical tests – 10,000 metres in a kayak canoe. The asthma will remain for all my time and no doubt worsen, but my mates paid a very much higher price. Even many who survived will never graduate from a dart board in physical effort, as a result of their war suffering, so who am I to complain?

   One small but unusual physical benefit I have enjoyed has been that, touching wood, I have not had any occasion to visit a dentist since being called up in 1939. The piece of ordinary cement filling I received at Moerbrike on the march from St Valéry has remained in position ever since. I wonder whether the absence of dental troubles may relate to the fact of having had an almost complete absence of sugar during those five years.

   As I say, I am not complaining; I would not have missed the experiences for anything, and I would not consider my life as complete without having tasted my fair share of adversity and being subjected to the testing trials of thirst, starvation, heat, cold and probably more particularly the mental trials which resulted from exposure to these and other physical discomforts. But above all, it was ultimately the behaviour of my fellows, be they my own comrades in arms or the enemy, which made the most lasting impressions. Somehow, the old chap in the dirty grey mac seems to say it all.

Index